Vertue

Treasures of
Merton College

Treasures of
Merton College

General Editor: **Steven Gunn**

III

THIRD MILLENNIUM
PUBLISHING, LONDON

LIST OF CONTENTS

A drainpipe hopper in St Alban's Quad bearing the College arms and topped with a gargoyle.

FOREWORD

A 750th anniversary is a truly remarkable event. It seems simply astonishing that we know that the Warden and Fellows took possession of the Manor of Malden on 14 September 1264: this was the birth of Merton College. In the first contribution to this book we learn that Walter de Merton provided three sets of statutes over the ten years following its foundation; the first was essentially a founding document and the next two developed the constitution of the College. I find myself particularly moved by the admonition that the Warden and Fellows were to preserve 'unity, mutual charity, peace, concord and love'. This is as true today as it was then!

This book provides a brilliant lens for seeing how Merton has grown and changed over the many centuries. The book conveys a deep sense of the history of the College by displaying different elements of the spectrum of events since its foundation. With their mix of text and beautiful photographic images, these 57 articles bring to life all manner of facets of College life in this huge time span – with the great majority of the articles containing completely new insights or discoveries about their chosen topic.

The articles are divided into three groups: Medieval Merton, Merton Maturing and Modern Merton. In Medieval Merton we see how Walter de Merton built up the College and developed its endowment. It is very moving to hear of the difficult situation of the Jews of that time and the role that they played in the early years of the formation of the College. We then go on to discover various fascinating and curious features in the new College: the stunning timber and ironwork door to the dining hall through which countless generations of hungry students have passed since 1274; the beautifully coloured stained glass in the eastern arm of the Chapel which goes back to the early fourteenth century; and the brasses in the Chapel, in particular the brasses of two of our Wardens from the fourteenth and fifteenth centuries.

In Merton Maturing we encounter some quite fabulous documents. The 1476–7 first edition of Chaucer's *Canterbury Tales* is simply breathtaking, with its superbly illustrated borders. The oldest book in the College Library is a ninth-century manuscript copy of Jerome's translation

Opposite: The Gatehouse (see p. 52) from Merton Street. **Right:** *An etching of the Gatehouse by M.L. Menpes, c.1900.*

of the *Chronicle of Eusebius*. This astonishing manuscript made it possible to synchronise dates in world history from the time of Abraham to the time of Eusebius in the fourth century. No account of Merton Maturing – however brief – would be complete without mention of Bodley and Savile who, as founders of the Bodleian Library and the Savilian chairs, profoundly influenced the development of Oxford University.

One of the most striking features of this book is the way that various facets of everyday College life are shown to have a surprising and wonderful story behind them. So, for instance, we learn that the lectern, from which we read in Chapel, was part of a major programme of lavish refurbishment in the Chapel in the period 1486–1517. The sculpture over the Gatehouse was part of a programme of building works first licensed by Henry V in 1418. The College has had bells right from its earliest days. Anthony Wood commented that Merton's bells 'rang for the content of Society'. I hope the good citizens of Oxford would still agree! Ever since I arrived at Merton I have been fascinated by the miniature portraits in the New Common Room and wondered about their origins; this is now made clear – as is the reason why the collection contains two portraits of Warden Barton.

A further hugely impressive and distinctive feature of this book is the cross-cutting themes which run through a large part of the entirety of the College's history. The College's relationship with the village of Kibworth in Leicestershire began in the 1270s and continues to this day through our management of land given to us by Walter de Merton. It is exhilarating to see how different academic disciplines have waxed and waned over the years. Mathematics rose with the Merton Calculators, had a second golden age under Henry Savile, and is enjoying a current resurgence. Medicine was one of the first scientific disciplines to be studied at Merton. Initially, the discipline was based on the works of Galen, but this was then completely revolutionised by the work of William Harvey, appointed Warden of Merton by Charles I in 1643. The Linacre lectureships, subsequently professorships, were endowed by Thomas Linacre, physician to Henry VIII. This post has been hosted by Merton for over 300 years and the Linacre professors have played a major role in the massive explosion in life sciences that followed the ground-breaking work of Darwin.

This then brings us to modern times and to Modern Merton, where we see some completely new phenomena. One of the most striking features of College life today is the international make-up of both the fellowship and the student body. In *Treasures of Merton College* we learn of life for Kuruvila Zachariah, one of the College's first ever Indian students. I was delighted to learn that he chose Merton over other colleges on the grounds that it was '"a working college" and, for one of his academic ambition, this was the clincher'! Some of the saddest and most tragic events of recent times have occurred in the two world wars, and we learn of their impact on the College through our war memorial. One of the most touching aspects here are the two German Merton students who died in the Great War – but who we learn were exempted by their commanders from direct combat with the British. The twentieth century saw the appearance of the two Mertonian literary giants, J.R.R. Tolkien and T.S. Eliot; Tolkien has been credited with inventing the modern fantasy genre and T.S. Eliot was awarded a Nobel Prize for 'his outstanding, pioneer contribution to present-day poetry'.

It has been a very great pleasure to see this project develop from a rather vague plan to this quite marvellous account of so many aspects of College history: it has hugely exceeded our expectations! This, of course, is due to the hard work of all the contributors, and I wish to express my great thanks to them all. However, special thanks are due to Alan Bott, who authored and co-authored no fewer than 12 articles. Lastly, and above all, I wish to express my very deepest gratitude to all of the members of the Board, Alan Bott, Matt Bowdler, Helen Kingsley, Helen Morley, Julian Reid, Julia Walworth and the General Editor, Steven Gunn, for all their hard work and commitment in this splendid project.

Warden

*Opposite: A carved panel of 1540 with the royal arms and Tudor badges, formerly in the Hall. **Right:** The companion panel with the College arms.*

INTRODUCTION

Steven Gunn

Merton College is a brilliant conception, an endowed and self-governing academic institution that has served as a blueprint for many others. It is an intellectual tradition, joining diverse and sometimes surprising scholars across the centuries from Thomas Bradwardine and John Wyclif to Theodor Adorno and Nikolaas Tinbergen. It is a warm community, reaching out from its earliest members and its current residents and staff to its many alumni and friends. It is a financial institution, helping to shape the physical, agricultural and commercial landscape for three-quarters of a millennium in the use of its resources to fund its communal life. It is a set of buildings which in their design, use and re-use embody its story from its earliest days to the present. And it is a collection of treasures, from rooms, books and paintings to monuments and curios, that, when put together, give a kaleidoscopic picture of its life over the centuries.

In this book we have grouped a selection of those treasures, somewhat artificially, under three ages of Merton. To set them in context we might take a tour around the College's buildings and reflect on the wider historical setting in which they came into existence. To start from the beginning takes us not to Oxford at all, but to the manor house at Malden in Surrey, which the College still owns. It was there that Walter de Merton first planned to site the administration of his new foundation. It was, as a donor put it in 1266, 'the house of scholars of Merton, which Walter lately founded at Malden'. Walter, born in Basingstoke in about 1205, had begun his career near Malden, as an administrator for the Augustinian Priory of Merton, where he was known, logically enough, as Walter de Basingstoke. From there, perhaps fitting in some study at Oxford in the 1230s, he had moved into the service of King Henry III, now as Walter de Merton. He worked his way up through the royal chancery – with a spell diversifying his experience in the service of the bishop of Durham – to become chancellor, head of the royal administration, in 1261. As he rose he not only collected posts in the church but also bought up land, planning to make an educational endowment.

His first attempt, granting the Surrey manors of Malden, Chessington and Farleigh to Merton Priory in 1262 so the profits could be spent supporting students at Oxford, misfired. Tensions between the king's men, Walter among them, and the party of baronial reformers led by Simon de Montfort, broke into civil war. Walter lost the chancellorship, his lands were ravaged, and the transaction fell through. The constitutional convulsions which had produced Magna Carta in 1215 and were shaping the growth of parliament had apparently choked Walter's project in its infancy.

In September 1264 Walter tried again. This time he gave his lands not to Merton Priory, but to a College based at Malden. This would be led by a Warden, under the watchful eyes of the bishop of Winchester and Gilbert de Clare, earl of Gloucester, feudal overlord of the Surrey manors. It was charged with praying for Walter's soul and maintaining 20 scholars at Oxford or elsewhere, among them the sons of his seven sisters. Political circumstances soon enabled him to expand on this beginning. The king defeated his opponents in 1265 and lent his support to Walter's scheme, as did Gilbert de Clare. Walter bought land for his College at favourable prices from supporters of de Montfort, who

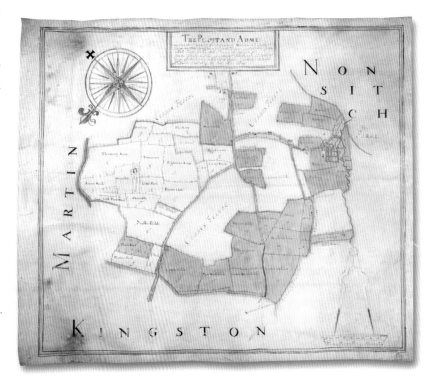

needed his help to clear their debts and make their peace with the king. King Henry, his brother, Richard, earl of Cornwall and king of the Romans, his son, the Lord Edward, and other aristocratic patrons such as Ela Longspee, countess of Warwick, also gave estates to the new foundation. Such was Edward's trust in Walter that, when Henry III died in 1272 and he succeeded as Edward I, Walter was re-appointed chancellor and left in charge of the kingdom for nearly two years while Edward made his way back from Crusade.

By 1274, when he stood down as chancellor, accepted the bishopric of Rochester and issued his final set of statutes for his College, the centre of gravity of Walter's foundation had clearly shifted to Oxford. He had managed to buy substantial properties in the south of the town along St John's Lane, now Merton Street. The Warden and the College administration were now based not at Malden, but at Oxford with the scholars. Though there was provision for a Visitor, a post soon entrusted to the archbishop of Canterbury, he was to intervene only in case of crises. Under ordinary circumstances the College was to be entirely independent and self-governing under its Warden, Peter of Abingdon, and his successors. All this was confirmed not only by the king but also, a few years later, by Pope Nicholas III.

When Walter visited the College in spring 1277, months before his death, construction work had been going on for about nine years. There was already a Hall and a Warden's House, parts of each of which survive today, and other buildings. In the 1280s and early 1290s the oldest recognisable buildings were put up. They prioritised the safekeeping of the College's records with a Treasury or Muniment Tower and the splendour of its religious life with the beginnings of a new Chapel, a chancel with high traceried windows glazed in vivid colours, to replace the parish church of St John the Baptist in which the College had at first held its services. By 1300 the attractions of the Warden's Lodgings had been increased with a new roof, now that of the Middle Common Room, solid accommodation for the scholars had been provided with the beginnings of Mob Quad, and the site had expanded to the far side

of Merton Street by the incorporation of what would later be known as Postmasters' Hall. The College's staff increased with its activities, and in this first generation the Bursars' accounts give us the names of William the head cook, John the assistant cook, Adam the kitchen boy, John the gardener, and Alexander Chivaler the porter.

The flexibility that Walter's foundation gave his College would be needed in the fourteenth century, as Oxford flourished intellectually amid economic, social and political turmoil: the Hundred Years War, the Black Death, the Peasants' Revolt and the depositions of Edward II and Richard II. The University on which the College and its scholars began to make an impact was a leading centre in diverse disciplines,

Opposite, left: The seal of Jacob the Jew, depicting the Lion of Judah, from his sale of a house to Walter de Merton for the site of the College in 1267 (see p. 24). Opposite, right: The chancel of the Chapel. Left: The Virgin Mary at the Annunciation, from the east window of the Chapel (see p. 38). Above: The thirteenth-century chest in the Library (see p. 72).

though they were not all classified as we would classify them today. Beyond the basic arts course – which included arithmetic, geometry and astronomy – lay higher studies not only in theology and philosophy, but also in law, music, medicine and natural philosophy, which included what later ages would separate out as the natural sciences.

Merton nurtured experts in almost all these fields. In philosophy there was Walter Burley, foil in debate to the more controversial William of Ockham. In medicine there was John Gaddesden, author of one of the great textbooks of the age, the *Rosa Medicinae*. In astronomy there was a succession running from John Maudith, who recalculated astronomical tables from Arabic sources to make them usable for observers in Oxford, to Simon Bredon, who bequeathed his astrolabe to the College. In mathematics there was a similar chain leading to Richard Swineshead, known simply as The Calculator. Robert Wickford, a lawyer, ended up as chancellor of Ireland. Particularly wide-ranging was Thomas Bradwardine, a trenchant theologian who also applied geometry creatively to problems in mechanics. Rewarded with the archbishopric of Canterbury, he died of the plague in 1349. Equally brilliant but more wayward, in the eyes of the powers that be, was John Wyclif, a junior Fellow in the 1350s. Starting as an extreme realist philosopher, he ended as a theologian who questioned central teachings about the mass, lay access to the Bible, the church's authority and the way to salvation, inspiring waves of Mertonian followers long after he had moved on to Balliol and Queen's.

Building work continued through the century. The great arches of the crossing were added to the Chapel in the 1330s, followed by the south transept. Mob Quad was completed with the two ranges containing the Library on their upper floors in the 1370s. Property acquisitions continued, extending the College site westwards, over what is now the site of Corpus Christi College, and eastwards towards Rose Lane. Endowment continued, now for specific ends. Several former Fellows gave money and books for the Library and in the 1380s John Wyliot founded the Postmasterships, five-year scholarships for undergraduate students. One of the Fellows was to oversee these students' conduct, as Principals of

the Postmasters have done ever since. But in the background it was the Warden and Fellows' careful oversight of Walter de Merton's legacy, the manors and churches with their tithe income or other profits, through a period of agrarian upheaval, that kept the College prospering.

The fifteenth century was a bad time for landlords, as lower population in the wake of the plague drove down rents and prices. The College, like others, turned from direct management to leases, sometimes for long or repeated terms, in the hope of a steady income. Profits were not sufficient to expand the number of fellowships, as successive Visitors urged the College to do. But together with donations from successful alumni such as John Kemp, cardinal, archbishop of Canterbury and chancellor to the troubled Henry VI, they sufficed to press ahead with building. First came the north transept of the Chapel, then, from 1448, the majestic Chapel tower. Expansion of the Warden's House in the south-east corner of Front Quad followed, and in the 1460s the Gatehouse, a reminder of the Wars of the Roses with its Yorkist badges. The political troubles of the time touched the College closely when a former Fellow, John Stacey, and a chaplain, Thomas Blake, were convicted of treason for making astrological calculations to predict the deaths of Edward IV and his son.

Fortunately Merton soon found it had friends close to the ascendant Tudors. Richard Fitzjames, Warden from 1483, Henry VII's almoner, put the king's arms and badges on the archway he built to join the Warden's House to the Hall and on the new ceiling of the Library. John Chambers, Warden from 1525, was one of Henry VIII's doctors. It was under his wardenship that the College arms were carved, surrounded by the Tudors' red and white roses, for display in the Hall. Richard Rawlins, elected Warden in 1509, was perhaps too close to the court for the College's comfort. He welcomed Katherine of Aragon on a visit in 1518 and accompanied the royal couple to the Field of Cloth of Gold. But he fell under the influence of the powerful statesman Richard Fox, bishop of Winchester, and negotiated the transfer to him of the western end of Merton's site for his new college, Corpus Christi. The Fellows certainly agreed at the time, but seem later to have held the sale against Rawlins, whose removal as Warden they secured in 1521.

Mertonians found themselves on both sides in the religious storms of the Reformation. Richard Smith served as Regius professor of Divinity under the Catholic Queen Mary and ended up in exile as chancellor of the University of Douai. John Jewel went into exile under Mary, to return as bishop of Salisbury under Elizabeth and write the *Apologie* in defence of her Protestant settlement. Those left in charge of the College did their best to steer it through unscathed, enabling Henry Savile and

Opposite, left: A physician's quadrant, c.1400–50, now kept in the Library. Principally intended for time-telling, it also carries an engraved male figure known as a zodiac man to provide astrological guidance for techniques such as bloodletting. Opposite, right top: The crossing arches of the Chapel. Opposite, right bottom: The ceiling of the Chapel bell-tower (see p. 88). The lantern aperture in the centre, when open, allows the bells to be lowered to the ground. Above: The Gatehouse vault, with the Virgin and Child and heraldic badges including the sun in splendour, a padlock and a ram's head (see p. 52).

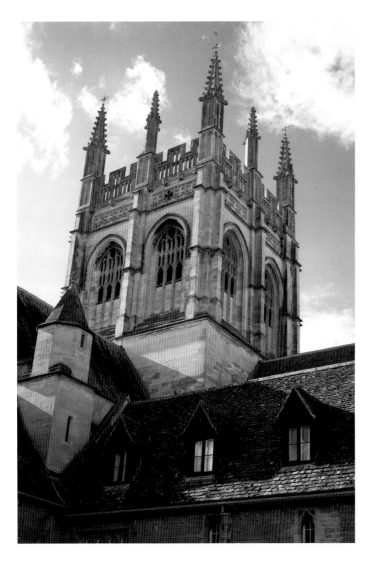

polish useful for a career in the world. The College's accommodation was greatly expanded by the building of the stately Fellows' Quad in 1608–10. Scholarship was turned to public service. Sometimes this met with resounding success: one of the committees working on the Authorised Version of the English Bible at the command of King James VI and I met in Savile's Warden's Lodgings. Sometimes it led to disaster: Henry Cuffe, the Fellow and Regius professor of Greek who gave political advice based on the classics to Elizabeth's over-reaching favourite, the earl of Essex, was executed for his pains.

Merton's next greatness was thrust upon it. Warden Brent, who installed the fine wooden staircase that now leads to the Breakfast Room, took the side of parliament in the Civil War. His Lodgings were thus conveniently vacant when Charles I made Oxford his capital and were commandeered for Queen Henrietta Maria, who slept not, it would seem, in what has become known as the Queen's Room, but in the Warden's dining room, in the warmer interior of the Lodgings. Brent was replaced at the king's command by the royal physician, William Harvey, thus giving the College its most renowned participant in the Scientific Revolution. Brent's return and the election of moderate successors ensured that Merton passed more smoothly than many colleges through the Interregnum and Restoration.

The building projects of the later seventeenth and eighteenth centuries suggest a fellowship that knew how to enjoy itself, whether contemplating the gardens from the Summer House of 1709, now the Music Room, or indulging in volcanic feuds with the Wardens. Those of the 1670s, chronicled by the former Postmaster, antiquarian researcher and long-time resident of Postmasters' Hall, Anthony Wood, formed the backdrop to the panelling of the Senior Common Room and Sir Christopher Wren's refurbishment of the Chapel. Those of the 1730s produced no buildings, but epic volumes of complaints by Warden Wyntle against the Fellows and vice versa, featuring unruly dogs in Chapel services, the controversial sacking of the College barber and a Library left in neglect as 'an old Ruinous Place'. The College's tone between the Glorious Revolution and the French Revolution was predominantly Whig in a largely Tory University. It harboured a series of comfortable clerical, legal and medical men but also researchers into antiquities, languages and literature, as well as John Wall, founder of the Royal Worcester Porcelain Works, Richard Steele, first editor of *The Spectator*, and David Hartley, who negotiated peace with the American Revolutionaries.

Thomas Bodley to lead it into a period of glowing good health in the later sixteenth and early seventeenth centuries. Rising population and rising prices were reflected in rising rents on the College estates, partly pegged to the cost of grain by a helpful act of parliament of 1576. The new studies of the Renaissance – Greek, Hebrew, ancient and medieval history from the original texts, geography and Copernican astronomy – were cultivated with vigour. The Library was refitted and restocked.

Undergraduate numbers increased with the admission of gentlemen commoners, studying under tutors not to gain a degree under the still largely medieval University syllabus, but to acquire knowledge and

The nineteenth and early twentieth centuries brought university reform, imposed by government and generated from within, new subjects of study, and new construction projects. While the High Church enthusiasm of the Oxford Movement led to a medievalising of the Chapel from the 1840s, the first University Reform Commission of 1852 brought in Fellows who were not clergymen, and from 1871 they were allowed to marry. It also introduced larger numbers of students,

....

*Opposite: The Chapel tower. Above: The bust of Sir Thomas Bodley in the Library, copied from that of 1605 in the Bodleian. **Right top:** The Summer House. **Right bottom:** The kitchen pump of 1785, now in the garden (see p. 105).*

for whom the Grove Building, with its coloured brick interiors, was put up in 1862–3 – only to be reduced in height and refaced in stone in 1930 – and the Hall rebuilt in 1872–4. By 1882 the 35 undergraduates of 1851 had become 111. In 1881 Merton absorbed the adjoining St Alban Hall, and in 1904–10 its buildings were replaced by St Alban's Quad. Sales of land to the University, other colleges and railway companies helped to finance new posts and new buildings, including a grand new Warden's Lodgings of 1908, now the Old Warden's Lodgings. Rowing, cricket and tennis were taken up and a Junior Common Room established.

The domestic and administrative staff increased and houses in Manor Road and Manor Place were built to accommodate them. Teaching in the natural sciences expanded and diversified and new humanities subjects came in too, with English literature and modern history. But older disciplines held their own, above all philosophy, where the idealist F.H. Bradley was a powerful force. Mertonians went into politics and the law, producing two lord chancellors, the earls of Birkenhead and Halsbury, and a chancellor of the exchequer, Lord Randolph Churchill, but also pursued a range of other careers. Overseas

students began to trickle in. During and after the First World War they provided the College with some of its most famous alumni, notably T.S. Eliot and Theodor Adorno, who were attracted by the philosophy teaching of Bradley's successors Harold Joachim and Geoffrey Mure. Literary interests were widespread between the wars – Edmund Blunden, Keith Douglas, Louis MacNeice and Angus Wilson all studied or taught in the College, and J.R.R. Tolkien arrived in 1945 – but the scientific tradition also remained strong, exemplified by Bertram Lambert, the chemistry tutor who made a vital contribution to the invention of the gas mask, and a succession of zoologists including the Nobel laureate Nikolaas Tinbergen.

The aftermath of the Second World War brought further expansion in student numbers, up to 255 by 1948, 388 in 1993 and 661 in 2012. The Rose Lane buildings, completed in 1940, stood ready to receive them and new tutors, funded by land sales in suburban London and new investments in equities, to teach them. More new subjects were taken on: biochemistry and computer science, modern languages and music, economics, politics and management. Further accommodation

was provided in Rose Lane V, built in 1964–5 at the same time as the new Warden's Lodgings in Merton Street, and by the adaptation of houses in Merton Street and Holywell. The 1930s had seen the first modern graduate scholarships and the body of graduate students grew steadily from a small proportion in the 1940s to the current parity with undergraduates. The physical symbol of their arrival was the Jowett Walk building (1993–4) and they made a large contribution to the internationalisation of the student body. In 1980 the College admitted women as Fellows and students, as most of the men's colleges had done, and now the proportions of men and women are similar to those across the University.

New challenges face the College and University in the twenty-first century, but it has striven to meet them without losing a sense of its past. That mood might be summed up in its newest buildings. The Finlay Building blends in with Postmasters' Hall, parts of which are older than the College. The T.S. Eliot Theatre, slid in among the Rose Lane blocks, looks back not only to a great alumnus, but also to the lectures which have been at the heart of Oxford's teaching ever since Walter de Merton's day. It is fitting that our collection of treasures culminates with them.

*Opposite, top: Ralph Carr, Fellow, by Lewis Vaslet, 1790 (see p. 98). **Opposite, left:** The Grove Building as it looked before remodelling in 1930. Before construction the Governing Body had already toned down the 'bands of coloured stone' in the original design by William Butterfield, who would go on to design Keble College. **Opposite, right:** The Old Warden's Lodgings. **Above, top:** The Rose Lane buildings. **Above, bottom:** An oar from the victorious Women's 1st VIII in Torpids, 2003. **Right:** The Jowett Walk building.*

SECTION ONE: MEDIEVAL MERTON

THE FOUNDER'S STATUTES

Roger Highfield and Steven Gunn

Walter de Merton gave his College three sets of statutes, in 1264, 1270 and 1274. While the first gave the College its corporate legal identity and is thus rightly regarded as its founding document, only the second and third gave it the constitutional form which has since become characteristic of all colleges in Oxford and Cambridge. The 1264 statutes were issued in a lull in the civil war between Walter's master King Henry III and the baronial reformers led by Simon de Montfort. They were made possible in mid-September of that year by two events. The baronial regime released Walter's lands from confiscation and his feudal overlord Gilbert de Clare, earl of Gloucester, came of age: he was now in a position to confirm the property transactions necessary to endow the College with the Surrey manors of Malden and Farleigh. These first statutes established the House of the Scholars of Merton as the embodiment of Walter's charitable provisions for the promotion of education and the maintenance of prayer for his soul. They gave it a Warden and two or three priests for his colleagues, and set it to support 20 scholars studying at Oxford. They lent it some features of the self-government which was to be characteristic of later colleges. The most senior of the scholars, who would have been studying for higher degrees, were to monitor the Warden's management of the College's resources and were to be involved in choosing future Wardens. But it was to be based not in Oxford but at Malden and overseen by the bishop of Winchester, in whose diocese Malden lay. The bishop and his cathedral chapter duly sealed the statutes together with Walter and the king, whose approval was shown by the charter's enrolment on the royal charter rolls.

Several years' experience of operation gave birth to the statutes of 1270, twice the length of the first set. The base at Malden was maintained for the Warden and priests, but there were now to be two Sub-Wardens, one to assist at Malden but the other to oversee affairs in Oxford. The scholars' studies were more closely defined. They were mainly to proceed through the arts course to philosophy and theology, though there was some provision for the more careerist path of Roman and canon law. The bishop of Winchester's role was reduced and the College tied more closely to the University. The royalists having defeated Simon de Montfort, Walter now had many more lands with which to endow the College, and arrangements for their administration were accordingly more complex. By 1274 circumstances had changed again. King Henry had been dead two years and Walter had been leading the government as chancellor while the new king, Edward I, returned from Crusade. His arrival freed Walter to retire from the chancellorship, take up the bishopric of Rochester, and concentrate on his College. His final statutes, sealed by Walter and the new king, built on those of 1270, but defined much more precisely the duties of the Warden, presumably with an eye to the need to replace the founding Warden, Peter of Abingdon, sooner or later. Three Bursars were now to take care of finances, meetings were to be held three times a year to conduct College business and an as yet unnamed Visitor – it would soon be the archbishop of Canterbury – was to help resolve crises in place of the bishop of Winchester. All was to be based in Oxford, and while horses would be necessary so the estates could be inspected, their provision was regulated to prevent waste.

The far-sightedness of the founder is evident at many points in the statutes, which, though revised at various times, have stood the College in good stead. From 1264 onwards there was an insistence that the College should increase the number of its scholars as its resources allowed and an encouragement that those who had benefited from the foundation should in turn remember the house in the days of their prosperity. By 1274 there was an awareness that, 'inasmuch as all future cases cannot be beforehand comprised in any certain law or statute', the fellowship should be empowered to cope with change by making new 'observances and statutes'. In place of excessive prescription, there was repeated exhortation to good practice: the Warden and Fellows were to administer the College with 'good faith and prudence' and 'with all skill and attention'. Above all – an admirable aim, though one not always attained – they were to preserve 'unity and mutual charity, peace, concord and love'.

....

*Insert: Walter de Merton's seal, with his motto 'Qui timet Deum faciet bona', 'He who fears God shall do good'. **Opposite**: The statutes of 1264, sealed by King Henry III, the bishop of Winchester, Walter de Merton, and the Winchester Cathedral chapter.*

HEBREW STARRS

Peter E. Pormann

ew documents have had a more interesting fate or testify better to the involvement of Jews in the early history of Merton College – and Oxford University more generally – than the two starrs (or Hebrew quitclaims) to be discussed here. At issue is a conveyance of land in Gamlingay, Cambridgeshire. One William de Leicester ran out of money in the early 1260s and turned to a Jew, Abram de Vives, for a loan, secured on his land in Gamlingay. Although he should have repaid his loan by 1263, William was still unable to do so in 1268. But Jews could not foreclose on Christian debtors, and their legal status was becoming more and more precarious. This is when Walter de Merton stepped in. Familiar with the court of the Exchequer of the Jews as chancellor, he bought up bad debts owed to Jews such as this. By 1268, Abram had died and his widow, Esther, had remarried Josce, son of Benedict. Their situation must have become quite desperate, because they ceded the debt to Walter de Merton.

The two starrs confirmed that Josce no longer had any claim on the land in Gamlingay that William de Leicester had pledged, while a corresponding Latin quitclaim confirmed that William de Leicester had ceded his land to Walter de Merton. To put it differently, in the Hebrew document, Josce, the Jew, confirmed that he no longer had any claim on the land in Gamlingay; and in the Latin document, the impoverished William confirmed that his land now belonged to Walter de Merton. Of course these documents, historical monuments that they are, still confirm the current legal status of the estate, as it is still in the College's possession.

Yet the starrs in question also followed a rather colourful itinerary away from, and back to, Merton. Originally, the two starrs were kept together with the Latin deed of conveyance in pyx (or box) V in the College archives. The Hebrew deeds were stitched into the larger Latin document. But at some stage, the Hebrew documents were separated from their Latin counterparts. In the early eighteenth century, the Lord Almoner's professor of Arabic, J. Gagnier (*c.*1670–1740), transcribed the Hebrew documents and translated them into Latin. Later, John Fowell

(1725–1803), who was the chaplain of Merton in 1750, sent both Hebrew deeds to Joseph Kilner, a Fellow of Merton, with the request to have them translated. He was particularly intrigued by the fact that the documents refer to 'Sir (שׂר) Walter de Merton'. Kilner must have passed them on to Benjamin Kennicott (1718–83), sometime Regius professor of Hebrew at Oxford, for from the latter half of the eighteenth century until the 1960s, they remained in Kennicott's estate. Only when Lambeth Palace bought the estate and its librarian, Dr Bell, sifted through the documents did he notice that these Hebrew starrs really belonged to Merton. In an act that seems inconceivable nowadays, he simply returned the starrs to Merton (more than a century and a half late). There I discovered them anew when I joined the College in 2001, and had the privilege to edit, translate and interpret them.

The College has a number of other Jewish documents, such as the deeds relating to the site of the College with two pendant seals representing the Lion of Judah (believed to be the earliest examples of Jewish seals in England). But two further starrs particularly deserve to be mentioned here: in one, William de Watville cedes land to Walter de Merton, and in the other, Stephen Chenduyt grants Walter de Merton the manors of Cheddington and Ibstone. Both were translated into Latin by Thomas Bodley. Bodley was himself a keen Hebraist, and his translation of the documents attests to the Renaissance interest in acquiring the 'third language'.

For me personally, these documents bring to life the early history of our College in vivid, yet also heartbreakingly painful ways. On the one hand, they show that Jews played a role, perhaps an important one, in the early history of the University. They lent money, rented out properties, and even produced bilingual Hebrew-Latin manuscripts to allow Christians to read the Old Testament in the original language. And yet, they also illustrate how a shrewd Christian, moving in the higher echelons of society, could exploit the legal uncertainty from which the Jews suffered and which, eventually, led to their expulsion from England in 1290.

....

Opposite: This charter, enrolled in the Exchequer of Jews in 1271, shows how Hebrew starrs were attached to Latin grants of property. By it Robert de Percy conveyed land at Barkby in Leicestershire to Walter de Merton for his College, unencumbered by any debt to Cok Hagin of London.

KIBWORTH

Michael Wood

I n the upper chamber of the Muniment Tower – the oldest custom-built archive repository in Britain – are two runs of tall varnished wooden cupboards. On the drawers are the stencilled names of manors, Ponteland north of the Tyne, Cuxham in Oxfordshire, Cheddington and Thorncroft in Surrey, and three drawers for Kibworth in Leicestershire. The association of Merton with Kibworth is one of those happenstances which are the fallout from great events in history. In 1264 Walter de Merton's plans to endow his College were interrupted by the revolt of Simon de Montfort. The rebels ran amok, looting and burning barns on Walter's estates around the village of Merton in Surrey. Among them was Saer de Harcourt, who held manors in Simon de Montfort's Leicestershire heartland, including Kibworth. When

the reckoning came after de Montfort's death, Saer was spared but bankrupted by his fines, and at that moment Walter stepped in with an offer Saer could not refuse.

Walter's purchase document of £400 (between five and ten million today?) survives in the archive: a small, folded packet of crisp cream parchment, still bearing Saer's seal. What Walter got for his money was a manor house with a mill, 11 free tenants, men and women, and nearly 40 families of tied villeins and cottagers, working around 1,000 acres of arable. Merton has been the landlord ever since. But for that reason Walter's purchase has also left Merton with one of the very best archives for any place in England; an archive that opens up the working lives of everyone who has lived in the village for most of the last 750 years. To

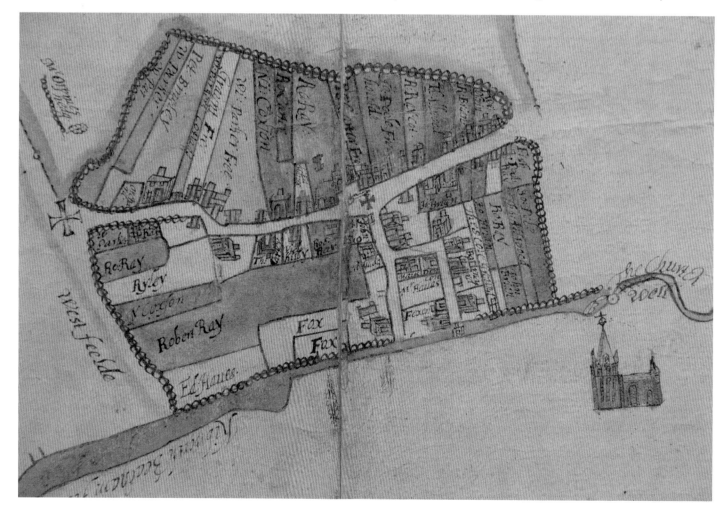

take at random the 1280 survey: along with the free and unfree tenants, the ploughmen, threshers and smiths, there are for example Alice the washerwoman and Robert *medicus*, a freed serf. So rich is the detail that it has even proved possible to define relationships, map inheritance, and to trace family trees of some families, such as the Sibils, Herings and Browns; the Polles in particular are here for 15 generations, from the 1260s to the 1600s.

The archive is a historian's delight whose riches are still only partially explored. Here are court rolls from the 1270s to 1700; bailiffs' accounts year by year from 1283 to 1682; rentals from Henry III to 1527, some still with their notched tally sticks inked with 'Kybbeworthe'. Here too is a vast miscellany of other records, terriers, lease books, tithing lists, repair bills, building accounts, letters, maps and miscellaneous bundles of deeds. There is even a letter from the village butcher to the Fellows from the 1440s, presumably written by the village notary or clerk, but a real rarity to have a peasant's letter so early. The beautiful hand-coloured maps of the village and its houses, the earliest from 1609, have proved invaluable in reconstructing the village morphology. Though the College's houses were mostly sold after the Second World War, it still owns the fields and one of the farms, and it still plays a role in the community with the Warden's visits every three years, and memorable concerts by the Merton choir which pack St Wilfrid's with enthusiastic Kibworthians.

The Kibworth archive gives a wonderfully intimate portrait of a very diverse peasant community as it was transformed over time by plague, war and developments in society and economy; above all by the slow almost imperceptible push of change from below by the people themselves. But the archive also shows how the local story always reflects the national narrative: the Great Famine of 1314–18; the Black Death; and the fascinating impact of Lollardy here at the grass roots in the countryside, where the seepage of ideas can be traced back to Fellows who frequently made their journeys to Kibworth to meet with local sympathisers, galvanised by Vicar Hulman, another Mertonian Wycliffite. Great events are no less marked in the later parts of the archive: the change from labour services to cash with the rent strikes of the 1430s; the religious tensions of the Reformation; the Civil War, when the village was occupied by both sides; the Enclosures of 1779 during the Agricultural Revolution; and the Industrial Age with the coming of the canals, railways and framework knitting. The films we made about Kibworth in 2010 excited the imagination of the British public, from Elgin to Devon, and from Antrim to Essex, and have brought American tourists and student groups to the village. The story of Kibworth is the story of England in microcosm, entwined with the story of a college which has itself played no small role in the history of the nation.

*Opposite: Estate map of Kibworth, 1609. **Above:** The survey of 1280. Alice Launder (the washerwoman) appears on the ninth line, paying rent for her cottage, below Roger Molend[inarius] (the miller).*

THE EARLY WARDEN'S HOUSE

Robert Peberdy

Between the late thirteenth and mid-fifteenth centuries Wardens of Merton College occupied a house at the north-east corner of Front Quad. Part survives as the Middle Common Room and its basement. It differed from lodgings at many later colleges, which were sometimes combined with fellows' chambers or else placed in a prominent position, usually over a gatehouse as if to symbolise a head's authority over his college. At Merton the early lodging was effectively a separate, modest building, possibly with its own garden, which was marginal on the main site. These characteristics appear to reflect the Warden's role in Walter de Merton's evolving educational schemes, his limited status within the academic community, and the related disposition of collegiate buildings.

The post of Warden predated the creation of an integrated college community, and may originally have been envisaged as an administrative office subordinate to a religious house. Walter de Merton's original idea, in 126?, was to establish an endowment for supporting university scholars vested in Merton Priory (Surrey). His intended gift comprised two manors in three parishes, and these would have required management. Such an arrangement would have resembled the organisation of some Benedictine monastic estates, when individual manors, or groups of manors, were entrusted to a warden or supervisor (*custos* or *supervisor maneriorum*). Though Walter de Merton's scheme was not implemented, a warden is recorded at one manor in 1263. When the Warden of Merton appears in the 1264 statutes, he was the administrator of a divided entity. He was to live at Malden in Surrey, receive manorial profits, and provide allowances to the scholars at Oxford or elsewhere, with the senior ones being required annually to investigate his management. The Warden's initial lodging was probably Malden manor house, where the first Warden, Peter of Abingdon, created a household.

Subsequent developments at Oxford provided a coherent group of buildings for the scholars and placed the Warden alongside them. Between 1266 and 1268 four properties were acquired in an area where the underlying plots originally had a street frontage of three perches (49½ feet). The first property, called a 'court', occupied three plots and contained a church (St John the Baptist). The others, to the east (Front Quad), consisted of three houses and gardens, each probably occupying a plot. Though the Warden's House is not mentioned until 1283, he was probably allocated the easternmost house at an early stage, perhaps in 1268–70, leaving space behind the other two, nearest the church, for a communal hall (built by 1277). A gateway was provided opposite the Hall entrance, and later a Treasury was built between the Hall and church (1288–91).

The Warden and his household moved to Oxford in about 1270. His new lodging, called Flixthorpe's House after its previous owner, was probably L-shaped, with a 'hall range' parallel to the street and a cross-wing on the eastern side. Its street frontage of three perches equated to the widest 'standard' post-Conquest urban tenement. Thus the Warden occupied a substantial town house, ranking him with wealthier merchants and parish clergy. By now he was required to supervise ten manors and several churches.

In 1299, after John of Wantage became the fourth Warden, the lodging was reconstructed. Merton College was now one of Oxford's grandest places, with its large communal Hall and a new church. Perhaps the new Warden thought that his lodging similarly deserved upgrading. It is unclear how much of Flixthorpe's House was rebuilt, but the work included removal of a street entrance, replacement of the hall roof, and insertion of new windows on the south side of the hall and on the west side of the cross-wing – similar in style to those of the new church. The work created a grander-looking frontage as seen from within Front

Quad. Inside, the hall (two-thirds of the street range – the surviving section) was enhanced by the new roof, which survives. Its construction is unusual, innovative and rich, including six vertical 'queen posts' on the cross-beams with moulded capitals and braces, and three higher 'crown posts', also with mouldings. The two-storied cross-wing probably included the Warden's chamber and a kitchen.

From the wardenship of Henry Sever (1456–71) onwards, some Wardens desired grander residences and extended the House round Front Quad and beyond. The trend culminated in the replacement, grandiose 'Old Warden's Lodgings' of 1908. But since 1947 Wardens have preferred more modest residences, akin in size and location to the first Warden's House in Oxford.

....

*Opposite: The west end of the Warden's Hall, now the Middle Common Room. **Above:** The roof of the Warden's Hall, looking west.*

MANUSCRIPT OF ARISTOTLE'S
METAPHYSICS

Julia Walworth

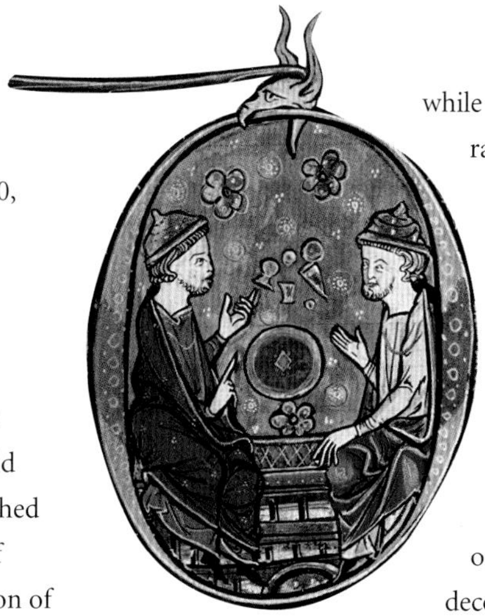

This manuscript book, now Merton MS 269, was probably made in Oxford between 1250 and 1280, in the same decades that Walter de Merton was devising and refining the plans for his new College. It is an academic volume containing a single text, Aristotle's *Metaphysics*, accompanied by a commentary by the twelfth-century Islamic philosopher Ibn Rushd, known to the Latin world as Averroes. Text and commentary are distinguished by the use of two sizes of script, with a section of commentary in small script following each section of text. Vertical and horizontal rulings in the margins provide space for the reader to add notes, and at least one reader also used the wide spacing of the main text to add interlinear explanatory glosses. Large colourful initials clearly mark the beginning of each major subdivision of the *Metaphysics*, with book numbers in Roman numerals in the top margin providing orientation for the reader. Among the relatively few surviving illuminated copies of Aristotelian texts from the thirteenth century, an illuminated *Metaphysics* is unusual. The historiated initials, use of gold and silver, and wide margins indicate that this would have been an expensive book.

At the time this manuscript was written Aristotle's *Metaphysics* had only been available in the west for a few decades. It was one of several key works by Aristotle that had recently been translated into Latin and spread rapidly: by the 1250s the arts faculties of the universities of Paris and Oxford had adopted them as textbooks. They generated a great deal of intellectual excitement and also, initially, fear of the spread of pagan ideas and of a philosophical structure not based on Christian cosmology. While Paris had for a time banned the teaching of some of Aristotle's works, Aristotelian studies thrived in Oxford, though they concentrated more on his ideas in natural philosophy – what we might think of as science – than on the *Metaphysics*, a difficult and abstract text.

The illustration depicted here shows how that text could find visual expression. In the initial 'D', two philosophers, identifiable by their Phrygian caps, long mantles and beards, are seated facing each other at either end of an elaborate bench. Their hands are raised as they gesture while disputing with each other. The man on the left has lifted his right hand with a raised index finger, perhaps to indicate that he is holding forth while the man on the right responds. In the space between them, rather mysteriously, is a large grey and white circle, above which several gold circles and other small gold shapes appear to float in mid-air. The artist has attempted to refer visually to the subject of debate, using imagery that was perhaps more easily understood by the medieval reader of the book than by the viewer today. This chapter of the *Metaphysics* (IX) deals with substance and potency (potentiality). It is possible that the circle represents matter and the gold objects above the forms or actualisation of potency. They were clearly not mere decoration, as they are included in the faint outline sketch to guide the artist that can be seen in the right-hand margin just under the modern folio number. Such sketches do not usually survive, as they were erased after the manuscript was completed.

The date at which this manuscript came to Merton is uncertain. It was associated with Mertonian Richard de Cleanger (Fellow *c.*1331–46), and it appears in the *electio* or borrowing lists of the Library in the 1370s. The monetary value of the book appears to have been useful for some of the later Mertonians, as partially erased inscriptions indicate that it was 'pledged' or pawned by several Fellows to raise ready cash.

The university context for which the manuscript was made is evident in its subject matter, the design of its pages and the iconography of the figural decoration in the initials. Training of advanced students involved participation in formal disputations, the student arguing one side or the other of a question or problem and the master acting as 'judge' in the debate. Like today's students in tutorials, scholars were encouraged to consider opposing views, to find evidence to support their arguments and to use conflicting evidence to reach new conclusions. Quiet study led on to vigorous and vocal exchanges and in manuscripts like this philosophical debate could continue across centuries, as students and scholars added their own comments and notes. Through text, commentary, marginal notes and the imagery of debate, this book is filled with many voices.

Insert: The philosophers in debate. **Opposite:** *The manuscript with text, commentary and reader's notes.*

e ente-
ctum ett
tribuun
tur ali
a p dic
entus u

t diftinguemus ⁊ loq
uemur de potentia ⁊
complemento ⁊ de pot
entia primo Et qd
dicitur magis uere in
illud quod non eft uia
re in hoc quod uolum
us nunc potenciam en-
⁊ actus dicuntur multi
magis quam illa qu-
e dicuntur secundu
modum modus tan
tum sz cum dicem
us de differentus in
actu tunc declarabit
ur ultima dra

ui dictum eft de fubftan
tia dicitur enim ena
a multa secundum qd
recipiunt diffinitione
fubftancie ut quantit
eas ⁊ qualitas ⁊ alia qu-
e dicuntur hoc modo o
mnia enim habent di
ffinitionem fubftancie
ficut diximus in prim
is fermonibz Et cum
dicitur aut enia hoc
aut quantum aut qu-
le aut enia eft in pote
ncia ⁊ ⁊plemento ⁊ actu

THE HALL DOOR AND OTHER MEDIEVAL DOORWAYS

Alan Bott

The College has six doors dating from the thirteenth to the fifteenth centuries. Besides those described below, there are also the south and north doors of the Chapel, both dating from before *c.*1425. There is also the little-seen inner door between the Treasury below and the Muniment Room above (1289–91). Locks for the windows of this building were acquired in 1289 and locks and keys were refurbished in 1291. The door still retains its three locks.

Hall Door (*c.*1274–7)

The first surviving reference to the Hall is in the Bursar's roll of 1277, when minor carpentry work was being done there. It is likely, therefore, that the great entrance door antedates this remedial work. The Hall,

it seems, has always had an undercroft below it, as shown in Loggan's print of 1675. This has meant that the entrance to the Hall has always been by a flight of steps, at least partly covered by a porch. In 1579, the porch was rebuilt, in part funded by a donation of £10 from the Warden. The long existence of a porch accounts for the un-weathered patina of the magnificent door. This is composed of four planks of timber. The delicate ironwork on it consists of two 'Cs' and a central strap, all of which form the hinges. The principal ironwork is elaborately adorned with scrolls, which terminate in leaves and stamped, eight-petalled rosettes. Originally the door had a pear-shaped handle, but this was replaced with the present fine, animal-headed handle, by Sir Gilbert Scott in his restoration of the Hall in 1874.

Library Door (*c.*1378)

The building of the Library to the south of the Chapel, by the erection of two ranges of buildings to the south and west of those already in existence, produced what was to be Mob Quadrangle. This, indeed, almost inadvertently, created the first college quadrangle in Oxford. The work was powerfully advanced by the donations of William Rede, Fellow and bishop of Chichester since 1369. In 1374, he gave the College £100 and 100 books. The building works were conducted by the Bursar, John Bloxham, who became Warden in 1375. His master mason was William Humbervyle, who was also employed by Edward III at Windsor Castle and by the Black Prince at Wallingford. The doorway to the Library, at the south-west corner of Mob Quadrangle, has moulded and shafted

jambs. It has a square head with delicate, traceried spandrels in stone surrounding the wooden door. This, which is of rather inferior quality to the surrounding stonework, is nail-studded and has strap-hinges. Part has been restored. John Bloxham's accounts (1372–5) speak of 'a new door bought from the Carmelite Friars for 6s 8d'. Perhaps this is it. The Carmelites had acquired a house (near the present Worcester College) where they remained until 1318, when Edward II in fulfilment of a vow made at Bannockburn in return for his safe escape, granted them his palace at Beaumont Fields, nearby. The Carmelites continued to receive benefactions and in 1373 Thomas Heathfield left them his tenement, on the death of his wife, to be sold by the Brethren for his 'soule's sake'. Perhaps the Library door at Merton originated in such circumstances.

The two corbel heads on either side of the door are much eroded. This is perhaps accounted for by the fact that with the building of Fellows' Quadrangle in 1610, the 'Little Quadrangle' (Mob Quadrangle) became the exclusive residence of the junior members of the College. The rooms to the east of the doorway, below the Library, were, until the end of the nineteenth century, undergraduate sets. Both Lord Randolph Churchill and Max Beerbohm were accommodated here in the 1860s and 1890s respectively. The origin of 'Mob Quad' most likely derives from its eighteenth-century description as 'the small quadrangle (vulgo, Mob)'. This in turn suggests occasional riotous undergraduate behaviour in this Quadrangle!

College Gates (*c.*1465)

Although the College was authorised by Henry V to construct a battlemented tower with a 'licence to crenellate' in 1418, the Gatehouse in fact dates from 1465. It was much restored by Edward Blore in 1838. All that now survives from the 1460s exterior are the carving of St John the Baptist above the lintel of the doorway and the great gates themselves. These consist of two leaves. Each has five cinquefoil-headed panels with vertical tracery in the four-centred head. In the east leaf there is a wicket gate. The keys are modern replacements, but the gates themselves have served the College for almost six centuries.

Opposite: The Hall door today and as drawn before 1872–4, when a new handle was made for it. **Above:** *The Library door.*

COLLEGE SEALS

Roger Highfield and Julian Reid

One of the distinguishing features of Walter de Merton's foundation was its corporate status as a legal entity that could own property and make decisions conjointly. For centuries the visual expression of this authority was the seal, used both to authenticate documents and to keep their contents private. Seals had been used by earlier cultures – examples survive from the Egyptians, Greeks and Romans – but were not widely used in post-Classical Europe until they appeared in royal chanceries in the eleventh century. By the thirteenth century their use had extended to the church – by bishops and heads of religious houses – to civic corporations, and across various strata of secular society. In 1449 Margaret Paston exemplified the potent authority of the seal when presenting her husband's claims to the manor of Gresham in Norfolk: the seals on the Pastons' title deeds were 200 years old while those of their counterclaimant were, she maintained, recent forgeries, their wax 'not yet cold'.

The statutes issued by the founder in 1264 were authenticated with four seals, including the great seal of Henry III, that of John Gervais, bishop of Winchester (in which diocese the College's earliest estates lay), and the dean and chapter of Winchester. The College was just coming into existence, and so the fourth seal was not its own but that of Walter de Merton. By the time that the second set of statutes was issued in 1270, however, the College had been in existence for five years, and in possession of its own seal. The image chosen was highly appropriate to a college or fellowship: five souls, represented by small human figures, gathered in a towel or napkin in the bosom of Abraham. The image was surrounded by the inscription, 'SIGILL[UM] SC[OLARIUM] DE MERTON'. The concept of the bosom of Abraham as a place of succour or repose first appeared in Jewish writing during the period of the Second Temple (*c.*500 BCE to 70 CE), but had its immediate origin in the parable of the rich man and Lazarus in the gospel of St Luke (Luke 16:19–31) and became established in Christian iconography in the twelfth century. It was sufficiently familiar in the sixteenth century for Shakespeare's audience to recognise Mistress Quickly's confused reference to the soul of the dead Falstaff being 'in Arthur's bosom'.

As the seal was pendant, that is, suspended from the document by means of a strip of parchment or length of cord, the wax was impressed on the back with a second image. The image chosen – the head of John the Baptist – was also highly significant, since the parish church of St John the Baptist was among the earliest Oxford properties acquired by the founder, in 1266. Oliver Sutton, bishop of Lincoln, gave permission for the church to be demolished and a new chapel built to replace it, provided that proper provision was made for the parishioners to worship. The new Chapel was in due course dedicated jointly to St John the Baptist and the Virgin Mary, whose statues still greet people approaching the College from Magpie Lane, and who remain the College's patron saints.

By the 1330s, however, this first seal had been superseded. The new seal abandoned both Abraham and John the Baptist in favour of a figure of the Virgin Mary holding the child Jesus, seated beneath a pinnacled canopy. The seal was no longer round but of a *vesica*, or pointed oval, shape; a shape often adopted by churchmen and religious communities. Both the shape and imagery had been adopted by the Augustinian priory of St Mary, Merton, with which the founder was closely associated, by the mid-thirteenth century, and it is impossible not to think that this had influenced the College's decision. The choice may also reflect the College's adoption of the Virgin Mary as a patron alongside John the Baptist. At the base of the seal is a kneeling figure with hands raised in prayer, reminiscent of the oft-repeated kneeling figures in the fourteenth-century stained glass in the Chapel. About the seal in Lombardic script is the inscription, 'S[IGILLUM] SCOLARIUM DE MERTONA AD C[AU]SAS'.

The College is fortunate in preserving not only several wax impressions of the seal attached to documents, but also the original brass matrix for sealing documents. Technology changes, and the matrix and sealing wax have been replaced by a press that stamps the College seal directly onto the document, but the design adopted by the College more than 600 years ago remains the official means of authenticating College business.

....

*Insert: The bosom of Abraham seal. **Opposite:** The brass seal matrix of the 1330s and a wax impression of it from a charter of the 1340s.*

THE TREASURY

Julian Reid

The medieval Treasury is one of Merton's oldest buildings, but few Mertonians or visitors ever get to see inside it. Mindful of the need to have somewhere in which to secure the College's portable wealth, as well as its title deeds and financial records, the early Fellows built a strong room in what is now the north-east corner of Mob Quad as proof as possible against the threats of theft, fire and flood. Like the Library, it is located on the first floor, both to restrict access and to

raise it above the risk of flood. A stair turret that projects from the west side of the building is entered from the vestibule to the Sacristy. Heavy oak doors at both the bottom and top of the stairs, each originally secured with three locks, bar access to the room. A separate key opened each lock, requiring different key-holders among the senior Fellows, limiting the risk of theft or embezzlement. The use of wood in the structure was kept to a minimum, with the walls, staircase, and the roofs of both lower and upper chambers supported by stone vaults. It is the stone arches of the vault of the Treasury that give the roof its distinctive pitch.

The Treasury was completed in 1291, when 14s 7d were paid for the laying of its tiled floor. The chequer-board of black and honey-coloured tiles still survives. The thick stone walls are pierced with small windows on the east and west sides, and high in the north gable; the broad splays of the embrasures make the most of the natural light, reducing the need for candle or oil-lamp. Lockable chests added extra security to the room's contents. A lock on one of the chests was repaired in 1294, and the chest in which the account rolls were kept was repaired in 1299. The title deeds were also kept in locked chests, with the different estates distinguished by a different letter of the alphabet written on both the deeds and on the chests in red or blue: A–G for Surrey, H–K for Kent, and so on. An inventory taken at the start of Richard Fitzjames's wardenship in 1483 gives us an idea of how much medieval plate was later lost to the cause of Charles I in the Civil War: ten salt cellars of silver or silver gilt, six standing cups, an ablution basin (a precursor to the Jacobean rosewater bowl), and more than 30 other silver dishes for various uses. The College's cash reserves also comprised £90 15s in gold, and 12s 5d in silver 'both good and bad'. The Postmasters enjoyed their own plate, with Wyliot's Chest housing eight matching silver dishes, four silver salts and a pair of silver spoons. It is likely that the rosary of jet and crystal beads had been left as a pledge against which money had been borrowed.

By 1587 the College records were in disarray, and the College appointed John Savile, barrister of the Middle Temple and brother of Warden Savile, to inspect the 'writings, deeds and muniments' and put them in order. It may have been at this time that the College decided to give up storing documents in chests and to replace them with cupboards of wood panelling ranged around the walls. Individual cupboards could be reserved for different estates, with the deeds stored in small wooden boxes, with the name of the estate written either on a slip of paper or parchment on the lid, or directly onto the side of the box. A joiner was

paid for making half a dozen such boxes between 1606 and 1607, and several examples are preserved in the Treasury to this day.

Ever creative in its use of space, in November 1826 the College considered converting the room under the Treasury into a bakehouse, with the Treasury itself being reserved for the storage of flour. Thankfully this conversion did not take place, and in 1842–3 the cupboards in the Treasury were altered; it may be from this period that the present cupboards date. The Elizabethan panelled doors were retained, but the shelves inside were replaced with rows of drawers, once again labelled according to the estate. This was the last major re-fit of the Treasury and, while a new archive room for more recent records was provided in the Finlay Building in 2004, the Treasury continues to house many of the College's early estate records; testament to the forethought of the earliest Fellows.

*Opposite: The Treasury seen from Mob Quad. **Above:** The interior of the Treasury, with document boxes on the table. **Right:** The nineteenth-century drawers, including that for Kibworth (see pp. 26–7).*

THE MEDIEVAL STAINED GLASS

Tim Ayers

The eastern arm of Merton College Chapel contains one of the best-preserved schemes of early fourteenth-century stained glass in England. Of the 15 windows, the glazing in the 14 three-light windows on the north and south sides is more or less intact. Typical of the period, the design allows in a great amount of light, comprising a brightly coloured band of figures under canopies, set against white glass boldly painted with scrolling foliage and decorated with coloured ornaments. In each window, the coloured band centres an Apostle or an Evangelist. In 12 windows, these figures are flanked by kneeling scholars, each with a Latin inscription claiming that 'Master Henry de Mansfield made me'; the two windows on the south side of the sanctuary include saints in these positions. The east window once formed the centrepiece of this planned scheme, but the main lights were replaced in 1651 and their figurative contents are not recorded. They may have included christological subjects, however, like their eighteenth-century replacements. The tracery retains its original glazing, in a dazzling display of colour, incorporating heraldry and the Annunciation.

Just as Walter de Merton's foundation established new standards for the graduate college in the late medieval university, in its statutes and fabric, so the church that was begun for it in 1288–9 was planned on an unparalleled scale. The windows of the eastern arm were, and still are, its most exceptional feature architecturally. The glass that filled them also expressed in various ways the character of this new kind of institution, in the place where its members gathered for worship and celebrated their place within the body of Christ, on earth and in heaven. In the east window, the arms of England and of the de Clares, earls of Gloucester, royal benefactors and overlords of the founder's lands in Surrey, respectively, marked the place of the College within the kingdom of England. Gathered around Christ, often shown ruling with him in heaven, the Apostles were represented in contemporary churches of many kinds. As the first Christian community, they were highly appropriate to a new kind of community of secular scholars, preparing for service in royal government or the institutional church.

Praying before them are shown 24 scholars, all in caps and gowns, and associated with the name of Henry de Mansfield. There is no equivalent for the extent of this commemoration in contemporary English glass. It has been observed rightly that the closest comparison is with the multiple images of Queen Eleanor of Castile (d. 1290) on the Eleanor Crosses and on her tombs, established by her husband Edward I. Mansfield was a Fellow of the College by 1288–9, graduating later as a master of arts and a doctor of theology. At the time when the glass was made, he was chancellor of the University of Oxford, so his career was flourishing. This commemoration of an alumnus is the first of countless examples in the stained glass of educational institutions around the world. The relationship between word and image is, in fact, ambiguous: the inscriptions proclaim Mansfield's donorship, rather than that the figures represent him. They may do so, but they differ strikingly in facial type and gown colour, leaving open the possibility that this is a representation of the College itself. Either way, they mark the choir as a space special to secular scholars of this kind.

The glazing of the eastern arm is also exceptional for the amount of documentation that survives for it in the College archives. The construction of the building is recorded between 1288–9 and 1296–7. Its subsequent furnishing included a delivery of glass for the church in 1305–6, from Thame (Oxfordshire). Then between November 1310 and May 1311, there are recorded deliveries by cart of a further 25 loads; in such quantities, and in the context of other activity, this must also have been for the church. No recipient is named for the payments, but in 1307 and 1310 other payments were made to a glazier called William de Thame. The recorded delivery of glass from Thame itself suggests that he was based in the town, and a glazier of this name is listed there in a tax roll for 1306 and a charter of 1317. So it is highly likely that the deliveries in 1310–11 were from this business. If so, William is – with the Master Walter who worked at Exeter Cathedral at the same time – one of the two earliest named glaziers in England whose work survives.

....

Insert: The rose in the east window. **Opposite:** *St Mark or St Matthew, holding a white palm and a scroll, with a scholar on either side, the heads of St Paul, a queen and a prince and a pelican feeding its young.*

THE BRASSES IN THE CHAPEL

Alan Bott

In his statutes of 1274 Walter de Merton provided that the Fellows, as they had enjoyed the society in their lives so, in death, they should each have the right of burial in the Chapel (*cum suis sociis atque confratibus ecclesiasticam in sua morte habeant sepulturam*). Of the 1,000 or more persons known to have been buried or commemorated in the Chapel and churchyard since 1300, nearly 200 were members of the College, including 17 Wardens. The remaining 800 burials were members of the parish of St John the Baptist (in which the College is situated). There now remain 70 College monuments in the Chapel. Of these, 23 originally had brasses with effigies and inscriptions. Although the matrices of these memorials can generally be identified, only seven figures in brass, including three Wardens, still survive.

Originally, the thirteenth- and fourteenth-century monuments were placed in the choir. From the fifteenth century, the graves of Fellows were placed under the tower or in the south transept. One exception was Warden Sever (d. 1471), who was buried in the choir. However, in the 1650s, disaster was to strike twice in the Chapel. In 1655, Anthony Wood recorded: 'Oct 17, Wednesday, in the vigil of St Luke, part or half of the roof of the south part of Mert. Coll, outer chappel, joyning to the tower, fell within the church, about 9 of the clock at night and broke all the stones laying in the floor, of which some were monumental stones.'

But, according to Richard Rawlinson, it was 'the sacriledge of an army of reprobates under the countenance of a rebellious Parliament' which was to be responsible for much further desecration. Wood elaborated, describing how, in 1659, it was decided to paint over 'in oyle colours the pictures of prophets, apostles, saints, etc on the backside of the stalls in the choir. While the workmen were performing this work, several of the brass plates, with inscriptions, on gravestones were most sacrilegiously toren, and taken away, either by sum of the paynters, or other workmen in the chappell.'

The great refurnishing of the Chapel in the 1670s included the laying of square black and white marble stones, arranged diamond-wise, throughout the choir. As a result, a payment of £2 1s 5d was made in 1673 for 'cutting & laying ye great marbles, taken out of Quire, at ye ascent to ye screen'. They were then placed in the north transept. The brasses of Warden Bloxham and John Whitton and of Warden Sever, however, were placed on either side of the steps leading up to the altar in William Butterfield's restoration of 1848–51. They were again re-set in their original matrices in the north transept in 1996. Three, at least, of the remaining brasses are of special importance. Richard de Hakebourne, 1322, Fellow, is the second-earliest surviving ecclesiastical brass in England. The monuments to John Bloxham, 1387, Warden, and John Whitton, *c.*1390–1400, Fellow, and the great brass of Warden Sever, 1471, are splendid examples of the fourteenth and fifteenth centuries.

*Left: Richard de Hakebourne, 1322, Fellow. **Above:** John Bowke, 1519, priest. **Opposite, left:** John Bloxham, 1387, Warden, and John Whitton, c.1390–1400, with the inscription from their brass below. **Opposite, right:** Henry Sever, 1471, Warden.*

THE BURSARS' ROLLS

Julian Reid

The College's earliest domestic accounts date from 1277, and are essential to our understanding of Merton in its earliest centuries. It is from them, for instance, that we know the names of early Fellows. They cover a wide range of activities and were maintained in several series. The Warden rendered an annual account for the income and expenditure of his household, and the Sub-Warden for various revenues and expenditure, in particular maintenance of the Chapel and Library. Three Bursars each year were appointed from the fellowship, each accounting for a four-month term for the income from College estates and all the regular household expenses. Founder's kin were entitled to be educated at the College under the direction of a Supervisor, whose annual accounts survive irregularly between *c.*1300

and 1459. The Principal of the Postmasters rendered an annual account for his administration of Wyliot's Foundation. Out of the 140 years until his separate accounts ceased in 1519, 108 rolls survive. As far as buildings are concerned, the single most important series is the 11 accounts kept from 1286 onwards by Walter Cuddington as Master of Works.

The accounts are written on parchment, and vary greatly in size depending on the office. The longest are those generated by the Bursars, which may be several feet long, sometimes made of several pieces of parchment sewn end to end, with supporting documents enclosed or bound to one end. None of the series is complete, but they are the oldest accounts of any college in Oxford or Cambridge. Rebuilding and relocation are often agents of destruction, from which colleges are not immune. The earliest accounts of University College (relocated in the 1330s) begin in 1381, while those of Balliol survive no earlier than 1544 and, even then, only in a later transcript. In contrast, Merton's existence on the same site for 750 years, and the preservation of its medieval Muniment Room, has meant the survival of over 800 account rolls.

The College Hall was already complete by the time the accounts begin, and the late 1280s saw attention turned to the building of a new Chapel, the accounts recording the process in minute detail: loads of stone and timber, glass and metalwork; carved stonework and doors; and the wages of craftsmen – masons, carpenters, plumbers, sawyers and labourers. We can almost picture the scene. A century later, it was the Library under construction, the process itemised in similar detail. Then as now, food was a central item of domestic economy. The church's imposition of a meat-free diet for much of the year must have challenged the most inventive of cooks, especially in a town so removed from the sea, where preserved fish was the staple. The many watercourses around Oxford, however, helped to provide variety, and the customary salt fish was occasionally supplemented with the likes of pike, tench and eel. But on high days the kitchen could furnish the best that local and distant markets could provide, with rice, almonds, sugar 'from Alexandria', pepper, ginger and saffron all making their appearance.

Fellows, who might be called on to serve as Bursar, had to be men of business as well as of books. They would be expected to be able to ride, and might spend many days in the saddle on College business. In the summer of 1336, John Vilers spent two weeks journeying to and from Lincoln and his itemised daily expenses survive rolled up in the relevant Bursar's account. He had celebrated his arrival in Lincoln with a wash

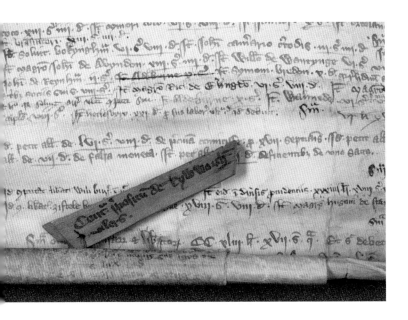

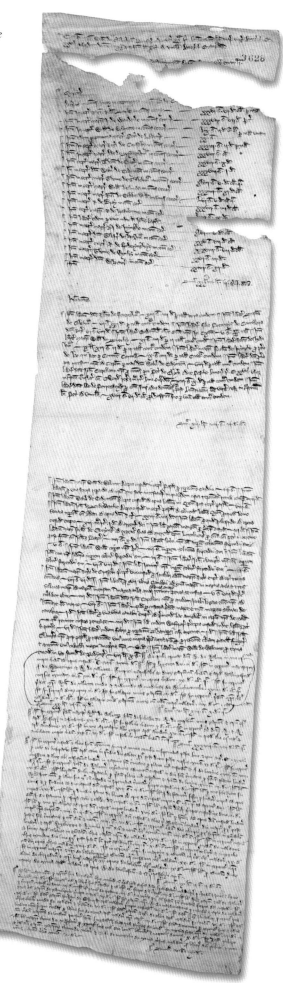

and shave. In an age when not all were literate, many sums of money were accounted for with tally-sticks, slips of wood notched to indicate the sums involved. Of the many hundreds that must once have existed, a sole example remains, sewn into the base of John Vilers' bursarial account of 1335, recording dues from Kibworth, Leicestershire.

Accounts written on strips of parchment, in paragraphs rather than in columns, with the numbers in Roman rather than Arabic numerals, are not the most transparent accounting medium, yet the practice proved remarkably tenacious. Separate account rolls of the three Bursars lingered until the advent of Warden Savile in 1585 when, for the first time, accounts were entered in a single book. An accounting system that had survived for 300 years was a thing of the past, but the rolls remain, a vital repository of College memory.

....

*Opposite: A selection of medieval rolls. **Above:** The roll of 1335 with its wooden tally for 'kybbworth'. **Right:** The account roll of William de Chelesham, Third Bursar, March–August 1299. The payments include 2s to John of Stanton for cutting out a gown and tabard for the Warden, 1s 4d for a pair of shoes bought in London for the Warden, and 13 marks (£8 13s 4d) for a palfrey or riding horse for the Warden. Wages were paid to the laundress, William the head cook, and John the assistant cook, and three swans for the feast at Malden cost 13s 4d.*

THE ASTROLABES

Stephen Johnston

Geoffrey Chaucer's 'Miller's Tale' is centred on the cuckolding of a carpenter, gulled by the astrological expertise of an Oxford scholar. The young clerk, Nicholas, is both quick-witted and learned, while also susceptible to worldly temptation. By his art he can predict the weather, and evidently resolve myriad questions of individual and communal destiny. The poet appears untroubled by the dangers of the powerful knowledge the youthful Nicholas has at his command – there is no Faustian bargain here. It is not Nicholas's soul but his body that ultimately suffers in the story. Admittedly the carpenter exclaims that men should not pry into God's secrets, but astrology was clearly a legitimate passion and delight for an adventurous scholar.

Chaucer fills out his portrait of Nicholas with the trappings of the art: on a bookshelf by his bed, pride of place goes to the ancient classic of astronomy, Ptolemy's *Almagest*, along with the most emblematic of medieval astronomical instruments, an astrolabe. This was no fanciful poetic licence. Surviving medieval lists show that the scholars of Merton College had access to a fine set of instruments as well as a rich astronomical library. Nor did Chaucer stumble on the appropriate equipment for Nicholas by lucky guesswork. By the later fourteenth century, astronomy and astrology were of much more than merely academic interest. Chaucer's own fascination led him to incorporate elaborate astronomical imagery in his poetry. He even compiled one of the earliest scientific texts in English – a clear and readable treatise on the astrolabe.

The survival of a particularly sophisticated astrolabe among several astronomical instruments now kept in the Upper Library demonstrates both the pleasure and power which such devices conferred, and Merton's leading role in the medieval science of the stars. To a substantial brass disc are attached two moveable parts: a rotating ruler (one end of which is now broken) and, underneath it, a more elaborate structure of circles and arcs, bands and pointers – a combination of geometric and organic forms known as the rete (Latin for net or web). The rete's off-centred circle carries a zodiac scale on which the sun can be located for any day of the year, while the tip of each of the pointers represents a bright star. Like the ruler, the rete rotates. Its centre is the celestial north pole – the fixed point around which the heavens

appear to turn. In one revolution of the rete the sun and each of the stars are rotated through a complete circle: a day of 24 hours has passed.

By capturing and mimicking the visible movements of the sky, the astrolabe literally provides a handle on the cosmos, a mirror of the heavens. The great dome of the sky becomes a disc which can be admired, contemplated, grasped and controlled. But it is also much more. With the help of the pair of projecting sights on either side of the suspension point, the instrument becomes a clock, telling the time by sun and stars rather than wheelwork and weights, a compass pointing out direction with no need for a magnetic needle, and a general-purpose measuring instrument for surveying and calculation.

This example is unusual in several respects. It is constructed only for the latitude of Oxford, whereas most contemporary astrolabes were made with several interchangeable plates so that the instrument served for a range of places. It is significantly larger and more precise than normal, reinforcing the impression that it was made for a scholar to use rather than just for prestigious display. Finally, the reverse carries a much rarer device, an equatorium – indeed the earliest example to survive engraved in metal rather than drawn on parchment or paper. Now unfortunately incomplete, this sophisticated addition expanded the reach of the instrument beyond the sun and stars to include the planets too. For an astrologer casting horoscopes or a physician determining the influence of the heavens on sickness and health, the equatorium was intended as a boon, abbreviating the laborious business of calculating planetary positions from astronomical tables. This Merton astrolabe reduces much of the practice of medieval astronomy into a single, exceptionally potent object.

The instrument is unsigned and its exact route to Merton is uncertain. But we can be confident of its date. The reverse carries a small table so that the equatorium can be kept in step with the longest-term cycles of astronomy. The table runs from 1350 to 1450, placing the instrument's origins firmly in Merton's period of mathematical pre-eminence and looking forward to at least a century of further use.

Opposite: The dense network of engraved lines in the upper half of the astrolabe provides a co-ordinate grid against which the sun and stars can be located when observed in Oxford. Insert: A detail of the equatorium on the reverse of the astrolabe.

LICENCE IN MORTMAIN, 1380

Julian Reid and Julia Walworth

The endowment of the College in 1380 by John Wyliot with discrete properties for the maintenance of undergraduate scholars marked an important development for Merton. Earlier financial accounts indicate that scholars supported by Merton were living in Oxford beyond the walls of the College. Housed in Pennyfarthing Street, they may have included both undergraduate and graduate students, but they disappear from the accounts after 1347.

John Wyliot gave the College property in Oxfordshire, Hertfordshire and elsewhere to maintain scholars already qualified in grammar to study arts for up to five years, thus establishing the admission of undergraduates to Merton on a permanent basis. One of those properties, Battes Inn, was in Oxford itself, on the site of what are now Nos 119 and 120 St Aldate's. By the late 1490s the property was known as the Fleur de Lys, and during the seventeenth century was leased to members of the family of the Oxford antiquary Anthony Wood, himself a one-time Bible Clerk of Merton. While No 120 was exchanged with the Corporation of Oxford in 1854, No 119 remains in College hands. In 1279 the property had belonged to Moses, son of Jacob, from whom Walter de Merton had purchased part of the site of the College. But it was not until 1374 that a group of current and former Fellows, including Wyliot and the Warden, William Durrant, acquired the property, apparently with a view to bestowing it on the College. In July 1378 the property was taken into the custody of the Crown, on a charge that the Fellows had failed to obtain the necessary licence to buy it, in order to avoid the statutes of mortmain. Property held in mortmain (literally 'dead hand') was property acquired by an enduring owner, such as the church or a corporate body like a college, so removing it from the property market and also removing its liability to customary or feudal dues. Statutes enacted in 1279 and afterwards banned grants of property in mortmain made without a royal licence.

By 1380 the king's officials were satisfied that the Fellows had not intended to defraud the Crown, and on 5 October Richard II issued a royal licence confirming the College's ownership. The importance of this transaction for the College is demonstrated by the unusually rich decoration of the licence document that was brought back to Oxford from London. The large sheet of parchment is dominated by an elaborate illuminated initial letter. The upright of the 'R' (of 'Ricardus') is filled by an image of the youthful and fashionably dressed king holding a sceptre in his left hand. He extends his right hand to give a sealed charter, the licence itself, to the kneeling Warden of Merton (John Bloxham, who had succeeded William Durrant in 1375), who reaches up to receive it from him. Clustered around the Warden are several tonsured figures in fur-trimmed academic gowns representing the Fellows of the College. The initial is further decorated with exuberant ivy and foliage extensions, while the bowl and tail of the letter are formed by the bodies of two dragons with entwined heads. The result is a striking composition that reveals something of the relationship between the monarch and the College. The contours of the letter 'R' form a distinct royal space, which the king breaches in order to hand the charter to the waiting members of the College. The Warden and Fellows, although kneeling well below the king, are larger figures. As a united group firmly planted on the grassy earth they outweigh the willowy figure of the sovereign.

Decorated royal documents such as this were not commonplace, since it was the recipient, not the king, who would have arranged for the decoration and paid the artist. The style and technique employed in the Merton licence suggest that the decoration might have been added in London just after it was written. This type of initial, in which the parts of the letter itself are formed by figures, and the technique of delicately modelled pen-and-ink drawing were at this time just being adopted in England and were probably inspired by examples from France. The Merton document was thus in the forefront of artistic fashion at the time it was made and as such has a place in the history of English medieval art. In distinction to many works of art, the document still has legal force, and in 2006 was produced as the College's proof of title for the St Aldate's property.

....

Left: The St Aldate's property marked on the Ordnance Survey map of Oxford, 1876.
Opposite: The upper left portion of the licence with its illuminated initial.

Ricardus dei gra et rex Anglie et Francie et dominus hibnie Omnib3 &c
dominis scolarium de merton in Oxon et eorum Willo Duraunt et
chamdour Thomas Gyne Waltus Brampton Johannes Ball
eis ptm vna cum celario shopis et solariis eidem adiacentib3 in Ox
degenciu pia misericordia comoti mesuagium siue hospiciu pd
in auxilium sustentacois pauprum scolarium in scolis degenciu ex licencia regia quouis
colore cum ca magnificois p Excecutorem dm E nup Regis Angl aui nri in com Oxon
Thomas Waltus Johannes et Ricus dam mesuagiu siue hospiciu cum ptm cum celario
ea maxim Oxon sibi et successorib3 suis ad opus de donis siue licencia regia in fraude
edit adquisiuerunt pdm hospiciu cum ptm captm sint in manu am ipm cupiata et siue
in Curia nostra allegauimus qd ipi dm hospiciu cum ptm in feodo sibi et heredib3 et assi
et collusionem statuti pda adquisiuerunt pnt pdcam magnificocem supponebat comptum
Beston Johem Thoma Waltum Johem et Ricm captam ipi pdci Johannes Wills Besto
absq3 fraude et collusione statuti pda adquisiuerunt et inde coram nobis consideratu
cium cum ptm vna cum exitib3 ppisienis medio tempore ppris pfatis Joh Wilto Best
coram nob hita plenius potit apparere Ac iam pmissis non obstantib3 colore cuiusdam in
quorundam emulor ipos Custodem et scolares suiare machinanciu capte p quam psentariu
pmeuacois felonie pda in villa Oxon vnu mesuagiu cu ptm vocatu Battesyn cum cela
Wills Duraunt quonda Custos donus pda et magr Johes Wilhot quenda socius eiusde
mippm siue licencia regia in fraude et collusionem statuti pda dam mesuagiu siue hosp
cio maliciose paisata ac minus vera existat p dcm Excecutorem nrm captu oit in manu nra
rio shopis et solariis adiacentib3 ut paisat laborib3 et expensis quos ipi circa psecucod
nram disimilit sustinuerunt p sonabili fine ni hac pte nob soluend p securitate domus pte
impetu vel magnieraji Nos ad fructum multiplicem quem collegiu donus pte de cuius sta
pinde p incremento fructuoso eiusdem domus ex beniuolencia regia gidose pvidere de cisi
et Ricio sub illa intencoe de gra nra confisi totum ius et clameum quos ipi in pdco mesuag
heie potint insuper nob et heredib3 nris relaxauerunt et ipe et heredib3 suis mippm amc
soluerunt deminus et concessimus p nobis et heredib3 nris pfatis Custodi et scolarib3
heien et teneren vna cu exitib3 inde a tempore capcois pte in manu nram ppris et
in scolis degenciu de nob et heredib3 nris p diuica inde debita et consueta mippm Ac et

CATALOGUS VETUS

Michael Clanchy

The *Catalogus Vetus* (meaning 'The Old List of Names') is the earliest list of members to survive from an Oxford college. It was started by Thomas Robert, who compiled the names of 509 Fellows (including himself), reaching back over 150 years to the foundation of the College. He may have started it when he was a Bursar in 1411–12, as his notes for it are found on the backs of the College's account rolls on which he worked. He provides no explanation as to why he took this initiative. It is strange that Merton, with its strong institutional foundations, had not possessed a register of its Fellows from the start. Robert seemed to know of no earlier list, as he had considerable difficulty extracting the individual names from hundreds of enrolments in the College accounts. He was undertaking the first piece of archival research to be done at Merton.

The *Catalogus Vetus* begins with the name of Peter of Abingdon. He comes first because he was the first Warden and also because his surname begins with the letter 'A'. Robert arranged the names of the Fellows alphabetically and within groups by the reigns of kings: from Edward I (1272–1307) through to Henry V (1413–22). The number of Fellows rose from around 30 in the 1280s to over 50 in the 1330s, but it fell back to 30 in the decades following the Black Death in 1348. Robert's list is unusual in providing the surnames only of the Fellows and in being arranged in alphabetical order, as this took no account of precedence or seniority. There are exceptions to the surnames only rule, however, as Robert designated his contemporaries in Henry V's reign by both baptismal name and surname and he preceded his own name with an embellished capital 'T' for Thomas. Ordering by surname distinguishes Robert's list from the books of remembrance in which churches (at Durham and Winchester, for example) recorded the baptismal names of those for whom they prayed. Robert's list is not religious but historical; this is what makes it so unusual.

In 1422 Robert retired to the major Merton living of Kibworth Harcourt, leaving the *Catalogus Vetus* with the College. Soon anonymous improvers began adding the names of Oxford's famous scholars: the polymath Roger Bacon, the

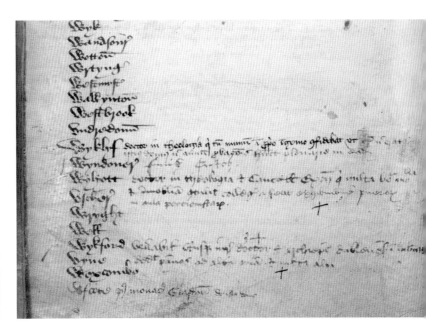

astronomer and horologist Richard of Wallingford, the philosopher John Duns Scotus and the logician William of Ockham. These additions are crudely done; in the case of Bacon the forename 'Rogerus' has simply been added in different ink before the surname 'Bakun'. None of the added names appear in the College accounts; but some accounts are missing and they cannot therefore guarantee that Robert had listed every Fellow. At the least, the added names indicate the high regard the Fellows had for the *Catalogus Vetus* and the distinction they expected their colleagues to achieve.

Robert's list lends itself to tampering because the names are written in the left-hand margin with the rest of each line blank, as if inviting readers to make additions. By the name 'Burley' for instance someone has added: 'doctor of theology and he was a profound philosopher'. This is the Aristotelian Walter Burley, who was a Fellow of Merton in 1305 and of the Sorbonne in 1324. A 'beloved clerk' of Edward III, he presented his commentary on Aristotle's *Politics* to Pope Clement VI in 1343. The most prominent Fellow to combine royal service with academic distinction was Thomas Bradwardine, 'doctor profundus', mathematician, logician and theologian. Late in life he recalled the companionship of 'his beloved brethren the Warden and Fellows of Merton hall', where he had been a Fellow from 1323 to 1335. A counsellor of Edward III, he preached the victory sermon celebrating

the battle of Crécy in 1346 and was rewarded with the archbishopric of Canterbury. The most controversial Fellow in Robert's list was John Wyclif; against his name someone has noted that he failed to complete his probationary year (and he had therefore not been a full Fellow).

The additional notes give the *Catalogus Vetus* a crude appearance which belies the achievements of the Fellows in royal service as much as in international scholarship. In 1417 the College recorded the names of the 'very many' Merton men, headed by the Warden, who were serving Henry V in occupied France. The *Catalogus Vetus* is a modest product of this triumphant time. Even in its contentious additions, it is a monument to the success of the College in its formative years.

....

*Opposite: The opening page. The list of Fellows begins with 'Petrus Abyndon', the first Warden, on the fourth line. 'Rogerus' has been speculatively added to 'Bakun' in line nine and Walter Burley comes two lines later. **Above, left:** Thomas Robert, the author, appears in line nine as 'T Robt', just below Thomas 'Rudborne', Warden in 1416–17 and later bishop of St David's. Further up the list is Andrew Newman, noted to have given the College a beautiful new missal and £6 towards building work in the Chapel. **Above, right:** John 'Wyklyf', the controversial theologian, is the ninth Fellow listed, followed by John 'Wyndover', Warden from 1387 to 1398, and then by John 'Wylyott', founder of the Postmasterships.*

THE MANOR OF HOLYWELL

Robert Peberdy

The Manor of Holywell is an area of Oxford which was part of Merton College's endowment from the later thirteenth century. It extends from Holywell Street northwards to the University Parks, and is bounded on the west by Parks Road and on the east by the River Cherwell. It was in two ways atypical of the early endowment: unlike the College's other manors, it was not received as an independent unit but attached to a church; and it was given by an outside benefactor rather than the founder. It was small compared with most manors in lowland England, but thanks to its location it has proved an advantageous resource.

The manor passed into Merton College's nominal ownership in 1266 with Henry III's gift of St Peter in the East Church (now St Edmund Hall's library). The gift doubtless rewarded Walter de Merton's long service to the king and Henry's prominent place in the foundation. In the College's 1264 statutes, Henry's soul had been specified as the first spiritual beneficiary, and Henry had confirmed the statutes with his seal. He donated St Peter's at an early point: soon after Walter de Merton's initial donation of two manors (1264) and the start of land-buying in Oxford (1266). It was the principal donation from the royal family, and one of only seven early gifts by outsiders. The others included a share in Holywell Mill.

St Peter's had been founded probably in the tenth century to serve a new eastern extension of Oxford, and Holywell Manor was created in the tenth or early eleventh century as a compact estate to the north and north-east. It was named after a well to the north-east of Holywell Street. Around 1100 a chapel dedicated to St Cross was built near the well, and a manor house was provided (often also called Holywell Manor and now occupied by Balliol College's graduate centre). In 1266 St Peter's and its endowment were under Henry III's ultimate control as patron, though they were held by an absentee rector. The church was served by a vicar, who received a small income and provided chaplains at Holywell and Wolvercote. After St Peter's passed into Merton's ownership, the College obtained permission from the bishop of Lincoln, in whose diocese Oxford lay, to 'appropriate' or legally acquire the rectory's assets. But this did not take effect until the rector's death in 1294. Holywell Manor then became a directly held lordship from which Merton College derived income and over which it had considerable jurisdiction. It held courts for its tenants until 1864, and in 1337 even hanged a thief.

Holywell Manor comprises about 235 acres (95 hectares). Until the nineteenth century it consisted of two contrasting parts: Holywell Street, which was lined with buildings and was effectively a suburb of Oxford, and the remainder, which was rural in character. Landholding within the manor was unusual, in that most land (possibly three-quarters) was 'demesne', land reserved for the lord's use rather than held from him by peasant tenants. The dominance of demesne meant that Merton could maintain extensive control untroubled by tenants' customary rights. The tenants were mostly 'cottagers' with holdings of a few acres who lived along Holywell Street or nearby. In the fourteenth century cultivation of the demesne lands, apparently open fields, was managed for the College by officers. Much of the corn crop was sold in Oxford, with fluctuating profits going to the College. Thereafter the lands were leased, which provided a steady income. From the fifteenth century pasture was increasingly prominent, and the lands were enclosed. In 1672, 152 acres were grassland.

From the mid-nineteenth century Holywell Manor changed into a built-up area. Unlike St John's in North Oxford, Merton did not promote development according to a comprehensive plan. It sold land mainly in response to academic-related initiatives, accommodating currents of change. The University bought land for its new Museum (1854–5) and Parks (1860–5); some was later used for expanding the science area. Other sales were made for the Holywell range of New College (1870s–90s), Mansfield College (opened 1887), Manchester College (1893), and playing fields (late nineteenth century). Non-

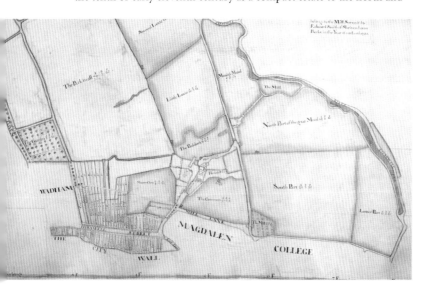

Dav. Loggan Delin. et Sculp. cum Privil. S. R. M 1675.

academic developments included sales for houses (1860s–70s), and provision of a garage in Longwall Street from which William Morris launched the Morris Oxford car (1912). Merton built houses for College servants (1890s), and in the late twentieth century accommodated Fellows and junior members, and built the Holywell Buildings (1995). By the early twenty-first century Merton owned little land in Holywell Manor, but more Mertonians than ever before were benefiting from Henry III's benefaction.

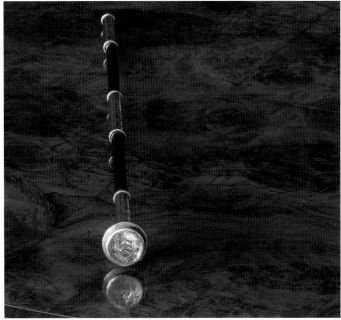

Opposite: An estate map of Holywell, 1758. Above: David Loggan's map of Oxford viewed from the north, 1675. Holywell Street is in the centre, outside the city wall, Holywell manor house and St Cross Church stand at the lower left and in the foreground are Civil War fortifications. Right: The reputed rod of the steward of Holywell Manor, topped with the College arms.

THE SCULPTURE OVER THE GATEHOUSE

Alan Bott

The College had been in existence a century and a half before attention was turned to erecting a Gatehouse worthy of the noble buildings within. On 4 April 1418, Henry V granted Warden Thomas Rodebourne a licence to build an embattled tower, but nothing further seems to have been done for half a century, as works on the Chapel consumed the College's financial resources. Between August 1464 and April 1465, however, a sum of £9 6s 4d was spent on 'the making of the great gate of the college' by master mason Robert Janyns, who had earlier been employed in the building of the Chapel tower. Two masons were paid for 'working on the stone of St John for seven weeks' and Janyns was paid 2s 6d 'for his labour concerning the positioning of that stone and of the Trinity about that same work'. In the statutes of 1264 the founder invoked the Trinity, the Virgin Mary and St John the Baptist. A demi-figure representing the Trinity appears in pictures of the Gatehouse in 1621 and 1675, but had disappeared by 1733.

Fortunately, the 'stone of St John' or, as Anthony Wood called it, 'the History of St John the Baptist' survives. This very interesting work in Taynton stone, brought down in 1838 by Edward Blore to its present position over the lintel of the Gate, summarises symbolically the major doctrines of the New Testament. On the right is St John the Baptist carrying a book, the harbinger of Christ. The life of Christ is variously represented: his incarnation and exaltation (the unicorn); his sacrifice (the Lamb of God and the pelican in its piety, feeding its young from its own breast); his Resurrection (the lion); the Holy Spirit (the dove); the sun of righteousness. In the centre is the Book of Seven Seals, described in the Book of Revelation and symbolic of the Day of Judgement. Above, perched in the foliage on the left, is another bird, which at least resembles an eagle, the symbol of St John the Evangelist, the putative author of the Book of Revelation. The seven trees in the background each represent a different species. John Pointer, chaplain, in his description of the carving in 1749 thought that they were a reference to Palm Sunday, but more specific symbolism can be identified. From the left, the foliage and fruit seem to portray the pomegranate (eternal life) or apple (tree of knowledge); the orange (fecundity); the ash (tree of the universe), box or hornbeam; the oak (fidelity); the beech (tree of nuts signifying the church) or sallow (medieval substitute for palm); the walnut (its shell standing for Christ's human flesh covering his divine nature) or myrtle; the poplar (humanity). In the foreground, the conies, which are being hunted by hounds, may represent the checking of

waywardness – or just be delightful decorations. Attendant upon these mysteries is the kneeling figure of Walter de Merton, bishop of Rochester. John Pointer's description does not completely accord with the present appearance of this carving, which may suggest that it has undergone some alteration during restoration. Certainly 'the Serpent, condemn'd to creep on the ground, whose head 'twas prophesy'd our Saviour should break' seems to have disappeared. Further, it seems curious now, that Pointer could have identified the two figures as 'the Baptist in the habit

of a monk and our Saviour himself coming after him with the Dove over his head'. The figure of Bishop Walter de Merton is certainly original. Anthony Wood, who noted that the carving was (erroneously) 'supposed to be a relic of the old collegiate Church of St John Baptist, Merton', records that the sculpture, having been defaced during 'Oliver's raigne' (1653–8), was 'repaired and new oyled over in white colours' in 1682. It was again repaired in 1897 after the head of a hound was knocked off during preparations for the Queen's Jubilee illuminations, and weathered details were re-carved in 1954–5 by the sculptor Edgar Frith.

Below, and contemporary with the sculpture above, are the great oak doors of the College. Within, the 17 bosses of the vault also include large representations of the Virgin and Child and St John the Baptist. Others refer to Yorkist and Lancastrian heraldic families, appropriate to the date of construction of the rest of the Gatehouse, between 1464 and 1465. The statues of Edward I and Walter de Merton were re-carved during the restoration of the front of the College, including the Gatehouse, by Edward Blore in 1838.

*Opposite: Walter de Merton, bishop of Rochester, with rabbits and unicorn. **Above:** The sculpture over the Gatehouse, 1464–5.*

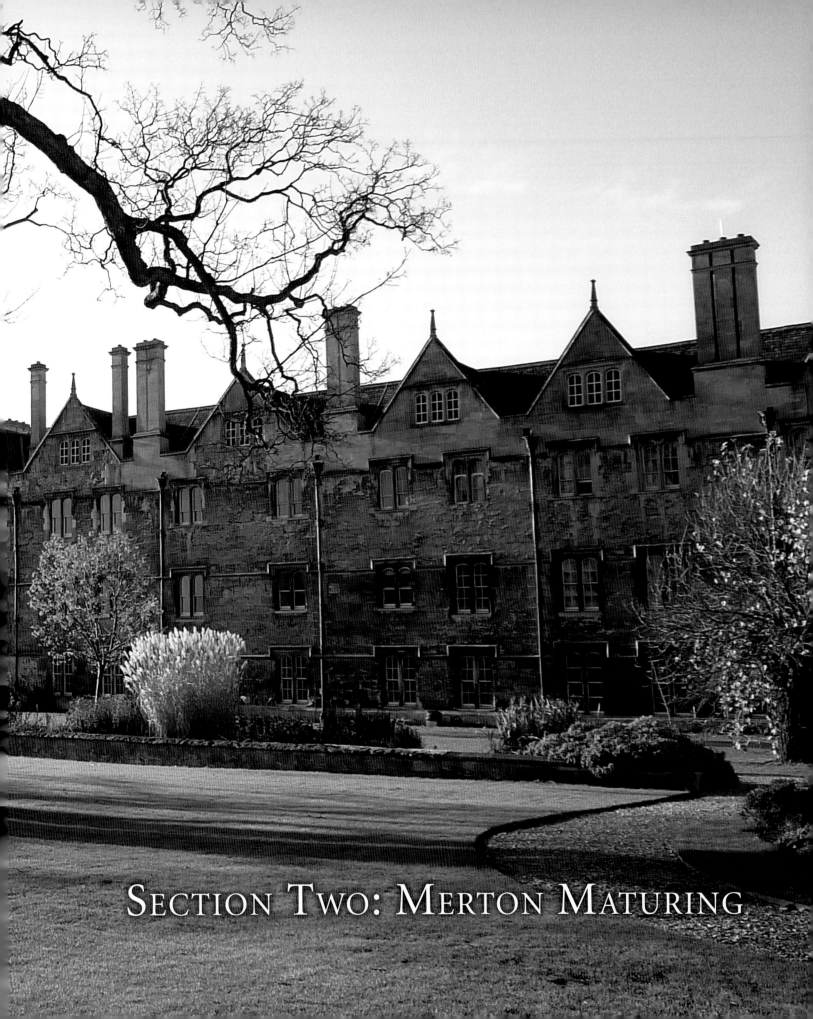

SECTION TWO: MERTON MATURING

Fifteenth-century Illuminated English Statutes

Jack Beatson

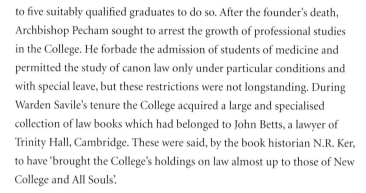

This beautifully illuminated folio, from *Vetera et nova Statuta Angliae*, a fifteenth-century collection of statutes, is one of over 200 books, including many rare editions, bequeathed to Merton by James Leech. Elected a Fellow in 1557, he served as senior Proctor and was a renowned disputant. He elicited loud applause from Queen Elizabeth when disputing before her in St Mary's Church in 1566. His will, proved on 15 February 1588, provided *inter alia* that the books 'shall be … put sett and chayned in the [Library of the College] within six monethes next after the delivery of the same books to the subwarden … And from thenceforthe for ever shall so remaine chayned in the said librarie to the common use of the students in that house.' The book contains Magna Carta and 107 other 'old statutes', and 40 statutes from 1 Edward III to 4 Henry VI in French and Latin. The folio reproduced shows a large pink and blue elaborately patterned 'A' in a gold frame enclosing Henry VI as a boy, seated and holding two crowns and two sceptres, inscribed '*Viuere pacifice michi sit et utrique corone*'. Other sections open with gold initials on gold and pink grounds, patterned and enclosing beasts, each with a coronet. An eagle possibly represents Edward I, a leopard Edward III, a hart Richard II, a dog Henry IV, and a horned, dog-like spotted animal, possibly an antelope, Henry V.

What part did legal study play in the College and the University? From the Middle Ages until the seventeenth century law at Oxford was taught as a professional subject to those who, having obtained a degree in arts, wished to prepare themselves for a career in diplomacy or in the ecclesiastical courts. That involved studying canon law and civil (Roman) law. Until the nineteenth century English (common) law was not taught in Oxford.

Walter de Merton spent the greater part of his life in the king's service as a lawyer and administrator, but wanted most of the Fellows of his College to take higher degrees in theology. The earliest statutes made only marginal provision for the study of civil and canon law. The 1270 statutes, however, made provision for up

to five suitably qualified graduates to do so. After the founder's death, Archbishop Pecham sought to arrest the growth of professional studies in the College. He forbade the admission of students of medicine and permitted the study of canon law only under particular conditions and with special leave, but these restrictions were not longstanding. During Warden Savile's tenure the College acquired a large and specialised collection of law books which had belonged to John Betts, a lawyer of Trinity Hall, Cambridge. These were said, by the book historian N.R. Ker, to have 'brought the College's holdings on law almost up to those of New College and All Souls'.

Interest grew in the study of English law after the creation of the Vinerian Chair in 1756. In the mid-nineteenth century the School of Law and Modern History was created. Although a number of distinguished people took and excelled in it, including Warden Brodrick, who obtained a first in 1854 and was called to the Bar by Lincoln's Inn, the marriage of the two subjects was not successful. In 1872 an independent school of jurisprudence was created. For the next 24 years, however, law teaching at Merton continued to be provided by those whose main interest lay elsewhere. It was not until 1896 that F.E. Smith, later Lord Birkenhead and lord chancellor, was elected as Merton's first tutorial Fellow in law. The College was aware that Smith was likely to leave for the Bar when he had paid his debts, but thought that before doing so he might 'arouse interest in law in the breasts of undergraduates'. They were correct. Until Smith resigned his fellowship in 1899, he took his tutorial duties seriously, made his pupils work, did not tolerate perfunctory essays, was a successful although *ex tempore* lecturer, and published on contract and international law. There have been eight law tutors since Smith left, including Warden Miles and F.H. Lawson, Oxford's first professor of comparative law. Since 1989 the College has had two law tutors.

The books that law students use now are not as beautifully illustrated as *Vetera et nova Statuta Angliae*. But the subject matter of many of the statutes in it is similar to much of the raw material that Mertonian lawyers have to grapple with today.

....

Left: Vanity Fair's *depiction of F.E. Smith after his successful maiden speech as an MP in January 1907, captioned 'Moab is my Washpot'.* **Opposite:** *The first folio of the statutes of King Henry VI's reign from* Vetera et nova Statuta Angliae.

Incipiunt statuta de Anno 33 Henrici sexti post Conqueste Anno

Un parlement tenuz a Westm le lun...
...thien devant la feste de seint Martin l'an du regne du Roy Henry
sisme puis le Conquest trimer me-
me nre s' le Roy del advis a assent
des s'gñrs esperituelx a temporelx a les
especial instance a request des comes
assemblez en mesme le parlement fist faire ordeigner a establir
certeins ordinances a estatutz en la
fourme ensuyt. En primes
ordeigne est p' le p'fit du Roy a l'ease
de son poeple q' les s'gñrs de la counceill
du Roy pur le temps esteantz p'ront
assigner p' auctorite du dit parlement m'istres a ovreors a faire moneie d'or
a d'argent a a tenir les eschanges de moneie sibien en la citee de Everwyk come
en la ville de Bristut a aillours es tantz des lieus come semblera as ditz s'gñrs
bon a necessarie solonc lour bones advis a discretions ascun estatut ou ordinance
fait au contraire non obstant. Item q' touz les estatutz a ordinances faitz des
purvoiours a achatours n'ient repelles soient gardez a executz en touz pointz a
ensi p'claimez en touz Countees p'my le Roialme p' mandement du Roy. Et
q' chm' visconts dengleterre apres ceo q'il ert vestu les ditz estatutz p'ent faire p'-
clamacion p' tiel mandement les face p'claim chm' an quatre fortz p'my sa
baillie sur peine de paier au Roy a chm' fortz q'il ent faille cent souldz. Et
q' sur mesme la peine chm' des ditz visconts face delivrance du dit mandement
a son successour immediate p' endentures entre eux affaitz p'ont il poet faire
semblable p'clamacion p' le temps q'il estoise en son office a l'ease a suerte de le
poeple a q' chm' tiel successour apres cell mandement a luy vestu face autieles
p'clamacions quatre fortz p'an a autiel delivrance du dit mandement a son
successour come dessus est dit sur la peine av'ntdit. Item pur tant q'
diu'ses homicides murdres rapes robberies a autres felonies riottes conventi-
cules a mahaitz ia tarde ount este faitz en diu'ses Countees dengleterre p' gentz
neez en Irland' repairantz a la ville d'Oxenford a illoesq'es demurantz desoubz
la iurisdicion del V'niu'site d'Oxenford a a grand' poure de tout maine de poeple
demuant la environ come p' tout sa cõe du Roialme assemblez en cest parlement
sinst av'rouusement de ceo complient en mesme le parlement. Le Roy de l'assent
av'ntdit a a la requeste de mesme la cõe ad ordeigne q' touz g'ntz neez en Irland'
soient voider hors du Roialme dedenz la iours p'ochien apres la p'clamacion
fait de cest ordinance sur peine de p'dre lour biens a d'estre emprisonez a la

THE FITZJAMES ARCH

Steven Gunn

Richard Fitzjames was one of Merton's most remarkable Wardens. Born into a talented Somerset family – his brother became recorder of Bristol and his nephew a judge – he came to Merton in 1465, gained a fellowship a few years later and a doctorate in theology in 1481, and was chosen Warden in 1483. From the start of his wardenship, he had a dynamic impact on the College. He instituted a register, kept in his own hand, of all the doings of the Governing Body, inaugurating a line of minutes unbroken till the present day and giving an insight into Merton's affairs unmatched by any other college. He presided over the decoration of the Chapel and the installation of the

new ceiling in the Library, to which he bequeathed attractive books. But he was by no means a stay-at-home Warden. As a royal chaplain from 1489 and king's almoner from 1495 he often preached at court, including at such grand occasions as the wedding of Henry VII's daughter to James IV of Scots in 1502. He served as treasurer of St Paul's Cathedral and preached regularly at Paul's Cross, London's most public venue. He sat on Henry's council and sometimes presided over its sessions. In 1499 he even negotiated a commercial treaty with the Netherlands.

His skills won him steady promotion in the church, first, in 1497, to the small bishopric of Rochester, then in 1503 to Chichester, and

finally in 1506 to London. It was at that point that he decided he had best give up the wardenship, as he did in the following year. In each of these posts he was as vigorous as at Merton. Unusually for the time, he ordained clergy, blessed newly appointed abbots, inspected his dioceses and tried to persuade heretics to recant in person. Unfortunately for his subsequent reputation, he fell out with the dean of St Paul's, John Colet, over his criticisms of clerical standards. Colet's friend Erasmus, the most famous humanist scholar in northern Europe at the time, denounced him as 'a superstitious and unconquered Scotist'. He also fell foul of Londoners' hostility to clerical privilege when his officials were implicated in the murky death of the merchant Richard Hunne under arrest in his episcopal prison. But some contemporaries admired him, the Italian humanist historian Polydore Vergil calling him 'a father of old family, great learning, and the utmost goodness'.

Fitzjames's energy combined with good taste in his artistic and educational patronage. At London he rebuilt part of Fulham Palace in brick with diaper patterning and moulded brick decoration in the current court style. He collected tapestries of high quality. At Bruton he founded a school to teach not singing or simple reading, but serious grammar. At Merton his greatest memorial is the work he did on what was then the Warden's Lodgings, and in particular the archway adjoining the Hall to the east. This was built in 1497, as a now lost window in the building explained. As a devotee of astrology, like Henry and others at his court, Fitzjames had a horoscope cast to discover the most propitious time to lay

the foundation stone: the answer turned out to be 10.20am on 12 March 1497, for which the window recorded the conjunction of the heavens. The arch was restored in 1905 and some of the exposed sculpture re-carved in 1973, but most of the original vaulting with its array of carved bosses survives. In the centre Fitzjames placed the arms of his royal master, backed with the double rose that signalled the Tudors' unification of the warring dynasties of York and Lancaster, crowned with the imperial crown that denoted their claims to supreme temporal power and supported by the dragon that spoke of their ancient British ancestry. Around it he placed the 12 signs of the zodiac, represented with great vividness and occasionally, as in the case of Scorpio, more imagination than observation on the part of the sculptors. One characteristic touch is that the fish standing for Pisces is the heraldic dolphin from Fitzjames's family arms. He made liberal use of his heraldry to mark his commissions and his dolphin can be found all over College. At their grandest, combined with the arms of the see of Rochester, surmounted by a doctor's cap and a bishop's mitre, and supported by two robed angels, his arms stand over the archway. More discreetly, moved from its original location, the dolphin still frolics with a crozier and mitre by the back door of the Old Warden's Lodgings.

....

*Opposite: The vault with the royal arms and signs of the zodiac. **Above, left:** Warden Fitzjames's heraldic dolphin as Pisces. **Above, right:** Leo.*

The Lectern of 1504

Alan Bott

By the 1450s, the construction of the Chapel had been completed. Between 1486 and 1517 the College embarked upon the lavish adornment of the furnishings of the interior. The lectern was an integral part of this programme and, sadly, is now the only part of it that survives.

Warden Richard Fitzjames (1483–1507) provided the inspiration and some of the funds for these very extensive works. He was also to undertake substantial construction in the Library (the ceiling) and the Warden's Lodgings (the arch). But the largest and longest undertaking was to be in the adornment of the Chapel. By 1484, there were already four altars there. In 1486, a contract was entered into for a roodloft (a screen with a gallery supporting a crucifix) and incorporating two additional altars. It was, in an early example of college competitiveness, to be like the 'Rodeloft of Mawdelen College' but with 'ferre better dorys'. The two new altars were to be dedicated to St Andrew and St Jerome. Some of the timber was to come from the College's estates. There was, on the new screen, to be a display of 'certeyn ymages in clene tymbre' two feet high over a distance of 30 feet, with the College specifying the subjects. The contract sum for these works was £27. The acquisition of a 'good & sufficient payr off organs' followed in 1488. Then in 1491, John Marshall, bishop of Llandaff and a former Fellow, gave £20 for the painting of the new stalls and pulpitum in the choir. These depicted apostles, saints and prophets, together with a kneeling figure of the bishop. In 1496, the bishop died and his legacy to the College of £20 was, with other donations, expended on the wainscoting of the ceiling of the choir at a cost of £90. The wainscoting of the roof of the Chapel continued, and in 1517 Richard Fitzjames, by then bishop of London, though having resigned the wardenship ten years earlier, contributed £5 towards its completion.

In 1504 came the donation of the great brass lectern from the executors of John Martock. He had become a Fellow of the College in 1458 and served as Bursar and Sub-Warden. He is described in the *Catalogus Vetus* as '*nobilis medicus*'. He was a notable benefactor to the College, giving silver ornaments for the High Altar and the St Andrew's altar in the new roodloft of 1486. At his death in 1503 he bequeathed to the College his better books, vestments and more silver. This lectern was not the first that the College owned. In 1300, when the Chapel was just built, the Sub-Warden's account enumerated expenditure on various necessary furnishings – containers for wine, incense, oil, candles – and a painted lectern. An eagle or pelican seems to have been a common form for medieval lecterns. An eagle was in use in Abbot Suger's St Denis in Paris in the twelfth century and Villard de Honnecourt in his *Carnet* of *c*.1230 shows an eagle lectern with a moveable head. Readings from the Gospel and the Epistle sometimes necessitated the provision of two lecterns. Although some 45 pre-Reformation brass lecterns remain in England, there is no record of any surviving from before the early fifteenth century. After the middle of the century, double-desk lecterns, facilitating the two readings from one lectern, rather than a

pair of ambos, came into being. Such a solution survives in at least four locations, including, as well as Merton, Eton College, King's College, Cambridge, and Yeovil. Many monumental brasses, chandeliers and lecterns were made in Flanders, especially Tournai, and Cologne, but there were also perhaps four separate workshops in England producing brass lecterns in the fifteenth century. The pedestal of the Merton lectern stands on four lions. Above the desk is open work cresting of geometrical design, the ends being pierced with a circle. In the centre of each of the sloping sides of the desk is the inscription '*Orate pro anima Magistri Johannis Martok*'. In the centre are the arms of Warden Fitzjames, *Azure a dolphin silver*. The dolphin is indeed made of silver, soldered on to the brass. The moveable branch candlesticks on the sides of the desk must be a later addition, as they do not appear in the careful drawing of the interior of the Chapel in 1813 in Ackermann's *History of Oxford*.

....

Opposite: The lectern standing in the Chapel. **Left:** *A rubbing of the brass to John Martock, Fellow, 1503, Banwell Church, Somerset.* **Above:** *The inscription on the lectern inviting prayers for Martock's soul with the dolphin of Warden Fitzjames. Unusually, some red pigment survives as a background both to the inscription and to the detail of Martock's cope on his brass.*

THE CAXTON CHAUCER

Kate McClune

The *Canterbury Tales* was the first major English work produced in England by William Caxton in his Westminster workshop. Although Caxton, who was born between 1415 and 1424 and died in 1492, is now famed for introducing the printing press to England, he was not primarily a scholar. Early records (which are sparse) show his mercantile background: he was an apprentice in the Mercers' Company, and spent much of the 1450s and 1460s living in the Low Countries, where he was a prominent figure, the 'governor' of the English mercantile community in Bruges. In this role, he was responsible for negotiations between local authorities and English merchants, as well as acting as representative of the English government when necessary. Such a position indicates high standing, as well as commercial success. In recognising the monetary potential of expanding into the innovative market of printed books, he demonstrated his financial shrewdness. His decision, upon returning to England in 1476, to make Chaucer's famous poem the first significant literary work to be produced at his press further indicates his business acumen: as his biographer Lotte Hellinga put it, he 'chose an English book with the widest possible appeal to begin his career in England', a work that would attract a broad audience.

Information provided uniquely in the pages of Merton's copy of that first edition provides some clues as to just how varied that audience might be. Patrons and purchasers of expensive prints comprised not just aristocrats and members of the nobility, but also merchants and burgesses. Caxton's second edition of the *Canterbury Tales* contains a series of famous woodcuts, but his prints tend not to include illustrations. The Merton Chaucer is exceptional in containing beautifully illuminated borders and margins, brightly coloured and well preserved, which tell us something about early readers. The images include the coat of arms and emblems representing the London Company of Haberdashers, incorporating, for example, the wheel that represents the haberdashers' patron saint, Catherine of Alexandria. It seems likely that these illuminations were added specifically for the haberdashers; certainly as a mercer (a seller of textiles and fabrics), Caxton would have had dealings with haberdashers, originally a branch of the Mercers' Company, who specialised in goods like ribbons, purses and gloves. However, no specific patron, or association, has been identified, and the print's history before it came to Merton in the seventeenth century is obscure.

The copy is believed to have been donated to the College in 1620 or 1630 by Alderman William Wright (*c*.1561–1635), a prominent Oxford figure. He was a goldsmith, a baker and mayor of Oxford (1614–15). The surviving evidence associating the book with Wright postdates the supposed date of donation, although Wright had connections with Merton – according to his will, he was a tenant of the College, and the Merton Register records that in 1627 he administered the funds for the junior Bickley exhibitioner, to whom he paid £6 per year. The book itself contains no ownership markers, although 'Homfraye Cole' has signed his name on one page, and other leaves contain marginal comments and corrections added by readers (the notorious inaccuracies of the first edition were acknowledged in Caxton's preface to his revised second edition). Merton's handsome copy, although well preserved, was imperfect: a handwritten note on one page records that 'this leaf was given to Merton College library by Lord Spencer 1815'. The College Register thanks Spencer for donating from 'his mutilated duplicate of Caxton's first edition of Chaucer any leaves that might supply the deficiencies in the copy belonging to the College Library'. Two other replacement leaves were purchased in 1820 for £21.

It is no exaggeration to state that the fifteenth-century print of Chaucer's *Canterbury Tales* – the first print (rather than manuscript) of the poem – held by Merton College Library holds a significance for book historians beyond its position as a precious early print witness to Chaucer's work. Although a number of these first editions (*c*.1476–7) are extant, the unique illustrative features of the Merton Chaucer and its history as a text with mercantile associations tell an invaluable tale of print circulation and of the composition of early audiences for Chaucer's story collection. Merton's copy of the *Canterbury Tales* is a key work in English literary and print history.

....

Opposite: The opening of the prologue to the Canterbury Tales, *with decorative features linked to the Haberdashers' Company.* **Insert:** *The start of 'The Tale of Melibee', decorated with a mischievous-looking monkey.*

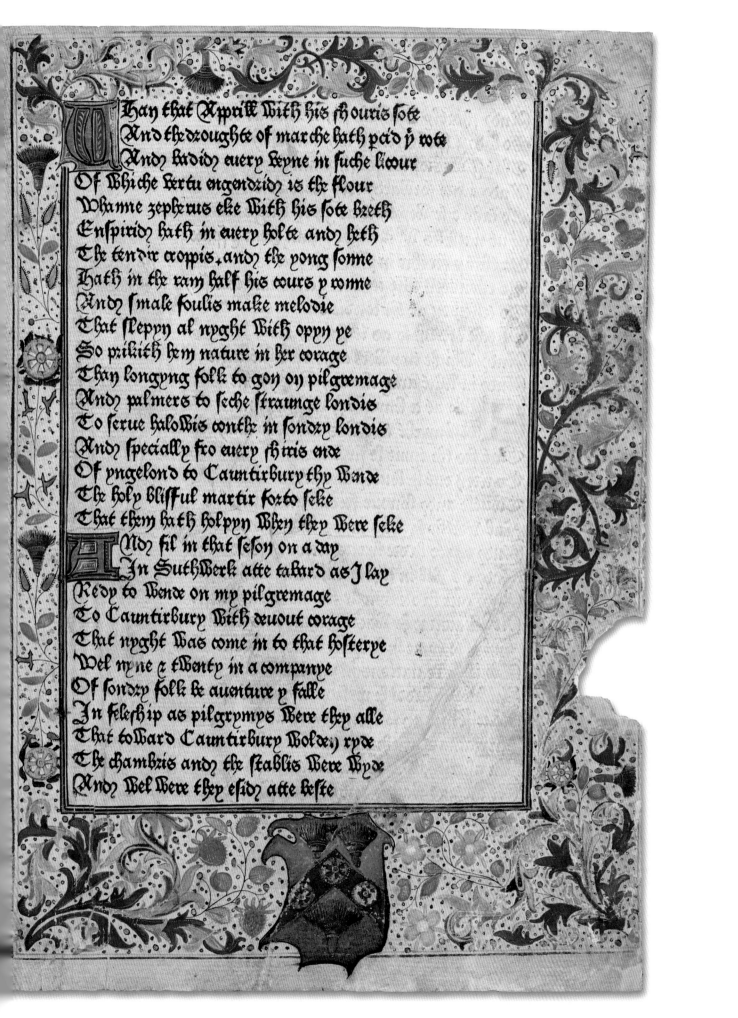

Whan that Aprill with his shouris sote

And the droughte of marche hath perced þ rote

And bradid euery veyne in suche licour

Of whiche vertu engendrid is the flour

Whanne zepherus eke with his sote breth

Enspirid hath in euery holte and heth

The tendir croppis, and the yong sonne

Hath in the ram half his cours y ronne

And smale foulis make melodie

That sleppyn al nyght with oppyn ye

So prikith hem nature in her corage

Than longyng folk to goon on pilgremage

And palmers to seche straunge londis

To serue halowis couthe in sondry londis

And specially fro euery shiris ende

Of yngelond to Cauntirbury thy wende

The holy blissful martir forto seke

That them hath holpyn when they were seke

And fil in that sesoy on a day

In Suthwerk atte tabard as I lay

Redy to wende on my pilgremage

To Cauntirbury with deuout corage

That nyght was come in to that hosterye

Wel nyne & twenty in a companye

Of sondry folk be auenture y falle

In felechip as pilgrymys were they alle

That toward Cauntirbury wolden ryde

The chambris and the stablis were wyde

And wel were they esid atte beste

JEROME'S TRANSLATION OF THE *CHRONICLE OF EUSEBIUS*

David Ganz

In 311 Eusebius of Caesarea wrote a Greek chronicle in a tabular format, which made it possible to synchronise the dates in world history from the birth of Abraham to his own lifetime. Before Eusebius the dating of notable events had depended on a wide range of different and often confused systems. Most nations dated events to the year of the ruler in which they took place: the Romans dated from the foundation of Rome, or by the names of the consuls, and some Greek cities dated by the cycles of the Olympic Games. Linking these dates to those in the Bible was especially difficult; did Moses live before or after the fall of Troy? Eusebius set out in parallel columns events in Persia, Israel, Greece, Rome, Syria, Macedon and Egypt. He recognised that many of the dates which he included were conjectural but his terse entries record the battles, treaties and earthquakes of antiquity and when prominent philosophers, playwrights and poets flourished. (Those are frequently wrong, but they are often the only dates we have.) The work showed that Moses was a contemporary of Cecrops, the founder of Athens and that Christ was born in the 42nd year of the emperor Augustus. Eusebius' Greek text is now lost, but an Armenian translation has survived. St Jerome (*c*.347–420) recognised the value of the work, and translated the second book into Latin with a continuation from the reign of Constantine until the defeat of the emperor Valens by the Goths in 378 AD. Jerome left careful instructions about how the book was to be copied with 26 lines per page, and with red as well as black ink, with the red linking events in different columns. Failure to do this correctly, Jerome stated, would insert a labyrinth of error.

Jerome's work is one of the small number of Latin texts which have survived in early copies. There are four fifth-century manuscripts, though none is now complete, and the work was copied and studied in the Carolingian age. The Merton manuscript was copied in the ninth century, most

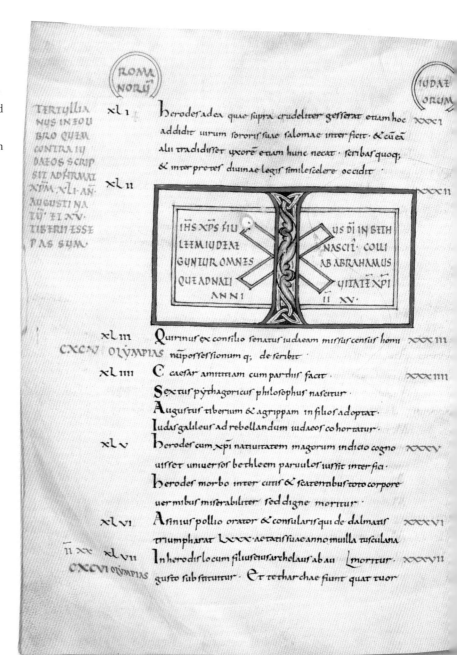

probably at the monastery of the Reichenau on Lake Constance in southern Germany, and it was corrected there by the scholar poet Walahfrid Strabo. He may have decided to add more historical and geographical material: a text on the names of different peoples, *Interpretatio sancti Hieronymi de nominibus gentium*, of which this is the only copy known, a text on the size of countries and a table of rulers. The Merton copy is thus an important witness to the ways in which people tried to locate their place in God's plan for human history. At the Council of Basel it passed into the hands of Pietro Donato, bishop of Padua, where it was copied in 1450. John Tiptoft, the humanist earl of Worcester, brought it to England around 1460 and it had reached Merton by 1556. It is the oldest manuscript book in the College Library.

Merton College MS 315, Jerome's Translation of the Chronicle of Eusebius. *This opening, folios 125 verso–126 recto, shows, among other events, the emperor Augustus' adoption of Tiberius as his heir, the death of King Herod the Great and Augustus' census of the population of the Roman Empire. The four-yearly cycle of the Olympic Games is marked in red and the birth of Christ is magnificently highlighted.*

THE CHAPEL TENNIS BALLS

Nicholas Richardson

In the west wall of Merton Chapel, three balls were found at some time in the past, lodged in putlog holes. These holes were about two feet deep and five inches square, and were designed to take wooden scaffold timbers. The balls are similar in size and construction to modern real tennis balls, though rather smaller. They measure from 17cm to 18cm in circumference, and are made of a woven fabric (either cotton or linen) tied round with a web of criss-crossed threads. Eight similar balls were found in the rafters of the hall at Wadham College: these are now on display in the Museum of Oxford. Many Oxford and Cambridge colleges had ball-courts within their walls in the sixteenth and seventeenth centuries. The print of Merton by David Loggan (1675) depicts the Merton ball-court in 'the Grove', next to Corpus Christi College, already mentioned in the College accounts for 1607. Two dons are watching undergraduates play. Their caps and gowns lie in a pile at the back.

The game known as real tennis evolved from a ballgame played originally with the hand (hence *jeu de paume* in French), and then with the glove (as in modern fives). In England the racquet, originally with loose strings, now with taut, gradually replaced the glove or hand. The peculiarities of the real tennis court reflect the forms of hand-ball played in the cloisters and courtyards of medieval monasteries and castles. At each end and on the server's left side are sloping rooves (penthouses), with galleries below the penthouse on the side wall, and an open space with netting behind the server (the *dedans*). On the right-hand wall at the receiver's (or hazard) end of the court is a projecting buttress (the *tambour*), and beyond this a square opening (the *grille*). The net dividing the court across the middle is not taut, but sags in the centre. The court is usually covered, allowing play in all weathers. Scoring is similar to that of lawn tennis, which derived from real tennis. But a major difference is the 'chase'. This gives a player a second chance, if he misses the ball. The point where the second bounce occurs is marked, and later in this game the players change ends and play the chase: the player who missed the ball has to improve on or equal the length of his opponent's previous shot, to avoid losing the point.

In fifteenth-century Oxford we hear of tradesmen being prosecuted for playing tennis or keeping a court within the city, for ballgames were illegal for commoners, being associated with idleness and gambling. The earliest mention of a member of the University playing tennis comes in the Merton Register for April 1492. Richard Holt, a young Fellow, is the subject of grave complaints: he frequented suspect places, often missed or was late for Chapel on feast days, was too familiar with his seniors, and instead of studying used to play dice at night in the town. Moreover, he played tennis, and in a public place! Holt withdrew from College for a time, and soon after resigned his fellowship and married. By 1584, however, tennis was being recommended by Thomas Coghan as the best protection against the plague for Oxford scholars, 'for that it doth exercise all parts of the body alike … and greatly delighteth the minde, making it lusty and cheerful'.

The public Tennis Court in Merton Street, which belongs to the College, is first mentioned in a lease dated 6 October 1595, as 'lately built'. Christ Church and Oriel both had courts older than this, but the Merton court is the only one still in use today. It was rebuilt in 1798, and is more or less the same as it was then. It is smaller than other courts, the penthouses are lower, and the angle of the *tambour* is exceptionally obtuse. In the 1870s the College commissioned plans to convert the building into studies and lecture rooms, but the idea was dropped when an agricultural depression set in. The Court is now leased by the Oxford University Tennis Club. Many leading players have begun their careers here, including some world champions. The club owes its gratitude to the College for allowing the game to continue to flourish in Oxford, over 400 years since it was first played on the Merton Street court. As J.K. Stephen wrote in 1891: 'Let other people play at other things; The King of Games is still the Game of Kings.'

....

Opposite: The tennis balls. Above: A game in progress on the Merton Street Tennis Court.

THE UPPER LIBRARY

Julia Walworth

When visitors pause at the top of the stairs in the Mob Quad Library the view of the oak book stalls extending in either direction under the great vaulted ceiling is so harmonious as to suggest conception by a single mind. Yet this unified ensemble was formed over more than six centuries. We are fortunate to know more about this process than is often the case with historic institutions because Merton has preserved remarkably rich sources for the Library's history. Records of expenditure on the building and on the collections, along with lists of donations and inscriptions in individual volumes all provide insight into the creation, maintenance, and evolving role of the Library, which is almost certainly the oldest academic library with an unbroken tradition in the western world.

In the first decades after it was constructed, the Mob Library was known as the 'new library'. The earlier library had its origins in the 'sturdy desk' to which Archbishop John Pecham, the College Visitor, required the College to chain three important grammatical reference

works in 1284. By the mid-fourteenth century there are recurring references in the College accounts to the care of the '*libraria*', which was clearly a separate room, although its location is now unknown. At this time the College had three distinct collections of books: those chained in the Library, those that circulated among the Fellows, and those needed for Chapel services. Medieval donors of books to the College sometimes specified that their gifts were to be 'chained in the Library', which undoubtedly helped to ensure their survival.

The construction of the new Library building in the 1370s was a major project led by Bishop William Rede (a Mertonian), Bursar (later Warden) John Bloxham, and master mason William Humberville. While still a Fellow serving as Sub-Warden, Rede's duties included the care of the College's books. In the course of his career Rede himself accumulated one of the largest private libraries of his day, which he then distributed by gift and bequest to several Oxford colleges, the greater part going to Merton along with a collection of astronomical instruments and the large sum of £100. His gifts encouraged Merton to become one of the first of several colleges to construct a prestigious library building in the 1370s. The Queen's College and Exeter also built libraries at this time, and a library was included in Wykeham's plans for the buildings of New College in 1379.

When completed, the Merton Library where Rede's books came to be housed formed the south and west sides of Mob Quad. The books were chained on lectern desks set at right angles to the walls on each side of a central aisle, forming study areas that made the most of the light from the windows. The junction of the two wings provided an open space that was at times used for teaching or College meetings. The original concept for the glazing of the windows can be seen today in the east windows of the west wing, which preserve the earliest window glass to survive from any English library. The decorative scheme combines grisaille (grey glass) panes that let in light with patterned borders and central roundels depicting the Agnus Dei. As the symbol of St John the Baptist, the Agnus Dei may have been an allusion both to the patron of the College Chapel, and also perhaps to John Bloxham. Another early stained-glass window once contained the English royal arms, although the royal shield was replaced by that of the Clare family in the mid-nineteenth century.

The next big alteration to the fabric of the Library was the installation of the magnificent oak-panelled ceiling in 1502–3. In keeping with

the taste of the period, the joints of the wooden mouldings were covered with brightly painted metal bosses depicting heraldic badges of the Tudor King Henry VII, the dolphin device of Warden Richard Fitzjames, and the earliest surviving examples of the College arms. These visual references to the College, the Warden, and to the monarch recall the imagery of St John the Baptist and the royal arms in the early glazing.

By the sixteenth century the Library was full. The College had gradually begun to acquire printed books and initially stored them flat on the lectern desks with the medieval manuscripts. The growing Library collections were not limited to books but also included additional astronomical instruments, maps and globes that were used for teaching and by individual Fellows. In 1589 Warden Henry Savile began a major refurbishment that was to update the Library while maintaining the existing overall arrangement of the space. Beginning in the west wing, Savile replaced the lectern desks with stalls comprising flat bookshelves above desks. As the seating was not altered, many of the medieval benches could be re-used. A separate circulating collection of books was no longer maintained, and all books large and sturdy enough to be chained were now stored upright on the shelves. At the time this was a new way of housing books, but it soon became the norm, as it is today. Savile's work was continued and completed in the south wing by 1623. Medieval floor tiles were purchased, second-hand, to pave the aisles. Dormer windows were set into the roof and a large window created in the east wall in order to admit more light. The upper walls at the end of each aisle were decorated with fashionable plasterwork incorporating the arms of the Warden and of successive College Visitors and archbishops John Whitgift and George Abbot, with the College shield in the centre.

Savile also actively updated the contents of the Library, encouraging donations and book-buying initiatives both in England and on the Continent. Many volumes had been given or bequeathed to the Library since 1276, when Archbishop Robert Kilwardby had first stipulated that a Fellow's books should come to the College on his death. The College had also been purchasing books from time to time since at least 1289. Although donations continued to play a major role in the development of the Library, as they do today, an ever-increasing number of books were purchased from College funds. During Savile's wardenship the holdings of the library tripled. Merton already had a sizeable academic library when in 1659 Griffin Higgs bequeathed more than 650 further books along with an endowment to provide a salary for a Librarian.

In 1792, at the same College meeting during which the Fellows agreed to donate £21 'for the use of distressed French refugees now in England', major changes to the Library were also approved: 'that the librarian be desired to add one shelf to each bookcase in the library, and to take down one of the reading shelves in each compartment, also that the chains be taken off from the books'. The books kept in the Library could now be borrowed, and during the course of the nineteenth century the Library, previously reserved exclusively for the use of Fellows and occasional academic visitors, was opened to students. The College approached this particular innovation cautiously, initially allowing undergraduates access for one hour per week. A generation later the interior of the Library was further enhanced by the stained-glass panels which were installed in the great seventeenth-century bay window. The glass itself was from the sixteenth-century Rhineland. Its exact provenance is unknown, but it somehow fits the atmosphere well.

Astonishingly, the Library was almost dismantled about two decades later. Disaster and irreparable loss were narrowly avoided in 1861 when, driven by the need to provide more student accommodation, the College agreed to 'the entire demolition (if necessary) of Mob Quadrangle'. There was strong disagreement among the fellowship and letters of objection in the *Times* from those outside the College. Fortunately three months later the decision was rescinded. Today the events of 1861 seem difficult to comprehend. F. Scott Fitzgerald took the Mob Library as a model of Old World elegance in *The Great Gatsby,* and its interior has become one of the most frequently depicted images of the College. Book historians study both the books themselves and what their arrangement tells us about the history of reading and scholarship, while visitors enjoy the tours conducted by graduate students during the summer. Most of the working collections for students were moved to the ground floor of Mob Quad from 1905 and then, between the 1950s and 1990s, to the Old Warden's Lodgings, yet the Upper Library retains its place in College life. It represents a uniquely enduring tradition of intellectual endeavour that continues to inspire both visitors and scholars.

....

Opposite: A book press and an Agnus Dei window. **Above:** *Heraldic bosses from the ceiling, showing Warden Fitzjames's dolphins, the Tudor rose, the College arms and the royal arms.* **Overleaf:** *The west and south wings of the Upper Library.*

THE LIBRARY CHESTS

Alan Bott

Two handsome chests, one dating from the thirteenth, the other from the seventeenth century, are deposited in the Upper Library. The thirteenth-century chest fits closely into a category of safe deposit chests of which more than 100 survive in the cathedrals and churches of England, many acquired under mandates of King Henry II and Pope Innocent III to collect alms for the Crusades. Its front, back and sides are made of single broad oak planks, nailed between uprights, which are extended to form the feet, each originally carved with a little column and capital in Early English style. Only the front right and back left feet survive intact. The ironwork consists of slender straps with split, curved terminals binding the chest ends and the underneath. The central strap incorporates a keyhole for the original single lock. Later, three square plates for flap locks have been added. Inside the chest on the left, there is a little compartment known as a till, formerly with its own pivot-hinged lid. The chest lid is a replacement of an original lid, which is also likely to have been pivot-hinged.

The chest was most likely provided either as a repository for the College's first books or, more mundanely, for its administrative records. Robert Kilwardby, archbishop of Canterbury, issued injunctions as Visitor to the College in 1276. In these, he ordered that the three Bursars should keep a strong-box or chest, with three separate locks and three keys. Herein should be kept the documents, muniments and books of the community. Several chests were acquired in the following years, one for the theology books and others for more domestic purposes. In the account of Mr Hamund Lincoln, first Bursar, 1288–9, the large sum of £10 was spent on the 'community's chest'. He also paid for repairs to a chest and three small locks for it. It is possible that the chest in the Upper Library, with its original single lock, replaced with three additional locks, is this same chest. At any rate, the replacing of the documents in their chest was sufficient cause for a celebration that 3½d was expended on wine for the occasion!

The purpose and uses of the seventeenth-century chest were made explicit in the will of its donor, Sir Thomas Bodley, who died in 1612: 'I doe give for ye founding & making of a new chest to ye selfe same use yt Reade's chest was anciently instituted … ye some of 200 marks in mony out of wch my meaning is that £13.6.8 or about that some shall be bestowed … upon some chiste or presse … with three locks of severall wardes and three different keyes to the same. The residue of 200

markes shall always continue as a stocke to be employed on ye like uses as ye aforesaide of Reade of ye studentes of ye college'. William Rede (d. 1385), bishop of Chichester, had bequeathed £100 for a loan chest in which Fellows could pledge their books in exchange for cash. Rede's and Bodley's bequests were to be amalgamated by 1745. The *Computus cistae Bodley*, preserved in the Library, begins in August 1614, and duly records the grants made. The Warden usually drew £8 annually, the 20 Fellows £5 each. Customarily, on 1 August, the beginning of the College year, three Fellows, each with a different key, were appointed as keepers of the chest. That practice continued until 1840, though no withdrawal is recorded after 1809.

Bodley's chest is made entirely of iron, strengthened with interlaced iron bands. The front has hasps for two padlocks and in the centre is a dummy keyhole, while the actual lock and intricate locking mechanism are under the lid. When the key is turned, 14 catches move under the rim of the four sides. There is some painted decoration on the exterior. Inside, there is another lockable compartment on the floor. Chests like these, sometimes known as 'Armada' chests (since three were found on Armada shipwrecks), were made in the Nuremberg region of Germany and exported all over Europe in the sixteenth and seventeenth centuries. In 1611, when Bodley began his permanent endowment of the University Library, he presented a similar chest to the University for the preservation of Library funds. It is painted with his arms and those of the University, flanked by two large padlocks. It has only 11 catches. It can be seen today in the Divinity School, where it is used, appropriately, for the collection of donations to the Library.

Opposite: The intricate locking mechanism of Bodley's chest. **Insert:** *One of the substantial keys necessary to unlock Bodley's chest and redeem the Fellows' loan pledges.*

THE BODLEY AND SAVILE MONUMENTS

Richard McCabe

The splendid monuments to Sir Thomas Bodley and Sir Henry Savile that now grace the north and south transepts of the Ante-Chapel commemorate not just the intellectual calibre of the two foremost Mertonians of their age but the crucial role that the Renaissance College played in the University's development. As the founders of the Bodleian Library and the Savilian chairs in astronomy and geometry, Bodley and Savile profoundly influenced the course of Oxford's academic history and it is entirely fitting that their memorials should so perfectly complement one another in style and form.

Designed by Nicholas Stone, the marble and alabaster monument to Bodley features a striking half effigy set in a recessed niche and surrounded by four of the liberal arts: music, arithmetic, dialectic and rhetoric. On the pediment above rest geometry and astronomy, while underneath lies the figure of grammar reclining before the stairs of the old public library that Bodley refurbished. To the right and left are two female figures, one holding an open book, the other proffering a spiritual crown in allusion to the three coronets that appear above on the blazon of Bodley's arms. Surmounting it all is the figure of Athena, the goddess of wisdom. The visual wit of the composition indicates that the monument is designed to be read as an allegory of the relationship between learning, public service and faith, and that is entirely appropriate to its subject. Bodley's father, a radical Protestant publisher, left for exile during the reign of the Catholic Queen Mary but returned on the accession of the Protestant Elizabeth. Educated as a boy in Calvin's Geneva, Bodley matriculated at Magdalen College in 1559, received his BA in 1563, and was elected Fellow of Merton the following year. He was the College's first lecturer in Greek, promoted the study of Hebrew, and served twice as Principal of Postmasters and three times as Bursar. He served the University with equal diligence, becoming junior Proctor in 1569 and frequently deputising for the public orator, Arthur Atye, secretary to the earl of Leicester, the University's chancellor. It was probably through Leicester's influence that Bodley entered the diplomatic service around 1576, serving in Denmark, France and the Netherlands. His record won great admiration but his career foundered on court factionalism. Despairing of politics in the late 1590s, he made the momentous decision 'to set up my Staffe at the Library doore in Oxford; being thoroughly persuaded, that in my solitude and surcease from the Common-wealth affaires, I could not busy my sclfe to better

purpose, then by reducing that place (which then in every part lay ruined and wast) to the publique use of Students'.

Bodley's great enterprise was largely inspired by the refurbishment of the Merton Library undertaken by Savile following his election as Warden in 1585. The two men had much in common. Elected to fellowship just one year after Bodley, Savile had served as Greek tutor to the queen and was a renowned polymath, equally proficient in the humanities and natural sciences. His lectures on Ptolemy and Euclid were celebrated and his edition of the works of St John Chrysostom remained standard for centuries. He was also an accomplished translator, expertly rendering Tacitus into English and serving on one of the committees for the King James Bible. His many benefactions to the College included the building of Fellows' Quad. Although his election as provost of Eton in 1596 occasioned considerable controversy, it also facilitated intellectual exchange between two of the foremost institutions of their day.

Savile's monument is elegantly sculpted in black, white and painted marble. At the centre is a sprightly half effigy with the left hand resting on a book, and flanking it on either side are the authors the Warden had made his own. Beneath are paintings of Merton and Eton embellished with their arms, and at the bottom, as if supporting the whole thing, a quarter globe mapping Magellan's route around the southern hemisphere. Directly above Savile's head, and beneath a frieze showing two astronomers gazing at the heavens, are his arms, and dramatically surmounting the whole monument rises the figure of Fame blowing her trumpet. A lengthy inscription beneath the effigy draws out the allegorical significance of the composition: Savile's mortal remains may lie in Eton, but his memory is imperishable because his benefactions to learning have left the whole world in his debt. And this, perhaps, is the keynote of both memorials, this sense of reaching out from Oxford to the world by establishing here an international centre for the advancement of teaching and research, a global vision inspired by local values.

Opposite: The monument to Sir Thomas Bodley. The inscription on the book reads, aptly, 'non delebo nomen eius de Libro Vitae' , 'I will not blot out his name from the book of life' (Revelation 3:5). Left: The monument to Sir Henry Savile.

THE PORTAL OF ST ALBAN HALL AND THE FRONTISPIECE IN FELLOWS' QUAD

Alan Bott

Italian Renaissance learning had reached Oxford by 1450. Duke Humphrey of Gloucester (d. 1447) had presented nearly 300 classical manuscripts to the University. Classical styles in furnishing were to arrive in London from 1512, with Torrigiani's tomb of Henry VII at Westminster. During the following century, the Gothic style gradually gave way to the Renaissance style in the architecture of the country, the court leading the way. Sir John Thynne's great house at Longleat of 1567–80 is a formal, classical construction. But at conservative Oxford the first Renaissance building was not constructed until 1599. It is the portal of St Alban Hall. How did this happen?

In 1576, Thomas Bodley, already a Fellow of Merton for 13 years, was granted leave by the College to travel to the continent. On his departure, he inscribed a copy of a Hebrew book to his junior colleague, Henry Savile, elected a Fellow in 1565. It remains with the Library. In 1578–82, Savile himself went on the Grand Tour, visiting France, Germany, Bohemia, Austria and Italy. The *Commonplace Book* he compiled in Venice is in the College Library. His exposure to classical scholarship and architecture was thus very considerable. On his return from his travels, Savile became tutor in Greek to Queen Elizabeth. In 1585, he was elected Warden of Merton.

Four years later, in 1589, James Leech, who had been a Fellow of Merton between 1557 and 1567, died and left the College 200 books. Among them were copies of Sebastiano Serlio's *Five Books of Architecture*, printed in Italian and French in Venice and Paris between 1544 and 1547. Here were demonstrated '*le cinque maniere degli edifice … Toscano, Dorico, Ionico, Corinthio e composito … concordano con la dottrina di Vitruvio*'. Bound in the same great volume are the *Ten Books of Architecture* of Vitruvius Pollio himself. In these works the perspectives, proportions and uses of classical styles are copiously described and illustrated. In the catalogue of books bequeathed to the University by Savile himself, *c.*1619, there is, among the works of Euclid, Tacitus, Ptolemy, Archimedes and Copernicus, a copy of *Vitruvii, De Architectura* in the edition of Guillaume Philandrier. Warden Savile thus had immediately to hand in the College Library and in his own collection all he might need in academic terms, for his classical furnishing of the Library itself (1589), the building of the

entrance portal of St Alban Hall (1599) and, to crown his classical essays, the building of the 'Tower of the Four Orders' in Fellows' Quad (1608–10). Taking advantage of a legacy of £250 from Benedict Barnam, an old member of St Alban Hall and an alderman of London, Savile turned his attention first to rebuilding the Hall, which Merton had acquired in 1549. For its doorway he used twin columns in the Tuscan order.

Who designed the 'Tower of the Four Orders' in Fellows' Quad? The first architectural displays of the classical Orders of Architecture in England were in ephemeral constructions at court, but variations on the theme in stone began with the gateway to old Somerset House in *c.*1548–60. The early examples are made up of single columns or pilasters, but coupled columns began in the 1570s, and in 1585 William Cecil built a classical 'Tower' at Burghley House. John Ackroyde, Savile's master mason at Merton and a fellow Yorkshireman, must also have brought advice to the enterprise. The Ackroydes were involved in the construction of several mansions in Yorkshire in the 1590s, each with Renaissance features, including Howley Hall and Stonyhurst. Sir Henry Savile was thus not without classical inspiration close to hand. Yet, with the exception of the pediment at the top and the four, paired, classical columns themselves, the remainder of the decoration of the 'Four Orders' in Fellows' Quad is, in the harsh words of *A Handbook to Oxford* (Parker, 1858), 'a good specimen of the debased style of James I'. It includes blank Perpendicular panelling, strapwork, finials and even Gothic pinnacles. The Gateway itself is four-centred, but with a classical keystone. Judging by the prints of Loggan (1675) and Williams (1733), classical obelisks stood on either side of the pediment and above the dials on the east and west wings. In a happy return of compliment, when Sir Thomas Bodley planned the Schools Quad in his re-founded University Library, he adopted his protégé's 'Four Orders' at Merton; but grandly enhanced them to produce the 'Five Orders of Architecture' which, including a statue of James I, was completed in 1624.

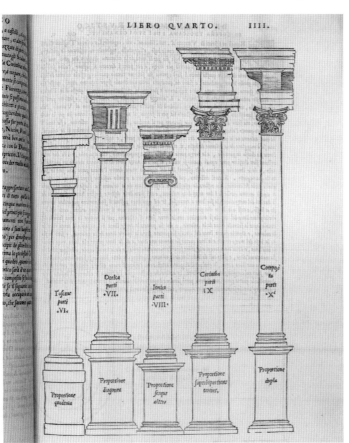

*Opposite: The 'Tower of the Four Orders' in Fellows' Quad. **Left:** The College Library copy of Sebastiano Serlio,* Five Books of Architecture *(1544–7), showing columns of the different classical orders.* ***Above:*** *The portal of St Alban Hall in Merton Street.*

THE SUNDIAL IN FRONT QUAD

Yang-Hui He

The casual tourist to the College on entering Front Quad would be perhaps too stricken by her medieval beauty to notice on the eastern wall of the magnificent Chapel a small sundial with the date 1629. The slightly more informed, in search of the 'Merton sundial', would perhaps head to Fellows' Garden for the charming armillary sphere from which 'Sundial Lawn' derives its name, or to the sundial on the west-facing wall of Fellows' Quad, made famous by the Time Ceremony, in which students walk backwards around the quad on the night the clocks go back, an invention of the 1970s. The former was a gift in 1830 from one George Tierney, Fellow. The latter was painted by Dr Geoffrey Bath, a Junior Research Fellow in astrophysics, sometime in 1974, though a print of 1733 shows that there were then two oppositely facing dials in Fellows' Quad.

It is on the sundial in Front Quad, in her unassuming position hidden on the edge of the north-east buttress of the Chapel, that our story will focus. We will see that behind the simple design of the timepiece lies a testimony to a great era. The gnomon of the sundial is a small brass bullet protruding from the Chapel wall to the left, projecting onto eight golden lines marking the hours 6am to 9am, together with

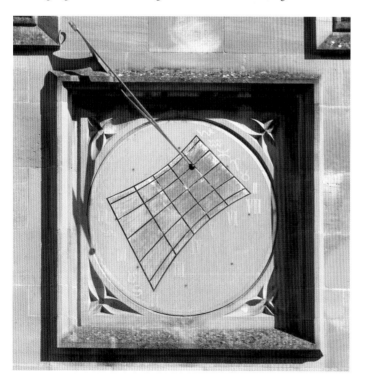

the intermediate half-hours. Being east-facing and in the shadow of the enormous Chapel, these are the only times which the dial could capture. There are five marked black lines which are slightly slanted, denoting the hours after sunrise. The remaining black lines consist of two types: four vertical, which indicate the angle of the sun (in 20-degree increments from left to right, ranging from 10 South of East to 20 North of East) and nine sharply slanted, which are local perpendiculars to the golden lines and indicate the lines of constant declination of the sun. At the bottom, the date 1629 is marked in gold. Thus is composed the sundial, occupying an area of the wall no more than nine feet by five, humble compared to some more elaborate instruments around Oxford.

That the carvings seem fresh need not trouble the visitor; the sundial has been repainted several times. In fact, both the *Oxford Almanack* of 1788 and J. Taylor's *Essays on Gothic Architecture* of 1802 show an earlier date of 1622. Thus, the present 1629 is an error due to a mis-transcription when the much deteriorated stonework was restored in the 1960s. One might wonder whether an ancient college like Merton might have had a time-keeping device much earlier than the 1620s. There was indeed mention of a horological expense in 1289–90, when 4s 4d was spent on a clock. Unfortunately, no remains of that clock or mentions of further devices survive.

The Warden at the time the sundial was created was the great Sir Henry Savile (1549–1622), mathematician, classicist, politician and biblical scholar. Of his many great deeds, the one most relevant for us was his beginning a great era of Oxford science – an era which could be called a second golden age of mathematics at Merton. In the fourteenth century, not long after the foundation of the College, Merton became a renowned centre for mathematics and astronomy, especially in the study of motion. Fellows in theology such as Bradwardine, Heytesbury, Swineshead and Dumbleton founded a school of mathematical science which is still known as the Merton Calculators.

Nothing rivalled them until the arrival of Savile, himself a geometer who gave well-loved lectures on Euclid and Ptolemy, while introducing the revolutionary ideas of Copernicus. He used his influence to attract to Merton Henry Briggs (1561–1630) from Gresham College, London, and John Bainbridge (1582–1643), a Cambridge man. These two distinguished mathematicians were to hold the Savilian professorships, respectively in geometry and in astronomy; chairs which continue to this day and the holders of which have included such figures as Christopher

The College Chapel holds lasting testimony to this great age. Briggs is buried under the tower, not far from the baptismal font, beneath a humble stone with no more than his name, and Bainbridge is commemorated with a beautiful monument to the south of Savile's marvellous memorial. The visitor to the College, after admiring the sundial, is highly recommended to pay homage to these great minds.

Wren and Edmund Halley. Whereas Briggs is famous for inventing the base-ten counterpart to Napier's natural logarithm, surely one of the most used functions in science today, Bainbridge is known for his description of the comet of 1618 and was, most likely, responsible for the construction of our 1622 sundial.

Opposite: The sundial in Fellows' Quad. **Left:** *The sundial in Front Quad, showing the time just before 7am.* **Above:** *The armillary sphere on Sundial Lawn.*

THE COLLEGE SILVER

Pippa Shirley

ollegiate plate collections are fascinating and highly important historical survivals, representing a cross-section of silver production over many centuries, and preserved because of their particular status as valued statements of institutional identity. Most college silver was presented by members, friends, visitors and servants and retained as heirlooms and for use. This giving of silver plate was a long and honourable tradition and an essential element of social obligation, percolating downwards from the very pinnacle of society. Gifts of plate were often preserved from the melting pot and treasured for their association. The fact that many of these objects were second hand was seen as an advantage, a mark of historical significance.

Not all gifts were voluntary. Custom dictated that members of Oxford and Cambridge colleges presented a beaker, cup, mug or tankard which were in daily use but also acted as a kind of financial buffer of plate which could be used in emergencies. Fellows were expected to present a piece of plate when awarded a fellowship. In the early seventeenth century, the colleges introduced a new category of undergraduate drawn from wealthy backgrounds, the 'gentleman commoner'. At Merton, they were required to give a piece of silver to the value of £8. This usually took the form of a distinctive two-handled cup, referred to in inventories as 'ear'd pots', 'pots with eares', 'college cups' or 'ox-eyes'. Merton has several of these, including one presented by George Pudsey, who matriculated in 1680, made in London in 1680–1 and marked for an unknown goldsmith, T.C., with fish above and trefoil below. It also bears the College arms.

Colleges, like livery companies, army and navy regiments and clubs and societies of all kinds, also needed plate for corporate life and ceremonial dining and drinking, and much of Merton's plate falls into this category. The Hall was the only place other than the Chapel where the whole College gathered together, and the rituals of the table were a powerful reinforcement of the College hierarchy. Silver plate used at table reflected both this and changing fashions in dining through the centuries. One of the undoubted stars of

Merton's collection is the magnificent silver-gilt rosewater dish, made in London in 1605–6, its maker identified by an animal head erased between the initials 'W.I.' (a mark which also appears on the Founder's Cup of 1601–2 at Magdalen College). Dishes of this sort, usually with an accompanying ewer, were carried to the table so that diners could rinse their fingers in warm, perfumed water. When not in use they would be set up on a buffet or plate cupboard to add glamour to the room. This one is decorated with engraved flowers, foliage, fruit and nuts, and grotesque dolphins, a nod to the watery function of the basin and an enduringly popular late sixteenth- and early seventeenth-century motif.

An example of standard late Stuart plate is the caudle cup and cover, presented by Sir John Barker, 4th Baronet Trimley, which was made in London in 1672–3, and marked 'T.K.' in a cinquefoil below with a plain shield. Barker matriculated in 1673 and was later MP for Ipswich in six parliaments between 1680 and 1696. Both cup and cover, which could be upturned to act as a small salver, are decorated with fine cut-card work introduced to England by Huguenot goldsmiths. Caudle, also known as posset, was hot, spiced, sweetened ale or wine, thickened with egg.

The vast majority of Oxford college plate is made and marked in London, so an intriguing addition to the collection is another early piece, a delightful, small silver-gilt tankard, bearing a medal of Martin Luther, alongside Melanchthon and several of Charles V, Holy Roman Emperor, all dated between 1500 and 1615. The body is engraved with flowers and foliage, and an inscription recording the donor as '*Edmundi Caroli Blombergi*', or Baron Charles Blomberg of Blomberg, who matriculated in 1706 and held a court appointment under George II. The tankard is unmarked, but its style, decoration and the incorporation of medals as ornament suggest that it was made around 1650 in southern Germany. Unusually, it retains its original leather case, the stamped decoration still bearing traces of gilding.

College chapels were another repository of silver for use on the altar and during services. Daily attendance at chapel was mandatory, and founders, Fellows and gentleman commoners would often present pieces of plate. Merton retains some interesting early examples, which survived the great purge of 'superstitious vessels' which afflicted most Oxford and Cambridge colleges during and after the Reformation. One such is the beautifully simple silver-gilt chalice and paten, made in London in 1568–9, by an unidentified maker whose mark is a hand grasping a hammer. They are without a donor inscription, but both are pricked with the College arms and the inscription 'Coll:Mert:'.

*Opposite, left: The chalice. Opposite, top right: Sir John Barker's caudle cup and cover. Opposite, bottom right: George Pudsey's ox-eye cup. **Above:** The rosewater dish. Left: Baron Blomberg's tankard.*

THEODORE GOULSTON'S
GALENI OPERA OMNIA

Michael Dunnill

These three volumes, translated from Galen's original Greek into Latin by Nicolas De Reggio and printed in 1516 in Pavia, were presented to Merton in 1635 by the widow of Theodore Goulston (1575–1632), along with some 120 of his other medical books. Goulston, an erudite classical scholar, first matriculated at Peterhouse then transferred to Merton, where he was elected a probationer Fellow in 1596. In 1604 he was appointed to the junior Linacre lectureship, a post with the specific task of propagating study of the works of Galen and Hippocrates. While holding the lectureship and qualifying for his MB and MD, he set up in general medical practice in Wymondham, Leicestershire and then in London, where he rapidly established a reputation as a celebrated and prosperous physician. In 1611 he became a fellow of the College of Physicians, where he served as censor, responsible for conducting the entrance examination, in 1615–16 and again in 1625–6. All three volumes have extensive marginal notes, most in Latin but some

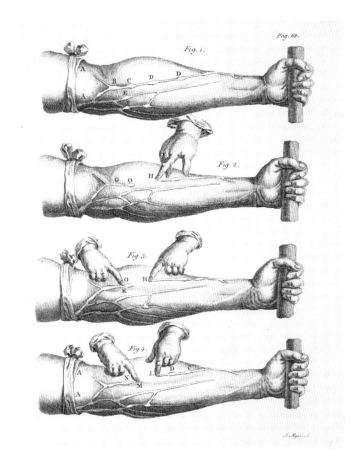

in Greek. Not all the writing appears to be of the same date or by the same hand, but some of these annotations may be by Goulston.

Galen was a prolific writer and more of his work survives than of any other ancient author. He was renowned for his experiments on animals. Yet his conclusions from the experiments were erroneous. Thus he thought that the liver was the source of the blood, that the venous system originated in the liver, that fever was the result of excess of bile and blood and that repeated blood letting was the therapy of choice for all ills, even for blood loss. His most important contribution to clinical medicine lay in his study of the pulse, on which subject he wrote five books. Yet even here some of his ideas were bizarre and this was especially true of his theory as to the cause of the pulse. Totally failing to grasp the concept of blood circulation, he considered the venous and arterial systems entirely separate. He postulated that there were two types of blood, venous and arterial, with separate pathways and functions. Crucially he thought that

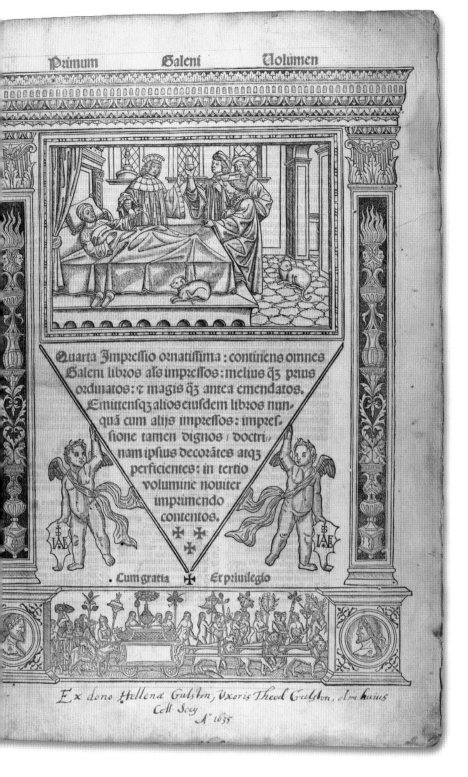

importance of studying function in the living subject. Returning to London in 1602 he sought entry to the College of Physicians, failing on two occasions before passing at the third attempt in 1604. It is not recorded that he was examined by Goulston, but they must have been acquainted, as he was appointed censor in 1613 and again, along with Goulston, in 1625. As early as 1616 Harvey demonstrated that the Galenic theory as to the flow of blood was false from a quantitative analysis in experimental animals of the amount of blood leaving the heart. He showed that the volume of blood leaving the heart in an hour exceeded the volume of the whole animal and deduced that the blood must circulate, otherwise the body would explode under pressure. Secondly, although he could not see the capillaries, he demonstrated in man that there must be a connection between the arteries and the veins. He placed a tourniquet around the upper arm so that no blood flowed into the forearm and hand; then, by loosening it to allow arterial blood to flow while still obstructing the veins, he showed that the latter became distended, proving that blood was passing from one to the other. He also demonstrated that valves in the veins ensured that blood flowed only in one direction towards the heart. He published his theory as to the circulation of the blood in his book *Exercitatio anatomica de motu cordis et sanguinis in animalibus* in 1628. Goulston and Harvey were part of a medical tradition at the College which went back far earlier, to scholars such as John Gaddesden (*c*.1280–1361), author of the highly successful medical textbook *Rosa Medicinae*, and has continued to flourish ever since.

blood leaving the heart was absorbed into the tissues and was constantly being reformed in the liver by conversion from food. It was this theory that blood was continually being produced and then absorbed by the body, presumably after each heartbeat, that led William Harvey, appointed Warden of Merton by Charles I in 1643, to formulate his own ideas on circulation of the blood.

Harvey (1578–1657) was born in Folkestone and educated at King's School, Canterbury, Gonville and Caius College, Cambridge, and Padua. He became sceptical of Galen's teachings and convinced of the

*Opposite, left: William Harvey, Warden, anonymous portrait. **Opposite, right:** Harvey's experiments on blood flow, from his* De motu cordis *(1766 edition).* **Above:** *The title page of Goulston's copy of Galen's works, showing physicians attending a patient, with an inscription recording its donation.*

THE WREN SCREEN

Alan Bott and Roger Highfield

The devastation that had been wrought during the Civil War on the Gothic stalls and Warden Fitzjames's screen of the 1490s, called in the 1660s for a rational, classical restoration of the furnishings of the Chapel. At his death in 1671, Alexander Fisher, senior Fellow, left £1,000 to pave the floor and make new stalls and a screen. The College Register, in unusually poetic style, described Alexander Fisher as 'a man of singular learning and prudence … and devoted to the College as he was in his piety towards God'. The work was entrusted to Sir Christopher Wren. As Savilian professor of Astronomy since 1661, Wren was already somewhat associated with Merton College. In Oxford, he had already built the Sheldonian Theatre (1664–9) and had designed chapel screens for both All Souls and St John's colleges. In 1670, after the Great Fire of 1666, he began to build at least 14 London churches and in the year he began work at Merton he initiated at least five others. In 1673, the year his work at Merton was completed, he submitted his 'Great Model' and design for St Paul's Cathedral. He was thus totally committed to classical architectural forms. The College Register had specified the work at Merton be executed '*ad regulam Corinthiacem exactum*'.

Regrettably, the classical style was to lose favour within the following two centuries. As early as 1814, Ackermann in his *History of Oxford* had pronounced that the design of the Wren screen was 'altogether foreign to the character of the building, displaying a defective taste, with which so many of our ecclesiastical buildings have been deformed'. The advent of Tractarianism in Oxford from 1833 onwards, with its insistence on the rejection of a pagan style in its buildings and a return by the Anglican church to its authentic roots in liturgy and furnishings, was to cause the ejection of Wren's stalls and screen in the following years. In 1842, persuaded by two Fellows, James Hope-Scott and J. Hungerford Pollen and perhaps, too, by Edmund Hobhouse (Sub-Warden and later to be the first bishop of Nelson, New Zealand), the College resolved that 'the wood-work in the choir of the chapel above the stalls' be taken down. William Butterfield was brought in to re-Gothicise the Chapel in 1848. By 1852, the Wren screen and pews had been replaced, the ceiling remodelled, the stonework at the south-east end re-carved and a new font and cover with a crane introduced. A low 'garden wall', consisting of stone, marble and metal work, was built at the entrance to the choir in place of the screen. By 1879 the wheel of taste had moved on yet again and T.G. Jackson (later

Sir Thomas) was invited to consider 'the possibility of restoring the oak screen to its original place', and drawings were prepared. But nothing more was done.

What happened to all the woodwork of 1673 in the meantime? Some has disappeared, some has found a good home. Panelling went to the library of Radley College, founded by William Sewell, a former Postmaster, in 1847, and to Cuxham Church, a college living, in 1923. Wren's pulpit, visible in the north-east corner of the Chapel in Ackermann's print of 1814, was, after a period at Kennington, placed on loan at the new church at Botley in 1958. Donations of woodwork went at various times to Wolvercote, All Saints Church, Oxford, and to Caversfield, although the latter may have been the remains of the Fitzjames furnishings of the 1490s. Fortunately parts of the screen itself were adapted to form the Brodrick Reading Room in the lower Library between 1904 and 1907. Most of the remaining fragments, together with what had been stored in the attics of Fellows' Quad, were splendidly restored to the Chapel in 1960, one bay west of its original position. The fate of two other victims of the diaspora of the Chapel's furnishings may be recorded. Butterfield's 'garden wall' went to Elham, a college living in Kent. It has since disappeared. Then there is the parish pulpit, situated according to Anthony Wood's plan of 1671, in front of the south-east pillar of the tower, thus 'speaking' to the parish congregation in the crossing, and apparently still there in Buckler's drawing of 1815. The tester of this pre-Wren feature now forms part of the large octagonal table in the Upper Library.

Opposite: The screen as restored in 1960. **Left:** *Wren's pulpit, on loan to the church in Botley.* **Above:** *The entry in the Bursar's accounts of 1673, showing in the third line expenditure on the honourable entertainment of Sir Christopher Wren. This provides the only documentary evidence that it was Wren who designed the screen.*

THE SENIOR COMMON ROOM PANELLING

Matthew Jenkinson

The Senior Common Room's wainscoting, completed in November 1680, was born out of two decades of tension between the Warden and many of the Fellows. Sir Thomas Clayton was chosen as Warden in 1661, with the help of his brother-in-law, Sir Charles Cotterell, Master of Ceremonies to Charles II. Yet, in April 1661, when Clayton arrived to take up his position, Fellows gathered at Merton's Gatehouse to block his entry. Clayton had the support of only one of the seven senior Fellows. The Sub-Warden and 12 Fellows wrote to the Visitor, Archbishop William Juxon, urging him to support another candidate, Sir Richard Browne. Clayton's humiliation continued for three weeks, before he could formally take up residence in the Warden's Lodgings.

This inauspicious start augured over 30 years of clashes between Clayton and the Fellows. Our view of Clayton is coloured by the waspish chronicles of Anthony Wood, who called him an 'impudent and rude fellow' and a 'common fornicator', but there were sufficient reasons for Fellows to look at Clayton with hostility. In 1665 Clayton took over Alexander Fisher's rooms in his absence, improving his own accommodation while exacting revenge on the man who, as Sub-Warden, had hidden in these same rooms instead of admitting Clayton in 1661. Lady Clayton allegedly insisted on the wholesale replacement of the furniture in the Warden's Lodgings, at great College expense, while a new summerhouse was built for her in the garden. Clayton also pursued a lawsuit against the City of Oxford, concerning the College's rights

in Holywell, which drove Merton into debt. In 1679 Clayton used the poor state of the College's finances as an excuse for Merton to elect five Fellows rather than six, declining to admit publicly his own animosity towards the potential sixth Fellow. Clayton compounded the situation by dismissing Fellows from the meeting before they considered it formally concluded. Then, even worse, the Warden suspended a senior Fellow,

William Bernard, because Bernard did not properly absent himself when delivering to the Visitor a petition against Clayton. The nadir was reached in 1681. William Cardonnel cried 'the Warden be hanged', when Clayton sent to him a gardener seeking payment for work in the Warden's garden. Clayton demanded that Cardonnel deliver a humiliating public apology. Cardonnel took his own life; Clayton expressed no remorse.

In the same year that Clayton was installed as Warden, Merton designated space above the kitchens as Oxford's first Common Room. It is tempting to view this increased communality of the Fellows as a reaction to an unpopular head of house. The walls were originally painted, but in 1678 Peter Nicholls left £200, partly for the Common Room to be panelled. Nicholls had been one of those Fellows who had stopped Clayton at the Gatehouse in 1661. His role as Sub-Warden in 1662 and Bursar the following year would have brought him into regular contact with Clayton.

The money Nicholls donated came from the tithes of Burmington, a parish of barely 750 acres, but enough to pay for 'well seasoned Flanders oake' for the Common Room. Arthur Frogley, who agreed to the commission on midsummer's day 1680, and who was given four months for its completion, crafted the oak. He had already worked on the staircases and upper gallery of the Sheldonian and the chapels of University College and Corpus Christi, while his Merton commission coincided with that for the south doorway of the Ashmolean. During the 1680s he also worked on the panelling of Brasenose College hall, as well as the first entirely classical chapel in Oxford, at St Edmund Hall. Frogley's wainscoting at Merton clearly impressed fellows in other colleges, as he went on to receive commissions for the common rooms in Lincoln and Trinity colleges.

Just as the designation of a formal Common Room might be viewed as the Fellows bonding in response to external forces, so we might see the panelling as further investment in that communality, as well as a rejoinder to Warden and Lady Clayton's feathering their own nest. It is not the coat of arms of Clayton, incumbent Warden, which appears in the carving, but the device of Nicholls himself: a pheon, or engrailed broad arrow. Perhaps Clayton was irked by this fine new decoration. Yet another clash occurred when Clayton attempted to stop payments to a senior Fellow of the Burmington tithes, the very source of funding that had helped Nicholls pay for the Common Room panelling.

....

*Opposite, left: Detail of the carving above the fireplace. **Opposite, right:** The Senior Common Room, hung with portraits from the sixteenth and seventeenth centuries including those of Queens Katherine of Aragon and Henrietta Maria. **Above, top:** The arms of the College. **Above, bottom:** Peter Nicholls's badge, the pheon.*

THE BELLS

Alan Bott

The College has had bells since its earliest days. Walter Cuddington's bursarial accounts for 1286–7 record expenditure on a wicket gate in a belfry and also work on three bells. Where they were located is not now known. Perhaps they belonged to the old church of St John the Baptist, shortly to be replaced by the building of the Chapel. The fact that there were three bells suggests they served a religious rather than a secular purpose.

During the wardenship of Dr Henry Abyndon (1421–37) work on the north transept was so far completed that the Chapel could be re-dedicated in 1425. Already in 1422 it was being recommended that the building of the bell tower should be expedited while those who had pledged support for its construction were still alive! £20 from the sale of timber from the woods on the College Surrey estates were allocated for the purpose. It was in this situation, evidently, that Warden Abyndon donated the tenor bell, which weighed 32cwt 1qtr 14lbs. The tower, however, was not completed until *c.*1450. Abyndon had died 15 years earlier, so if the bell had been cast in his lifetime it must have been hung from a temporary wooden structure, perhaps within the present belfry.

Although the College authorised the re-casting of the third bell and other necessary maintenance work in 1575, nothing material is known further about the bells until the seventeenth century. The events leading to the installation of the present eight bells in that period are well recorded by Anthony Wood. He noted that in 1657 he, his mother and brothers gave £5 'towards the casting of their five bells into eight. These five were ancient bells and had been put up into the tower at the first building thereof in the time of Henry Abyndon. The tenor or great bell (on which the name of the said Abyndon was put) was supposed to be the best bell in England being as 'twas said, of fine metall silver sound'. However, when the new bells were cast, 'severall were found to

be ugly dead bells for the truth is that (Michael) Darby who cast them stole a great deal of mettle from them … By the knavery of Thomas Jones, the sub-warden who they say was complice with him (the Warden being absent).' On 14 May the eight new bells rang. They 'did not please the curious and critical hearer. However, he plucked them often with some of his fellow-colleagues for recreation sake.' The College Register corroborates this account, giving the total weight of the five old bells as 85 hundredweight and the re-cast eight bells as just under 75 hundredweight.

In 1680, the College engaged Christopher Hodson, bell founder of London, to re-cast the bells, taking advantage of his presence in Oxford for the purpose of re-casting Great Tom at Christ Church. In February 1681, Anthony Wood noted these bells 'rang to the content of the societie'. All eight bells bear the name of Christopher Hodson, the second and the tenor the name of Henry Abyndon, and the third that of Thomas Milbourn. He was a Fellow of Merton, who had died in 1676 and had bequeathed £100 to the College. The eight bells then weighed just over five tons. The tenor, which is in E♭, weighs 28cwt 1qtr 10lbs. It is therefore smaller by 7cwt than Henry Abyndon's great bell.

The hanging and ringing of Merton's bells has a tortuous history and their ringing continues to challenge the most competent ringers. The bells are located some 80 feet from the ground, from which they were originally rung. With the restoration of the Chapel by Edward Blore in 1843, the sixteenth-century square panelling of the ceiling of the transept was removed and a new gallery for the ringers was installed. This has the advantage of revealing the original (*c.*1450) ceiling of the tower, which is located above the ringing gallery. It also provides a daunting challenge to the ringers, as there is a 60-foot drop below them! The massive oak frame of the braced king-post type that supports the bells was re-made in 1885 by Messrs White of Appleton, to the pattern of the former seventeenth-century frame. In 1982 the bells were sent to Whitechapel Bell Foundry in London for re-tuning. Apart from this, the Merton bells remain as re-cast in 1680 and have the distinction of being the oldest complete ring of eight bells in existence.

Left: The inscription on one of the two bells bearing the names of Henry Abyndon and Christopher Hodson. **Opposite:** *Four of the bells hanging in the tower.*

THE MULBERRY TREE

Anthony Fletcher

The Black Mulberry (*Morus Nigra*) is a rugged picturesque tree, often growing to around 25 feet, forming a dense spreading head of branches. This spread is usually wider than the height of the tree. The oblong fruit, about an inch long and an intense purple, resembles a large blackberry or raspberry. It is very juicy with a refreshing saccharine taste. It was much esteemed in the classical period and appears on mosaics at Pompeii. Mulberries reached England in the sixteenth century, a great age of experimentation in growing new plants coming into Europe from around the world.

The purchase of mulberry plants by many Oxford colleges in the early seventeenth century was undoubtedly prompted by an edict from James I in 1608. He was hoping by encouraging their planting to rear silkworms in England but he chose the wrong tree, since it is the White Mulberry on which the silkworm flourishes. It was no matter, for the positive response to the king's exhortation in Oxford may be explained by college fellows planting the tree as an exotic import. In the summer months, as it aged, it yielded a good supply of a delicious new fruit for their tables. It is interesting that the surviving mulberry trees at both Balliol and Merton were planted in their Fellows' gardens. There were certainly mulberry trees in Christ Church and University College gardens in the seventeenth century too. Anthony Wood recorded that, in 1655, an incautious 'chorister of New College fell off from the mulberry tree' there and 'broke his neck'. Shakespeare's celebrated mulberry at New Place in Stratford, planted in 1609, was said to be 'cultivated for its fruit which is very wholesome and palatable'.

No documentation has been found about the purchase or planting of the Merton tree in the accounts of the Bursars for the period 1585 to 1633. Yet it undoubtedly became a flourishing tree during its first 400 or so years of growth. Many Fellows of the College over this period must have enjoyed the fruit, which was presumably carefully collected and served regularly at High Table, for dessert or in cordials.

The recent history of the tree is well recorded. In 1987 the Garden Master and his staff were alarmed to find that a twisting gale appeared to have destroyed the mulberry. But inspection revealed that only half of it had been lost and the rest was in good shape. Knowing that mulberries regenerate readily even from old wood, rescue measures were put in hand: 'we were faced with the choice of starting again, wasting decades of growth, or severe pruning', recalls the Garden Master, Dr Edward Olleson, 'and we cut back savagely to mature wood. The result looked terrible for a year or two, but it soon became quite a shapely mop-headed tree and now no one would know'. One branch of the tree has been discreetly supported by an iron stanchion. Those who know the tree well will have noticed that this stanchion has been changed in length periodically, to allow the tree the support it actually needs as it ages gracefully.

An informal survey of current Fellows has shown that, while some distinctly recall tasting mulberry fruit at High Table, others have no memory of doing so. The quality and size of the crop has certainly varied year by year. Mulberries have often over the centuries been used for making various conserves and wines. The present chef, Michael Wender, remembers an experiment, when there was a particularly good crop, in making mulberry vodka, which he served as an aperitif before dinner. But over the last few years it has been observed that the main beneficiaries of the tree's fruit have usually been local jays and woodpeckers. Cleaning staff in the College, taking a morning break, have also sometimes enjoyed the fruit. But undergraduates and postgraduates appear to have shown less initiative in getting their fingers thoroughly stained by mulberries at their ripest. The quantity of grape sugar in the mulberry is surpassed only by the cherry and by the grape itself.

Notes on *Morus Nigra* in a modern herbal declare that 'mulberry trees are not easily killed' and that old examples may be rejuvenated by careful pruning and cultivation. The Merton garden staff deserve congratulation for the skill with which they have conserved the oldest tree in the garden, which has been enjoyed as a landmark on Sundial Lawn by many generations of members of the College.

*Opposite: The mulberry tree and the east side of Fellows' Quad. **Insert:** Ripening berries on the mulberry tree.*

THE PAINTED GLASS OF 1702

Alan Bott

The great east window of the Chapel dates from *c*.1295. It was originally filled with contemporary glass. The glorious tracery of the upper lights survives and contains a very beautiful 'Annunciation' on either side of the central rose. This, in turn, displays the coats of arms of Henry III, the Lord Edward (Edward I) and the Clare family, the original patrons of Walter de Merton. Apart from the 12 coats of arms of illustrious benefactors in the lower lights, recorded in a drawing by Sir William Dugdale in 1644 but now sadly gone, there is no record of what else was there. However, it must have been found obnoxious to the puritanical mind, for in 1651 it was all replaced with white glass at a cost of £7 3s 6d.

This wretched situation was to be remedied through the munificence of Alexander Fisher, senior Fellow of the College, who bequeathed £1,000 in 1671 for works on the Chapel. Some 30 years later Warden Lydall, at the age of 83 years, discharged his final duty as Fisher's executor by installing the painted-glass windows in the east window from the residual proceeds of Fisher's estate. The work, 'in which are represented the chief parts of our Saviour's history in six compartments', in the words of John Gutch, the editor of Wood's *History and Antiquities of Oxford*, was entrusted to William Price, senior, of Holborn, London. The six Scenes from the Life of Christ were arranged in the seven lights of the east window as follows: in the centre, occupying three lights each, the 'Crucifixion' and the 'Last Supper'; on the north and south sides, occupying two lights each, were the 'Resurrection', the 'Nativity', the 'Ascension' and the 'Baptism'. Above, in the heads of the seven lights, were placed the arms of the College, those of the donor, Alexander Fisher, and of the Warden, Richard Lydall. The individual numbers of the date 1702 were placed in each of the four outer lights. Below is an inscription reading '*W. Price pinxit. Expensis Mri. Alexand. Fisher hujus Coll. quondam socii. Ao. Dni.MDCCII Custode Ricardo Lydall M.D.*'

In 1934, Professor H.W. Garrod encouraged the College to remove Price's glass – 'a blare of yellow' – which was considered, at that time, an offence to the splendid medieval glass above it and the Henry de Mansfield glass alongside. In its place was put heraldic and figure glass brought from the west window, the Queen's Room and the Breakfast Room. At that time,

Professor Garrod noted that Price's glass might be placed in the east windows of the transepts. However, it was instead stored in the Chapel roof and in Mob Quad until it was loaned to the Stained Glass Museum at Ely in 1976. In 2000, the glass was returned to the College and installed in the north transept by Keith Barley of York. As the panels are so broad, they are placed in manganese bronze frames which stand inside the original fenestration.

Perhaps hardly anyone would claim that the eighteenth century was one of the greatest periods of stained glass production, but the Merton glass of 1702 is one of the largest and finest surviving examples of its manufacture in that period, made at the height of his powers by William Price, senior (*c*.1647–*c*.1709), founder of the preeminent family of painted glass makers continued by his son Joshua (1672–1722) and his grandson William (d. 1765). He was reportedly paid £260 for the work. Some £213 was left from the Alexander Fisher estate and Lydall also contributed generously. The depictions of the sacred scenes were derived from the many available engravings of works by Raphael and Tintoretto in the Vatican and in Venice.

Although now placed within the north transept, which dates from before 1425, the glass of 1702 has some more or less contemporary companions on the surrounding walls in the monuments to Sir Thomas Bodley (1612/13), Anthony Wood (1695) and Henry Jackson (1727). Beyond the crossing are the monuments of the principal *dramatis personae*, Warden Lydall and the donor himself, Alexander Fisher. But let the opinion of a discerning, though a trifle unlikely critic, Max Beerbohm, conclude the matter. He, of course, saw the glass in its original position in the east window. In the first letter that the young Max wrote dutifully home to his mother, in Michaelmas term, 1890, he reported: 'I went to a short service at Merton Chapel (where there is a fine stained-glass window!) at 8.30 and then there is not another service till 5.00, which I (also) went to.'

....

Insert: A detail of the 'Last Supper' showing Christ and St John. **Opposite:** *The 'Crucifixion' with the arms of Alexander Fisher, the College and Warden Lydall.*

THE GLOBES

Sarah Bendall

Two of the striking features in the southern range in the Upper Library are the globes at either end. This was not the first pair that Merton owned. In 1577 a terrestrial and celestial globe, possibly by Mercator (1541–51), were acquired in exchange for the organ in the Chapel, in a deal with William Smith, rector of the College's living of Cuxham and a former Fellow. These remained in the College until they were lent in 1645 to the tutor of the Duke of York (future James II), then at Christ Church, and alas never returned.

Colleges owned globes for both decorative and educational purposes, and several had a pair from the late seventeenth century. After John Senex had advertised in 1740 27-inch globes (the largest produced commercially in England at that time) as 'fit to adorn the Libraries of the Curious' for 25 guineas, Merton acquired a pair, as did All Souls, Queen's and St John's colleges. In owning globes by John Senex, Merton had objects made by an esteemed globe-maker with an international reputation. He had been apprenticed to a bookseller and became a publisher, bookseller, and map-, globe- and scientific instrument-maker. He was elected a Fellow of the Royal Society in 1728, was a skilled engraver and became the leading scientific publisher of his time. On his death in 1740 his widow Mary continued the business until 1755.

As was usual at the time, both globes have inner shells made from several layers of paper pasted together. In each, an inner support of a turned wooden pillar runs north–south, with four branches extending from the centre. The two hemispheres were attached to the support with staples and, like other English globes, joined at the equator (Dutch globes were commonly joined longitudinally). The papier mâché was coated with plaster, covered with copper-engraved and hand-coloured paper half-gores, and varnished. The globes are on their original stands; each has a horizontal horizon ring and a brass meridian ring with an hour circle and pointer.

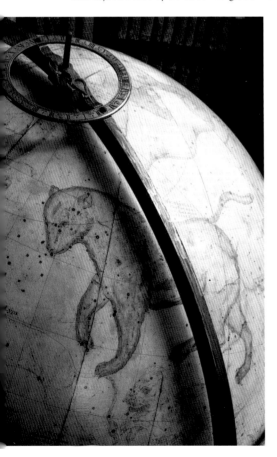  

One can spend hours poring over these globes. Both have notes on them in Latin, unusual for an English globe and perhaps indicating that Senex intended them for use in universities. The terrestrial globe has many notes on discoveries, for example of America (showing California as a peninsula), South Africa and South America, and remarks on navigation. The prime meridian runs west of the Canary Islands, not through London, perhaps reflecting Senex's intended academic market. The monsoons and trade winds are marked, along with the loxodromes for 32 compass points. The horizon ring has scales (from inside to outside) for degrees, 32 compass points, the Gregorian calendar, the zodiac, and the Julian calendar. We know the globe was made after 1722, because when the pair were conserved in 1999 it was possible to see that the shell was made from alternate layers of rough brown paper and uncut pages of a work by Nathaniel Marshall, *The case of the erectors of a chapel, or oratory; in the parish of St Andrew's Holborn*, printed in that year.

At first glance the celestial globe is easier to date because the title gives the year 1740, but this might have indicated the epoch of the stars shown and not necessarily the year of production. Senex also records the epoch 939 BC, which is based on ideas by Newton published posthumously in 1728. He advertised that on this globe 'are placed all the Stars in Mr Flamsteed's Catalogue, as published by Dr Halley, etc., being above 2000 more than ever were inserted upon any Globe'. Senex was one of the first globe-makers to mark the stars by their Bayer notation (a Greek letter followed by the genitive case of the constellation) and he introduced the name Ramus for the apples of Hercules. The 48 Ptolemaic constellations are shown along with four others, the four southern constellations and those of Plancius and Hevelius, all with attractive and colourful drawings filling in the fantastical creatures and figures.

Unlike the other Senex globes in Oxford and at the National Maritime Museum, the titles of Merton's have 'R.S.S.' (Fellow of the Royal Society) written in manuscript rather than printed, and 'Londini' printed at the end on the celestial globe. On this globe the meaning of the manuscript label 'Coll: Merton: Oxon D.C.D.' underneath the title is mysterious. It might refer to a gift, with the second 'D.' an abbreviation for 'dedit', but no likely donor with initials 'D.C.' has been identified. These beautiful treasures still have secrets to uncover.

....

Opposite, left: Ursa Major on the celestial globe. Opposite, centre: California and the Pacific on the terrestrial globe. Opposite, right: The title and label on the celestial globe. Above: The celestial globe standing in the south-east end of the Library.

JOSEPH KILNER'S COIN COLLECTION

Ben Zurawel

In 1951 the College loaned its collection of 676 coins, medals and tokens, mostly contained within a small eighteenth-century tortoise-shell cabinet, to the Ashmolean Museum. The collection is now incorporated in the University's wider collection, itself the oldest in England, five cabinets of coins having been donated to the Bodleian Library by Archbishop Laud in 1636. The Merton collection included 49 Roman coins (a mixture of silver and bronze), around 350 English coins, the majority covering the Tudor and Stuart kings, 30 Scots coins, 20 Irish coins and 10 or 20 each from Louis XIV's France, Colonial Spain, Portugal, Italy, Germany, Denmark and the Netherlands, together with a few interesting and unusual Early American specimens. The most interesting piece is probably an impressive gold coin of Cunobelin, the pre-Roman 'King of the Britons'.

As interesting as the coins themselves, some of which are quite striking, is the very existence of the collection. It was in large part bought for the College by the Reverend Joseph Kilner (*c*.1721–93), Fellow from 1741. Described by a contemporary as 'an accurate enquirer', who, on account of his poor health, 'had much time to use, which he employed chiefly as an antiquary', Kilner's tombstone records that 'after a life of infirmity most graciously alleviated and wonderfully lengthened out to more than seventy-two years he died 3 June 1793'. He funded his studies by holding a number of church livings: he was rector of Farleigh, vicar of Lapworth and held the sinecure of Gamlingay.

An expert on the history of the College, Kilner was preoccupied by the study of antiquities, what one might now today call archaeology or local history. In this he was not unusual among the College's eighteenth-century Fellows. Rogers Ruding (1751–1820), matriculated 1768, Fellow from 1775, wrote a seminal numismatic treatise, *Annals of the Coinage*. He was the nephew of Walter Ruding, who had been Kilner's patron

as a Postmaster. Family ties within the fellowship were not rare in the eighteenth century: Kilner's brother, Samuel, was himself elected Fellow in 1753. Joseph Kilner's work included four volumes of materials on the history of the College and an *Account of Pythagoras's School in Cambridge* (1790). The school, an early medieval stone house in Cambridge which pre-dates the earliest university buildings in the city, was owned by Merton from the 1270s.

The enlightened idea that the past could be studied using physical objects as well as texts was just beginning to take hold in the mid-eighteenth century, a process helped by the advent of the Grand Tour, travel to the classical sites of Italy which was increasingly *de rigueur* as part of the education of aristocratic gentlemen. Coins were a natural favourite of the antiquarian and Grand Tourist: they are portable, easily dateable, valuable, mass-produced objects which combine text and image, travel over a wide geographic area and survive well. John Evelyn, a contemporary of Samuel Pepys, wrote, in *Numismata: A Discourse of Medals, Ancient and Modern* (1697):

> *Every one who is a lover of Antiquities, especially of Marbles and Inscriptions, may yet neither have the faculty to be at so vast a Charge, or opportunity of Collecting them at so easy and tolerable an Expence, as he may of Medals [coins], which well and judicially chose have always been esteemed (and that worthily) not only an Ornament but an useful and necessary Appendage to a Library.*

Together with Kilner's cabinet, the 1951 donation included a small hoard (a collection of coins either lost or deposited and not recovered) of 12 gold coins found during excavations by the Chapel in 1903. It must have been deposited after 1723, the date of the latest coin. It comprised ten

guineas and one half-guinea ranging from Charles II to George I, and a Brazilian 'half-moidore' of John V of Portugal, minted in Bahia in 1715. The fact that the Portuguese coin, the same weight as a half-guinea, was found in the hoard has been used to support a theory that foreign coins of equivalent weight to English gold coins were frequently to be found in circulation in the eighteenth-century English economy. A College Order from 1903 records that one coin from the hoard was given to Mr Axtell, the builder, 'in consideration of the trouble he took in recovering the hoard'. The Merton coins remain accessible to scholars in the Heberden Coin Room, and the Ashmolean archive includes various manuscripts which accompanied the Kilner cabinet.

Opposite: Gold stater of Cunobelin and London rose noble of Edward IV, 1465–70.
Above: Half-guinea of George III, 1797; third-guinea of George III, 1799; marriage medal of Charles I and Henrietta Maria, 1625; Shrewsbury penny of Edward the Confessor; 'broad' (20 shilling piece) of Oliver Cromwell as Lord Protector, 1656.

LEWIS VASLET PASTEL PORTRAITS

Beth Williamson

Merton's 14 pastel portraits of Fellows by Lewis Vaslet (1742–1808), a fashionable Bath miniature painter, represent about one-quarter of the artist's 55 or so known pastel paintings. There are no mentions of Vaslet, or of these portraits, in the College Registers or accounts. Therefore it seems unlikely that the paintings of Fellows were commissioned as any kind of a College enterprise, and probable that the individual Fellows themselves were responsible for commissioning them.

The Merton collection comprises three groups of paintings, carried out around 1779–80, 1789–90, and 1795–6. Those definitely in the early group are a portrait of Walter Ruding (d. 1789), which bears the date 5 June 1779, one of Giles Rooke (d. 1808), inscribed 'Painted at Oxford, 1780 by Mr Vaslet of Bath', and one of Thomas Sainsbury (d. 1787). Two undated portraits of Henry Barton (Warden 1759–90, d. 1790) and a second portrait of Walter Ruding are harder to date. All three might belong to this early group, or Barton and Ruding may each have commissioned one earlier and one later portrait, though the portraits of Barton are very similar except in dimensions (one being 12 x 9.75in and the other 8 x 6.25). Perhaps he had a second portrait made to give as a gift to a friend or family member, but for some reason the copy stayed at Merton as well. Also hard to pin down is a portrait of Rogers Ruding (d. 1820): he became a Fellow in 1775, and it is possible therefore that he, along with his uncle, Walter Ruding, had a portrait made in 1779. But equally his portrait might belong with the second group, or the third.

The definite 'middle group' portraits begin with the portrait of David Hartley (d. 1813), inscribed 'L. VASLET FECIT 1789'. Three more, of James Boulter (d. 1822), Ralph Carr (d. 1837), and Henry Anthony Pye (d. 1839), each bear a similar signature and date of 1790. These three might have been commissioned to commemorate the fellowship

elections of those three individuals (1789, 1790 and 1790 respectively), but there is no general pattern across the rest of the dated portraits that links the date of an individual's becoming a Fellow with the date of his portrait. A fourth painting, without a subject's name inscribed, also bears a similar signature to the other 1790 portraits. Judging by the apparent age of this man, it might possibly be Peter Vaughan, who later became Warden. 1790 was the year of Vaughan's BA, though, so he would have been rather precocious in his commissioning of a Vaslet portrait at that date. There is one more dated painting, of Lewis Way (d. 1840), bearing Vaslet's signature and the date 1796. The final painting of the 14 is that of Robert Richard Pigou (d. 1823). This is undated. It may have been painted in 1795 to commemorate his fellowship in that year (or, perhaps painted in 1790, to commemorate Pigou's BA in that same year).

The Merton Vaslets are mostly of fine quality, with some of very high quality indeed, such as those of James Boulter and that which might be the later of the two depicting Walter Ruding. That of David Hartley is certainly among the best. It is also rather unusual, in that it was rare to depict a sitter wearing spectacles at this time. David Hartley himself was a distinguished character. Having served as MP for Hull, and working (with William Wilberforce) to end the slave trade, he was sent to Paris in 1783 as 'Minister Plenipotentiary'. There he helped to broker the Peace of Paris, which effectively ended the American Revolutionary War. Hartley may also distinguish himself among the group as the possible conduit by which Vaslet came to be working for the Merton Fellows. None of those who had a portrait painted in Vaslet's first Oxford period had obvious Bath or North Somerset connections that might have led to their knowing Vaslet and suggesting that he come to Oxford. However, David Hartley had, since 1757, owned a house in Bath, and it may be that Vaslet's Oxford work resulted from an introduction by Hartley. However the connection between Vaslet and Merton came about, it resulted in a unique collection. No other college in Oxford (or Cambridge, for that matter) has a comparable set of such paintings.

....

*Left: The portraits in the New Common Room. **Opposite, top left:** Walter Ruding. **Opposite, top right:** David Hartley, who, in addition to his political career, studied the fireproofing of theatres and ships. **Opposite, bottom left:** Robert Pigou. **Opposite, bottom right:** James Boulter.*

PARKER'S OF OXFORD SALES LEDGERS

Julian Reid

'Parker's of Broad Street' is a name familiar to older generations of Oxonians, but few realise that Basil Blackwell had acquired a share in this long-established bookshop in 1937, or that it had an even more venerable history than Blackwell's. Parker's traced its origins to the late eighteenth century when, following the death of his father-in-law and business partner James Fletcher in 1798, William Hanwell went into business with Joseph Parker. It was as a result of the acquisition by Blackwell's that the surviving records of Parker's came to Merton in 2003 as part of the Merton Blackwell Collection. A rare survival among these records are four ledgers recording trade conducted by Fletcher, Hanwell and Parker with members of the University between 1794 and 1800, giving us a glimpse into the reading habits, or at least book-buying practices, of late Georgian England.

The volumes measure approximately 48cm x 20cm, written on heavy paper and bound in cream parchment-covered boards. Three of the volumes run to over 600 pages each, and collectively record many thousands of sales. Frequent customers are assigned a page to themselves; less frequent customers share a page. Each is identified by title, surname and college and, in some cases, their academic status. Within their pages we encounter the nervous freshman, the dilettante gentleman commoner, the connoisseur bibliophile, the industrious Fellow and the impecunious scholar. The contemporary undergraduate curriculum can be reconstructed. Within days of matriculation the freshman is often to be found making essential purchases: a copy of Napleton's *Logic*, Xenophon's *Memorabilia*, and Simson's *Elements of Euclid*. To these Charles Garth of Merton, in November 1796, added 'a small case of instruments' with which to master Euclid better. The freshman could also add other essentials: paper, notebooks, ink, pens and, for those all-important letters home, sealing wax and wafers.

Industry, success, failure or waning enthusiasm are revealed as the years progress. Charles Garth progressed to the study of Hebrew in his second year, being awarded his BA in 1799, at which point he drew breath by taking up French (a grammar, book of exercises and works of Molière were among his purchases of 1799) before proceeding MA in 1802. His near contemporary Thomas Holt started with the same promise, tackling Xenophon, Quintilian and Aristotle in the

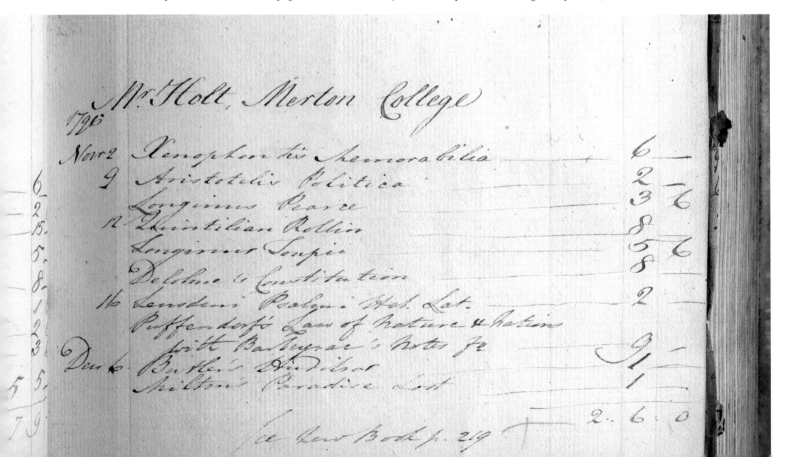

Michaelmas of 1796, but he did not progress to the study of Napleton's *Logic* until his second term. His purchases fail after the acquisition of an Italian dictionary and the works of Tasso in March 1797, and he went down a year later without taking a degree. Thomas Goddard of Corpus Christi, however, exercised the privilege of a gentleman commoner of not having to read for a degree, and his sole expenditure in 1797 was 11 shillings on nothing more taxing than the monthly *Sporting Magazine*.

By the 1790s, Oxford was shedding its reputation for sloth of earlier decades, and Oxford booksellers were able to cater for more than the traditionally narrow curriculum of classics, logic and theology. If his book-buying reflects his reading, George Williams, doctor of physic and professor of botany, kept abreast of developments in his fields and beyond, buying works on plants, fungi, insects, cow pox, and diabetes, as well as light, electricity and magnetism. It is doubtful, though, whether Scrope Berdmore, Warden of Merton 1790–1810, could ever have read the contents of his ever-expanding library. A connoisseur of books, with the exception of the long vacation rarely a week went by without at least one visit to Messrs Fletcher, Hanwell and Parker, spending over £50 on 31 purchases in the 12 months from February 1794. His tastes were catholic, encompassing theology and patristics, classical and English literature, history, natural history and law. Although he had little taste for science, he appreciated a fine edition, spending 11 guineas on a 15-volume edition of the works of Shakespeare bound in Russian leather, and a 1670 edition of *Paradise Lost*.

College libraries too drew on the stock of Fletcher, Hanwell and Parker. In 1795 Merton College spent £10 on two volumes of Stuart and Revett's monumental *Antiquities of Athens*. Exquisitely illustrated, they are still preserved in the Library, another of the College's hidden treasures. And when, at last, it came time for a student to go down, he could apply to Parker's for packing cases and cords, in which to stow his precious purchases. If he did not plan to graduate, he could whirl away from Broad Street, trailing a string of unpaid bills that might not be settled for years to come.

SECTION THREE: MODERN MERTON

THE KITCHENS

Alan Bott

Between 1264 and 1268 Walter de Merton acquired the principal properties which were to provide the site for his foundation at Oxford. In some cases, suitable buildings already existed for immediate use by his College, among them the houses of Halegod, Herprut and Flixthorp, which provided some accommodation for the Warden and scholars. By 1280, according to a Bull of Pope Nicholas III, confirming the foundation of the *Domus Scolarium de Merton*, there were already established 40 scholars, four chaplains and some laymen serving as Bursars and stewards. The construction of facilities for communal feeding must therefore have been an immediate priority. These were to consist of the Great Hall and the Warden's Hall, each with its own kitchens.

Unfortunately no formal College rolls remain before 1277 (if they ever existed), so there is no written evidence about the first kitchens. Bursars' rolls, however, survive from April 1277. Work on the Great Hall had doubtless begun some years before, because in 1277 an expenditure

of 1s 2d was made to Geoffrey the carpenter and his assistant for two days' work in the Hall and 1d for keys for the pantry. In 1296–7, expenditure was made for vats and other vessels for the kitchen and cellar. The second hall, the Warden's Hall, existed by 1283 and probably rather earlier. A major fitting out of the little kitchen was in progress in 1286. The little kitchen probably lay due south from its Hall, which was splendidly rebuilt in 1300. In 1300–1, some pigs were received from the College estates at Gamlingay for the Warden's table.

The earliest surviving picture of the kitchen of the Great Hall is that of Ralph Agas, a drawing of 1578, published in 1588. It shows a building running out from the screens passage at the west end of the Hall, southwards and occupying (as it still does) an area equal to almost half of the west side of what is now Fellows' Quad. There are, however, four corbels high on the outside west wall of the Hall, which perhaps suggest a penthouse or that some other building was planned there originally. Lower down, to the south of the Rawlins Arch there is a drip

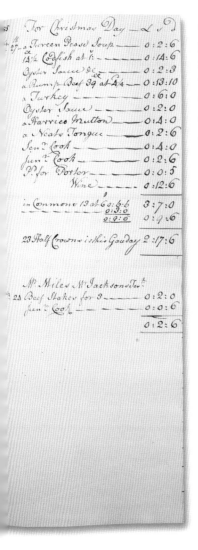

course, which suggests the former presence of a lean-to building. Judging from Loggan's print of 1675, there were two louvres on the roof in the area of the Hall, one towards the centre and one over the kitchen area, to allow the emission of smoke.

The admission of a new Warden was often accompanied by the compilation of an inventory of the College's furnishings, particularly of the Warden's House, but also sometimes of the Chapel, Hall and kitchen. Full lists of the contents of the kitchen are recorded in the sixteenth century, on the admission of Wardens Chambers (1525), Tyndal (1544) and Savile (1586). These lists include some 20 different objects, some running into many items. They include, for example: five brass pots, a cauldron, a chafing dish, a brass pestle and mortar, seven spits (three long, two short, two round), two gridirons, an axe, a pair of tongs, two chopping knives, a colander, two frying pans, two dozen platters and a brass custard ladle. In the same century, two queens dined in Merton Hall: Katherine of Aragon in 1518 and Elizabeth in 1592.

The building of Fellows' Quad in 1609–10 necessitated the clearing of the buildings on the south side of the Hall. In the accounts, there is an entry for two workmen, 'Deerlove and Gammon for demolishing the Kitchen, as agreed £5 10s'. This must have been substantial work for, in the same account, 'Whitehead the stone cutter' received only £20 0s 9d for 463½ tons of freestone. The Hall underwent a major rebuilding in the years 1790–4 at the hands of James Wyatt, and again between 1872 and 1874, more sympathetically, by Sir Gilbert Scott. The kitchens, however, were completely gutted and rebuilt in the early 1960s, under the supervision of Robert Hodgson, the Estates Bursar.

This formed part of the reconstruction of the Senior Common Room and Savile Room above. Some of the former furnishings of the kitchen, the stone mortar and the well-water pump of 1785 were saved and are now relocated in the garden, by the Summer House. The stainless-steel appurtenances of the present kitchen have succeeded the cockroaches of an earlier period and the kitchens are now regularly awarded a congratulatory first by Health and Safety inspectors!

....

*Opposite: The kitchen in 1960, with oven, frying pans and giant pestle and mortar. **Left:** College Christmas dinner in 1785 featured pea soup, beef, mutton, neat's tongue and cod as well as turkey, all dressed with plenty of oyster sauce and washed down with porter and wine. **Above:** The kitchen mortar, now in the Fellows' Garden for the benefit of the birds.*

ROWLANDSON'S DRAWINGS OF MERTON

Susan Skedd

Among Merton's many treasures that are not on public display are two watercolour drawings by the celebrated Georgian artist and caricaturist Thomas Rowlandson (1756–1827). These undated drawings depict two picturesque and indeed picaresque views of the College, the first looking along Merton Street, with the Lodge in the foreground, and the second looking south towards the Chapel from Magpie Lane. Animating these views are wonderfully vivid and characteristically rumbustious vignettes of College life. In 'View of the Lodge at Merton College', a group of rotund dons stand outside Postmasters' Hall to inspect the latest delivery of wine barrels, a female fruit seller waylays Fellows just before they duck through the wooden door into the College, and three figures on horseback prance down Merton Street at some pace, led by a fashionably dressed woman who cracks the whip, with two dons trailing in her wake. By contrast, a coaching scene dominates the foreground of 'View of the southern end of Magpie Lane': passengers on board a stagecoach parked on the left of Magpie Lane are getting ready to leave for a journey, a soldier kisses a woman goodbye, while a don and his lady in their carriage drive through an entrance into Oriel College on the right-hand side.

The two drawings certainly convey an image of College life that seems to conform to contemporary attitudes towards eighteenth-century Oxford, namely that the dons and students were pleasure-seeking and indolent and that the University was valued as much for its social life as for its academic excellence. From the particular perspective of a Mertonian, it is hard not to be surprised at the busy and bustling scenes presented in these two drawings, which seem at odds with our experiences of the quietness and intensity of life in Merton Street and Magpie Lane. How accurate and truthful is Rowlandson's portrait of College life? In order to answer this question, it is important to understand how the images were created. While it is not possible to date these views precisely, they form part of a series of watercolours of Oxford and Cambridge undertaken by Rowlandson between about 1810 and 1815. What has become apparent in recent years is that the architectural settings of these views were copied from prints that had previously been published in the annual *Oxford Almanack*. For example, the 'View of the Lodge at Merton College' is clearly based on the view by Michael Angelo Rooker (1746–1801) that had been published in the *Almanack* of

1772. The difference, however, lies in the depiction of the human and social elements in the scene for, whereas Rooker's figures are sober and non-controversial, Rowlandson's comic characters are clearly providing a satirical commentary on University life. After all, Rowlandson achieved great popular success with his series of illustrations to Dr William Combe's *Three Tours of Doctor Syntax* (London, 1812–21), which offered an overtly comic view of academic life in Oxford that had appealed to his largely non-Oxford public.

Several of Rowlandson's University views were published as aquatints in 1810 by the highly successful London publisher Rudolf Ackermann (1764–1834), who had already collaborated with him on a number of publications, including *The Microcosm of London* (1808–10). This established the practice of Rowlandson providing the figures against an architectural backdrop drawn by Pugin. It has been suggested that Rowlandson relied entirely on the *Almanack* prints for his visual depiction of Oxford life and that he may have never visited the city which he appears to depict so persuasively. It seems telling that when Ackermann later commissioned a full set of views for *A History of the University of Oxford, its Colleges, Halls and Public Buildings* (London, 2 vols, 1814), he chose Pugin to draw the architectural settings and William Henry Pyne (1769–1843) to sketch in the figures. While it is disappointing to speculate that Rowlandson may never have seen Merton College with his own eyes, this thought in no way diminishes the attractiveness and appeal of these two wonderful watercolours, which offer us amusing and intriguing insights into what he perceived was the everyday reality of College life.

The drawings were generously donated to the College by two former students, though it is no longer known who donated which drawing: one was given in 1938 by A.B. Burney, who had helped to fund the remodelling of the Grove Building with a gift of £10,000 in 1928, and the other in 1961 by G.T. Davis.

*Opposite, top: The view down Magpie Lane. **Opposite, bottom:** The view along Merton Street, showing the carving on the Gatehouse in the higher position it occupied until 1838 (see p. 52).*

THE SHUTE BARRINGTON PORTRAIT

Matthew Grimley

In 1956, the art historian Kenneth Garlick was visiting Merton when he took refuge from a shower of rain in the Hall. His Mertonian host apologised that there were no noteworthy pictures hanging on the walls, but Garlick, who was the leading expert on the society portraitist Sir Thomas Lawrence (1769–1830), recognised a 'lost' Lawrence portrait of Shute Barrington, bishop of Durham. In his own catalogue of Lawrence's work published a few years before, Garlick had listed the portrait as 'untraced.' Merton was unaware that it had such a treasure in its midst.

The portrait depicts Barrington be-wigged, and seated on a bishop's throne (though he was reputedly one of the first Anglican bishops to abandon wig-wearing). It was exhibited at the Royal Academy in 1796, by which time Barrington had been bishop of Durham for five years; a later picture by Lawrence of the bishop hangs at Auckland Castle. The artist was the leading English portrait painter of the Regency period, his reputation unrivalled at the time of his sudden death in 1830. But by 1881, when the College Bursar, William Esson, bought and presented the portrait to Merton, Lawrence's stock had declined. His subsequent twentieth-century rehabilitation owed much to the work of Kenneth Garlick.

The career of Shute Barrington (1734–1826) exemplifies both the 'Old Corruption' of English political culture before the 1832 Reform Bill, and the paradox that this was compatible with strenuous movements for social, moral and political reform. Barrington matriculated as a gentleman commoner in 1752, became a Fellow on graduation in 1755, and was ordained the following year. By 1759 his elder brother, Viscount Barrington, Secretary of War in the Duke of Newcastle's administration, was petitioning Newcastle on Shute's behalf for preferment, saying that 'anything in the church not under £300 would make both him and me completely happy'. Through Newcastle's patronage, and later that of King George III himself, Barrington landed a series of plum jobs – canonries of Christ Church, St Paul's and Windsor, and the bishoprics of Llandaff (1769) and Salisbury (1782) – culminating in his appointment to the fabulously endowed prince-bishopric of Durham in 1791. In spite of enjoying Newcastle's patronage, though, Barrington seems to have remained his own man; when the duke sent him to Merton in 1759 to instruct the seven voting Fellows not to elect Henry Barton as Warden because of his Tory connections, Barrington ended up switching sides, and Barton was duly elected.

Two details in the portrait – the academic cap in Barrington's hand and the Gothic arch behind him – point to two of the bishop's enthusiasms, scholarly patronage and architectural improvement. Though not himself a great intellect, he became a considerable patron, gathering around him a literary circle that included the literary scholar and Merton Fellow Thomas Tyrwhitt. Sir Walter Scott was also a frequent visitor to Mongewell Park, his house near Wallingford. Barrington built up a notable library of his own, and paid for the acquisition by the Bodleian of books from two great Italian collections, the Pinelli and Crevenna libraries. As bishop of Durham, he bestowed the wealthiest living in England, Bishopwearmouth, on the theologian William Paley, who returned the favour by dedicating to him his greatest work, *Natural Theology*.

Barrington's contribution to architecture was less beneficial. At Salisbury Cathedral, he employed the architect James Wyatt (dubbed 'Wyatt the Destroyer' by later critics) to demolish two medieval chantry-chapels and a bell-tower to tidy up the Cathedral Close. The duo's proposed 'improvements' to Durham Cathedral (including the addition of a spire) were never completed, owing to a public outcry. Less controversially, Barrington built new churches in the newly populous industrial areas of Durham diocese.

But it was for his benefactions to the poor and his association with the anti-slavery cause that Barrington was most celebrated. He supported the Sunday schools movement and endowed a large number of schools in County Durham. He also championed agricultural improvement, allegedly originating the 'three acres and a cow' slogan later used by Victorian land campaigners. With his close friend, William Wilberforce, he set up the 'Society for Bettering the Condition and Improving the Comforts of the Poor' in 1796 to conduct research into social improvement. Barrington also helped to fund Wilberforce's campaign against the slave trade, and warned fellow peers in 1807 that, unless they supported abolition, Britain would 'look in vain hereafter for the glories of the Nile or Trafalgar'. According to Wilberforce, Barrington was 'a very sun, the centre of an entire system'.

Insert: One of a pair of candlesticks presented to the College by Shute Barrington.
Opposite: Shute Barrington, bishop of Durham, by Sir Thomas Lawrence.

RUSSIAN TREASURES

Mikhail Kizilov

Merton College houses several highly interesting objects related to the visit of the Russian emperor Alexander I the Blessed (1777–1825), who was perhaps the most enigmatic tsar Russia ever had. Alexander's visit to England, which took place after the defeat of Napoleon in the Battle of the Nations in Leipzig (1813) and a short while before the Congress of Vienna (1814–15), formed an important event both in Alexander's life and in the history of the development of British-Russian relations. In June 1814 Alexander, together with his sister, Ekaterina Pavlovna, the duchess of Oldenburg, visited Oxford in order to get an honorary doctorate at the Sheldonian. They spent the night of 14 June in the Queen's Room at Merton, though Edward Nares, Regius professor of Modern History at the time, recorded that the emperor slept on a mattress on the floor in preference to the bed offered him by the College and that four of his servants 'slept in their clothes on the landing place of the staircase, and did no small damage, by their foreign habits, and disregard of the value of the furniture'.

Alexander and his sister's stay in the Queen's Room is reflected in several valuable inscriptions and objects currently kept at Merton. Peter Vaughan, the Warden of the College, was highly excited by the fact that Merton was selected to receive the mighty Russian emperor, 'the deliverer of Europe' from Napoleon's tyranny. After Alexander's departure he, at his own expense, installed in the Queen's Room two stained-glass windows with the image of the Russian imperial double-headed eagle and a lengthy inscription in Latin commenting on the emperor's visit to Merton. The inscription mentioned that Alexander and Ekaterina Pavlovna were content to stay in the Queen's Room because Henrietta Maria, the wife of Charles I, had lodged there during the English Civil War. Both windows still can be seen in the Queen's Room. Another monumental marble tablet with a Latin inscription in honour of

Collegii Mertonensis	Коллегіи Мертонской
custodi sociis que	Попечителю и Сочленамъ
vv doctissimis et sanctissimis	Мужамъ ученѣйшимъ и
a quibus	достопочтенѣйшимъ
cum oxonium inviseret	за оказанное
liberali hospitio receptus erat	при обозрѣніи Оксфорда
hoc vas	гостепріимство
e lapide siberiano factum	сей сосудъ
memoris grati que animi	изъ камня Сибирскаго
specimen	изсѣченный
d[onum] d[edit]	въ знакъ признательнаго
Alexander omnium russiarum	воспоминанія
imperator	даровалъ
anno sacro MDCCCXVI	АЛЕКСАНДРЪ
	ИМПЕРАТОРЪ Всероссійскій
	въ лѣто благодати
	1816

Both inscriptions may be translated as follows: 'In the blessed year of 1816, Alexander, Emperor of All the Russias, donated this vessel, made of Siberian stone, to Merton College, its warden and fellows, most enlightened and venerable men, as a token of pleasant memory of the hospitality accorded during his visit to Oxford'.

Archival sources attest that it was only in February 1822 that the vase reached the College. The classicist Samuel Parr (1747–1825) is said to have composed the Latin inscription, while its Russian variant (apparently a translation of the Latin inscription) seems to have been written by Count Christopher Lieven, the Russian ambassador to Great Britain. The vase has always attracted the attention of Russian and Soviet visitors to Oxford, including important Soviet officials and the famous poetess Anna Akhmatova. It seems to be perhaps the most important object ever donated to Oxford by a Russian visitor and another highly valuable treasure among those kept at Merton.

Alexander was installed in Merton's dining hall, in the most honourable place, right beneath the portrait of the founder. Its text was supposed to remind future generations of Mertonians and visitors to the College about the fact that Alexander and his sister stayed at Merton. At the end of the nineteenth century, however, when relations between England and Russia deteriorated, the tablet was removed from the Hall at the suggestion of Merton historian and critic, Andrew Lang. At the moment the tablet is kept in the College sacristy.

However, it was not only Peter Vaughan who wished to immortalise Alexander's visit to Merton. Alexander himself also wanted to thank his Oxonian hosts. In about 1816 Merton College received a plaster bust with Alexander's image; today it is exhibited in the Upper Library. Likewise, as a sign of monarchical gratitude, Alexander sent to Merton a vase of enormous size made out of Siberian jasper, which nowadays stands in the transept of the Chapel. Two iron plaques with Latin and Russian inscriptions were later attached to its sides:

*Opposite, left: The Russian plaque on the plinth of the vase. **Opposite, right:** The stained-glass windows in the Queen's Room. **Above:** The jasper vase standing in the north transept of the Chapel.*

– 111 –

THE PAINTED CEILING OF THE CHAPEL

Alan Bott

In 1842, John Hungerford Pollen (1820–1902) was elected a Fellow of Merton College. He had been educated at Eton and Christ Church. During the following four years he was to make journeys to France, Germany and Italy (including Ravenna), where he studied both the pastoral successes as well as the great range of styles in the buildings of the Roman church. These were important influences on his later work at Merton and proved an antidote to what he later described to Cardinal Newman as 'the weak and mannered features of the Gothic of the Pugin school'. Returning to England, he was ordained by Bishop Wilberforce of Oxford in 1846.

From 1833 onwards, Oxford had been absorbed in the ferment of Tractarianism, with its architectural preference for the Gothic rather than the classical style in building. Thus, Pollen had supported the appointment of William Butterfield to re-Gothicise Merton Chapel between 1848 and 1851. This included the substitution of the Fitzjames ceiling of the 1490s with a sharply pointed, strongly ribbed design, based on the thirteenth-century ceiling at Trumpington Church in Cambridge. In 1850, Pollen undertook the decoration of this large, newly created space. His *Journal* (for 1850) simply records 'Paintpot, paintpot, paintpot.' The area to be covered was about half that of Michelangelo's ceiling of the Sistine Chapel in the Vatican.

There had been an early *contretemps* with the anti-Tractarian Warden, Robert Bullock Marsham, when he discovered that Pollen's cartoons included a representation of Pope Gregory the Great, crowned with a tiara. Pollen's diary entry noted: 'Dined with Warden, tremendous fight with him and the *signora* (his wife) about Gregory the Great.' The matter was thrice referred to the committee but Pope Gregory remained in the design. On 5 November 1850, the scaffolding was removed. J.H. Pollen's brother, John, described the scene:

> Examined Merton roof. A really beautiful work and worthy of the better times of art. Along the ridge of the roof are medallions with angels in choir amongst which are portraits of (my) Dick and Mary opposite each other. Round wall: the Four Evangelists, the four great Doctors of the Church (Saints Jerome, Augustine, Ambrose and Gregory the Great), the four greater Prophets and the Founder, Walter de Merton. St Gregory the Great is an excellent portrait of the Warden!! Dr Pusey is Jeremiah, the Prophet of the Captivity and Manning is Daniel, the Prophet of Doctrine, the whole is altogether extremely successful.

The scaffold had been shared by Pollen during the painting with the young John Everett Millais. In the following years the ceiling was to be admired by William Morris, Edward Burne-Jones and D.G. Rossetti. This led, in 1858, to their all collaborating on the murals of the Oxford Debating Society. Although Rossetti pronounced that Pollen 'was the only man who has yet done good mural painting in England', his experience proved inadequate and the pictures quickly degenerated. In the same period, Pollen's next artistic challenge was offered by John Ruskin, who commissioned him to design the carvings for the façade of the new Natural History Museum at Oxford.

In 1852, Pollen had been received into the Roman Catholic church. He noted that 'Every doubt is at rest and I have found that kind of calm which one needs repose and reflection to enjoy to the full.' This decision meant he had to resign his Merton fellowship. He continued, however, to have a varied artistic career. On the recommendation of W.M. Thackeray he was appointed assistant keeper of the newly founded South Kensington (later the Victoria and Albert) Museum and was to produce foundation catalogues for the collections of furniture, sculpture and metalwork. In 1876, he was to join Lord Ripon's staff as his private secretary. A recent

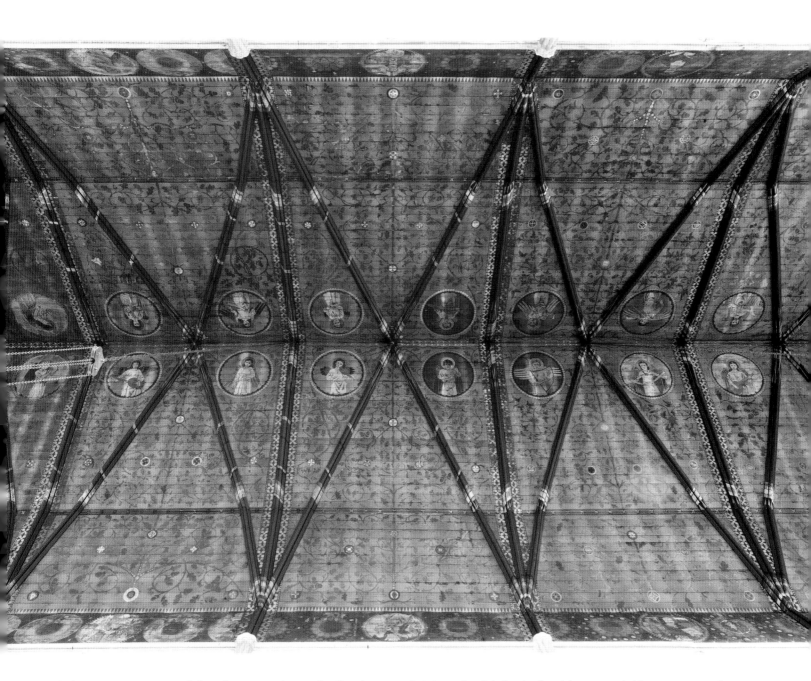

Catholic convert, Ripon succeeded Lord Lytton as Viceroy of India, where Pollen was briefly posted. But in 1877 he found time to revisit Merton Chapel and to adorn the spandrels between the windows and below the ceiling, with further painted decoration including foliage and birds in the style much associated with William Morris. Time and damp have dealt unkindly with these painted additions and also those on the west wall of the choir. In the 1960s they were whitewashed out. However, the ceiling of 1850 remains, faded and reduced, but a remarkable monument to the religious and artistic taste of High Victorian Oxford.

*Opposite: St Jerome, doctor of the church and translator of the Vulgate Bible, with quill pen and book. **Above:** The ceiling viewed from the centre of the Chancel.*

HOLYWELL MEADOW

Katherine J. Willis

Holywell Meadow is situated on the land bordering the River Cherwell (and associated ditches) running behind Magdalen deer park and St Catherine's College. As a 'Treasure of Merton College' this is probably unique, because it is not so much the land, which at first sight looks like flooded muddy field, but the biodiversity that it contains that makes it interesting. The biodiversity of the Holywell Meadow currently includes several badger setts, resident foxes, deer and a diverse bird fauna. In 1980, for example, a letter in the College archives reported that blue tits, sedge warblers, a whinchat, a sparrowhawk and a tree pipit had all been recorded in a survey, the latter three being rare for the region. Today, it is common to see woodpeckers in the willow woodland and the sparrowhawks are joined by the occasional red kite. It is for the flora of this low-lying alluvial meadow, however, that Holywell Meadow is probably best known; a feature distinctive enough that a number of the early British naturalists mention it, including Druce in his 1926 book *Botany of the Upper Thames*, Church in his *Introduction to the Plant life of the Oxford District* (1922–5) and Tansley in his book *The British Islands and Their Vegetation* (1939).

All three describe the distinctive herbaceous flora of Holywell Meadow (and neighbouring Magdalen Meadow), in particular the presence of *Fritillaria meleagris* (common fritillary), a bulbous plant of the Liliaceae family. According to Church these beautiful chequered purple-headed plants, known colloquially as snake-head fritillaries, were once numerous on these water meadows, flowering by the beginning of the University Summer term (the last week in April). Their collection by small boys to sell on the streets of Oxford for '2d or 3d for a bunch of a

dozen poor blooms' was a pastime deeply frowned upon by Church, who stated that 'a score of small boys taking home large bunches of buds with little colour, at estimate of 500 per child, will thus denude a couple of acres in an afternoon'. Church would be pleased to know that these fritillaries and the meadows in which they occur are now protected by law.

Counter-intuitively, these plants require some human-mediated disturbance to thrive; in this case, a grazing/cutting regime that is characteristic of managed water-meadows. The College archives provide some important pointers to understand the management required to ensure biodiverse water meadows such as Holywell Meadow. Holywell Meadow originally formed part of the manor of Holywell, which was given to the College in 1266 by King Henry III. The meadow was used for pasturing animals: an inventory of the stock of the manor survives

from 1331, which records that it then included ten horses and a herd of 29 cattle, including a bull, milk cows, beef cattle and calves. Since the stock of the farm also included dairying equipment, presumably the milk could either have been drunk or made into butter and cheese. Some of this might have ended up on the College table. The meadow was also an important source of hay. The bailiff's account for 1366, for example, records the mowing of 34 acres of meadow at Holywell for 26s 11d. By January 1501 the manor was being leased out to William Clare, a butcher, and it is very likely that he used the meadow to fatten up beef cattle. This was common in and around Oxford at this date and later. Christ Church Meadow was (and still is) used for grazing cattle and mown for hay.

It is, therefore, a management regime of grazing (deer or cattle) in autumn and winter, no grazing or mowing in spring and early summer (mid-March to mid-June), followed by cutting for hay in the summer months (July–September), that enables this distinctive flora to develop. Too much grazing (especially by sheep) and/or cutting of the meadow in March when the fritillary shoots first appear causes, according to

Tansley, a mixed grassland without fritillaries; too little grazing/cutting in the summer months will result in rushes and thorn-scrub becoming dominant. The skill, therefore, appears in the timing of the grazing/cutting regime.

Over the years, the meadow has often been mown in early spring, reducing its biodiversity. Likewise there are plans in the College archives to indicate that landscaping of these meadows was proposed in the early 1980s, including drainage and tree-planting. Thankfully these plans were never implemented and Holywell Meadow and its potential to grow fritillaries and other wild flowers, with the right management, will remain for future generations to enjoy – although Merton perhaps ought to invest in a few cattle.

....

Opposite, left: Bees help maintain the rich plant life of the meadow. **Opposite, right:** *Common fritillaries (Fritillaria meleagris) at Kew Gardens; they were once a common sight in the meadow.* **Above:** *A view of the meadow along the Cherwell.*

THE BEERBOHM ROOM

Stefano Evangelista

The first number of the *Yellow Book*, the most iconic literary magazine of the 1890s, contained an ironic essay entitled 'A Defence of Cosmetics', which praised the modern use of make-up as an antidote to Victorian earnestness and prophesied the beginning of an era when artifice would be the hallmark of culture. The author of this curious piece was Max Beerbohm, then an undergraduate at Merton and soon to become one of the most representative and discussed figures of his age. In 'A Defence of Cosmetics', Beerbohm makes fun of the then-popular Decadent cult for artifice by exaggeration and paradox. And indeed, Beerbohm – or simply Max, as he was chiefly known – would build a career on his remarkable talent for making fun, which he exploited in his parallel activities as writer and caricaturist.

Merton today remembers Beerbohm in a very special way. At the far end of one of the reading rooms in the Old Library an inconspicuous door leads into a little-known room, the 'Beerbohm Room', which was first opened in 1961 and then refurbished in 2000, thanks to the generosity of old members. There is something utterly appropriate about this location. If the Old Library, with its imposing collections of old tomes, symmetrically arranged, reminds students and visitors that scholarship is the product of hard work, the Beerbohm Room, with its intimate atmosphere, celebrates the fact that learning can also lead to laughter and pleasure. Its presiding genius is the figure of the dilettante rather than the scholar; its mood, in keeping with Beerbohm's own, is one of gentle irony towards the ethos of earnest application that reigns next door. The Beerbohm Room is like a secret museum within Merton, a *Wunderkammer* which recreates Beerbohm's taste and the

eclecticism of his work. Among its holdings are paintings and drawings by Beerbohm, caricatures by him depicting Mertonians and well-known people of his day, and various items of furniture that belonged to the author. The most striking presences in the room, however, are two wall paintings made by Beerbohm himself, which were detached from his house in Rapallo and re-plastered here, adding to the enticing incongruity of the environment. One of them immortalises a scene from Beerbohm's celebrated Oxford novel *Zuleika Dobson* (1911), which features an erotically charged exchange of glances between the heroine and the duke of Dorset.

The Beerbohm Room is just the visible part of a vast Beerbohm archive that is housed at Merton. The collection comprises autograph letters to and from Beerbohm, books from his library and books and articles by Beerbohm and about Beerbohm, as well as plenty of drawings. Especially evocative are a number of 'relics' of this near-mythic figure, including, among other things, the symbol of symbols of the 1890s dandy: Max's top hat, inscribed on the inside with verses in Beerbohm's own hand, which reflect on his passage from English to Italian life in 1910:

> *I used to perch on Max Beerbohm's pate,*
> *But now he's become Italianate;*
> *And I, in neglect and disregard,*
> *Languish forever in Apple Tree Yard.*

The inscribed top hat exemplifies a characteristic of Beerbohm that amounted almost to an obsession: he liked to personalise his belongings by leaving traces of his own life and art inside them. Many of the books in the Merton collection, for instance, contain sketches and drawings made by Beerbohm,

often caricatures of their authors. Beerbohm referred to this practice as 'improving' books. This was his unique way of commenting on what he read. But the improvement was also a way of appropriating the book as object: by leaving these idiosyncratic records of the act of reading, Beerbohm claimed the ownership of the text as reader. The improved books show us that all books are actually unique objects, inasmuch as they embody the unique relationship between an author and an individual reader.

Particularly fascinating in this respect is Beerbohm's copy of Oscar Wilde's *Lady Windermere's Fan* (1893), in which he drew a caricature of a bloated and self-satisfied Wilde, cigarette in hand and green carnation in his buttonhole. The drawing remembers an episode that has become famous in theatre history: after the premiere of the play, Wilde, wearing a green carnation like several of his friends in the audience and, outrageously, smoking, mounted onstage and thanked the audience for their impeccable performance as appreciative public. Beerbohm's copy of *Lady Windermere's Fan*, 'improved' in 1895, is, like almost everything in this archive, both art object and historical record.

....

Opposite: Max Beerbohm, self-portrait of c.1893, sporting the high collar, top hat and cane of the Victorian dandy. **Left:** *Beerbohm's caricature of Oscar Wilde from his copy of* Lady Windermere's Fan. **Above:** *One of the frescoes from Beerbohm's villa in Rapallo, 'Swinburne Warning Dante Gabriel Rossetti not to Tamper with the Blessed Damozel'. Algernon Charles Swinburne is on the left, Dante Gabriel Rossetti on the right, and the 'Blessed Damozel' is probably Elizabeth Siddal, whom Rossetti met in 1850 but did not marry until 1860.*

A CHINESE INCENSE BURNER

Jessica Rawson

The smooth rounded bronze basin sitting on the octagonal table in the Upper Library is a Chinese incense burner. Underneath the base is a six-character mark of the emperor Xuande (reigned 1425–35), but this is largely for decoration. Very many incense burners of this type carry such a set of characters. But they do not belong to that time. The incense burner dates, as do most others like it, to the late seventeenth or early eighteenth century. It has an openwork, wooden lid and a decorative jade knob, which was probably made around the same time, or a little earlier. Such incense burners would have held sand in which stood incense sticks. Accompanying it on a small altar would have been pairs of candlesticks and flower vases.

Jades are well known as some of the most precious items in the Chinese canon. But bronzes too have an exceptionally important role in Chinese culture of most periods. Bronze came late to China, around 2000 BC. But once they were familiar with the techniques of alloying and casting, the ancient Chinese craftsmen made some of the most complex and beautiful bronzes in the world as containers for food and alcohol to offer to the ancestors. The history of these ritual bronzes starts in around 1700 BC, and they had begun to disappear as the first emperor unified China in the third century BC. A very fine example of such a basin, the

Teng Hu gui, dating to the tenth century BC, or the Middle Western Zhou, as the period is known in China, is in the Art Gallery at Compton Verney, in Warwickshire, founded by Sir Peter Moores, also a generous benefactor to the College.

At first sight, the ancient bronze does not seem at all like its later descendants. It is a grand piece, and to show off its importance to its owners, the vessel was cast with a base that elevates it. Inside the basin is also an important dedicatory inscription. If we ignore the base and the handles, then it is evident that its soft, sweeping contours are very like those of the incense burner on the Merton Library table. Just as, in the West, Renaissance or eighteenth-century artists and craftsmen revived and reworked classical architecture and figure styles, so the Chinese venerated, collected and reworked the shapes and decoration of ancient bronzes. Many of these later versions were used on altars for family shrines for ancestor offerings, or in Buddhist and Daoist temples. And there are many such incense burners.

However, the bronze at Merton has its own special history. It was presented to Merton, probably around 1911, by Sir Aurel Stein (1862–1943). Stein is famed for his exploration and archaeological investigations in the Tarim Basin, in what is today China's western province of Xinjiang. The famed 'Silk Road' runs either side of this basin skirting the desert. Marc Aurel Stein was born in Hungary but became a British subject, working in Central Asia from a base in India. He died in Kabul and is buried there. Aurel Stein was a dedicated scholar, well

versed in many of the languages of the ancient peoples of Central Asia, from Indo-Iranian Kharoshti to different forms of the Turkic languages. During his expeditions in the Tarim Basin, Stein made collections of ancient manuscripts in these languages. He also brought back manuscripts and paintings from the Buddhist caves at Dunhuang on the eastern edge of the deserts of Central Asia. These collections are now divided between institutions in Delhi and London.

Many of Stein's works are scholarly reports on his exploration and archaeological investigations. He wrote one book of a more general kind giving an overview of his many, often dangerous, journeys across some of the worst deserts in the world. This is the *Ruins of Desert Cathay* (1912). At the end of the preface are the words: 'Merton College, Oxford, November 3rd, 1911'. Aurel Stein had a great friend among

the Fellowship, Percy Stafford Allen (1869–1933), who was at Merton from 1901 until he became president of Corpus Christi College in 1908. Allen, best known for his edition of the letters of Erasmus, had taught in Lahore from 1887 to 1901 and must have met Stein there. At his invitation, Stein came to Merton for a period to write the book. He is said to have worked in the Summer House, now the Music Room. And he left at Merton the incense burner, as a gift.

Opposite, left: The Teng Hu gui from Compton Verney. **Opposite, right:** *Aurel Stein's camels being loaded for departure from the site at Lop Nur in the Tarim Basin he excavated in December 1906, from* Ruins of Desert Cathay. **Above:** *The incense burner.*

THE LETTERS OF KURUVILA ZACHARIAH

Philip Waller

'It perhaps does seem rather useless, at first sight, to spend three years in England at such cost of money for an ordinary Arts Course in History. And yet I cannot think it is anything but worth doing … [W]hat Oxford stands for is not really the actual work done but the spirit, the tone, the atmosphere. It has taught me more than one can measure or write down, and I can never cease to be thankful that I had this chance of coming to Oxford.' So wrote Kuruvila Zachariah in 1914, mid-way through his time at Merton. The eldest of seven children of the headmaster of the Basel Mission School at Calicut, where Vasco da Gama landed in 1498, Zachariah had shone at Madras Christian College and won an Indian Government Scholarship worth £200 per annum. The 174 letters he sent home between 1912 and 1915 depict an undergraduate's life at Merton in unrivalled completeness.

The significance of this collection is even greater when the historical context is recalled. In 1909 Indian political terrorism made a debut at the Imperial Institute, South Kensington, when a Hindu Punjabi engineering student at London University shot dead the India Office's educational adviser Sir Curzon Wyllie. Abhorrence led several Oxford (and Cambridge) colleges to debar Indian students; a government inquiry also heard testimony about friction between Indian and other students at Oxford, blamed in part on a supposed race prejudice of American and South African Rhodes Scholars and class pride and race aloofness of British public schoolboys. This was far from the whole picture: countervailing evidence emanated from women's colleges and

from Balliol, which had taken many Indian students since the 1870s. Nor was it Zachariah's experience at Merton; moreover, he recognised that a resistance to intermixing was no monopoly of one particular race, class or creed. The idea that Indian students were all alike and irreproachable he found farcical: 'it is no use denying that as a community (as we delight to call ourselves) we are subject to serious faults which hinder real progress'. He was astonished to learn in March 1913 that Oxford contained 84 Indian students; he knew only about a dozen. Most others were non-collegiate, and it was this group who was generally least integrated and capable of benefiting from Oxford academically. As for those with college places, preponderantly they were 'rich and therefore free to pursue a fast life'.

Zachariah was not Merton's first Indian student – that was the grandly titled Prince Moorut Ullea Moorut-Meerza in 1897 – and Girja Bajpai (later Sir Girja, agent-general to Washington and governor of Bombay) was reading history when he arrived. That Zachariah came to Merton was adventitious. Balliol, his preference, and New were full, as was Lincoln, which also featured in his reckoning. National Indian Association officials originally directed him to Keble, where he would have been its first Indian student; but he cooled when he enquired about its standing and deployed as excuse that he was not High Church. Merton he was told was 'a working college' and, for one of his academic ambition, this was the clincher.

Once at Merton, Zachariah embarked on the most fulfilling period of his young life. How did he settle so happily? That he was naturally affable with a gift for friendship is manifest. He was continually interested in and entertained by human variety, and he relished that Merton was already international. He befriended a Chinese, Wan Yu, who arrived in 1913; previously, he also toured Italy with an American Rhodes Scholar, Thomas Means, a Connecticut classicist, and smiled when the German Rhodes, Carl von Wurmb, 'asked me whether I had shot elephants in India. No. Had I then shot antelopes, internal outburst of laughter in me; for to the best of my remembrance if I have shot at anything it was only a pigeon or a coconut palm!'

Zachariah cheerfully deployed varsity slang, of which 'Pragger Wagger' (prince of Wales, future Edward VIII, then at Magdalen) is pick of the bunch. Zachariah's English was practically flawless. Such was his familiarity with its literature that he readily summoned an apt reference on encountering peculiarly English scenes: not just Tennyson's *In Memoriam* 'which everybody knows', when visiting Trinity College,

Opposite: Zachariah (pictured left, c.1923) describes his rooms in St Alban's Quad, 'quite nice' though 'too large for me', and his tutor, 'the Johnner', whose lectures are 'rather amusing, though not exceedingly profitable', but who 'calms down & grants half your points' when you resolve 'boldly to argue with him' in tutorial.

Oxford.
Feb. 20. 1913.

My dear Apachen,

Your letter, Kunju's and George-Kutty's on Saturday. Many thanks for all of them. I might answer a few points in it first. My rooms are quite nice but I have two objections to them: that they are expensive and that they are too large for me. One feels much cosier in a small room where everything is at your elbow than in a big one where you have to walk a dozen paces to get a book. It is something like what GeorgeKutty would feel if he had No. 18 for to himself and as a bedroom no. 22. I am sure in a month he will be rather tired of the vast expanses. But I shall not quit the present room unless I can go up to some rooms on the second floor, smaller but quite nice and quiet, and cheaper by about £4 a year. They are in St. Alban's Quad too - as a matter of fact all the second floor rooms are in that style while all the first floor rooms are like mine. I shall not go to any other quad, because this is about the quietest and nearest the baths and the

---

2 J.C.R, which are great advantages. Besides in a new quad the rooms are ever so much finer than in a 14th century one and the staircases are not specially constructed with murderous intent. Of course I miss the divine chance of living in a room thick, perhaps, with memories of Duns Scotus, but I would barter all those musty associations for a wide grate and a pair of windows with a chance of seeing the sun if it is there.

[It is easy to talk of Johnson - familiarly called 'old Johnner' or 'the Johnner'. He comes from Eton but I cannot remember his Oxford college - since 1872 or thereabouts he has been a fellow at All Souls (and his rooms there have never been cleaned since). He was in his day a fine athlete, a great long-distance runner and a man who was at Eton years after told me his reputation still survived. He was one of the old school of riding and hunting parsons, one of his fellows being the master of Balliol. His early achievements account for his still being so hale and hearty, though now he pretends to grumble (with strange inconsistency) at the excess of athletics at the present day. He was a great tutor, & has had many men, now dons themselves, under him. But now he has mannerisms and talks like this - "Hobbes was a pessimist, look at this idea of his, pessimism, pessimism, pessimism, pessimism" with a chuckle between each

---

3 reiteration. When we go to read essays he usually stands in front of the fire and lights his pipe with pieces of paper at least a dozen times an hour. Sometimes when it is cold and I go alone - as yesterday - he makes me sit near the fire and we have a sort of semi-talk. Sometimes he drinks tea when we read our essays. Mrs Johnson is a great person in Oxford, having done many things - on the Poor Law Board & so on. He is Curator of the Parks and was Ford's Lecturer four years ago. The way to get on easily with Johnson is boldly to argue with him, when he calms down & grants half your points. In his lectures he tells us all sorts of stories and the hour is rather amusing, though not exceedingly profitable.]

[Oxford is the place for Kunjunju. There are only about two lectures a day & even those one can cut with impunity & hardly any scruple of conscience. One lecturer thus began for instance yesterday - "When I told you last time that I would lecturing on the church today, I expected that you would all take the hint & stay away. But since you are here I will try & make a dry subject as interesting as I can." There is no attendance or anything like it - people come or keep away as they please. And in most lectures they even come

---

4 in after the lecturer has begun.

We had fun today in Barker's class. He had been down with influenza for a week & when he came in was greeted with clappings & stampings in which I, remembering old days, took a prominent part. Then he talked of feudal tenures etc. & came to 'wardship' which he said was due to military reasons. 'A woman with the fragility of the sex' etc - tremendous applause (there were a score of women students present). Then Barker smiles & says. 'I am glad you understand the sex'. Loud stamping. From this it is not to be understood that stamping is a common feature in lectures here; on the other hand it is very unusual. Partly because lectures are four times out of five held in dining-halls, there are few proper lecture rooms in Oxford & those are very small; so that for all large lectures you go to a hall. Everything is informal. You sit as you please, anywhere at a table, & take down the notes if you want to. The lecturers usually talk in the ordinary way and not orate like Kochukutty.]

Anyway I am glad to hear Kunjunju is growing - by the time I return he may be a giant & unrecognizable. I am extending laterally and my weight has gone up. It

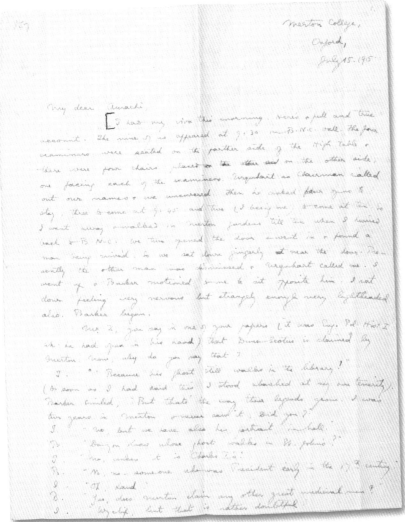

also villainously bad at golf – but he improved on the river, and ran and played tennis well, and the children of dons whose homes he visited rejoiced in his sense of fun. He was also an enthusiastic spectator of University and College sports, even rugby, which he cared for least.

Importantly, Zachariah most appreciated Oxford for its scholarly challenges and excitement. His popularity partly derived from respect for his intellect and application. At Warden's Collections, nicknamed 'don-rag', in Hilary 1913, Arthur Johnson lavished praise on him, which Zachariah thought absurdly overblown; yet 'I am rather glad that they are pleased … for that may mean that they'll take more Indian students now'. He would leave with the best history first in 1915 but, on the day before his viva, he set down what Merton and Oxford meant to him, in an emotional outpouring characteristically checked by wryly noting that the College garden was now opened all day to nurses, 'who also have the cheek to play tennis in Fellows' Quad'. If he couldn't stay, then Oxford must go to India: he served as professor of history at Presidency College, Calcutta, and twice as a college principal, always seeking to strengthen the critical spirit in Indian higher education. Above all, he was appointed by post-independence India's first foreign minister, K.P.S. Menon, to begin a Bureau of Historical Research, Zachariah insisting on complete freedom from interference: he would not connive in slanting the record to favour particular parties or governments. Zachariah refused several ambassadorial postings, but came to London in 1954 as historical adviser to the High Commission, in large part for family reasons. He had married in 1929, and their five children would all pursue careers in medicine or teaching, including a namesake who matriculated at Merton in 1955, the same year Zachariah died in Hammersmith Hospital. Merton has never ceased to be enriched by its overseas students, among whom Kuruvila Zachariah is outstanding.

Cambridge, but Meredith's *The Egoist*, a more strenuous test, having 'remembered the description which I had fancied imaginary and idealised … [yet] when I saw my first white tree in the [Oxford] Union gardens I knew at once it must be the double blossom cherry'. His mood at Abbotsford was rather of 'exaltation and awe than the tourist's curiosity – for this had been a half cherished dream of early days … [when] Scott was my first great hero in literature'. Culturally, he was more English than most natives. After a last bicycle ride through the Cotswolds, his favourite haunt outside Merton, he mused: 'Why do people go to great garish seaside resorts … when they can … holiday in a paradisal place like Stanton or Bibury?'

Zachariah acquired a bicycle in his first term; he determined too to try out all manner of games and recreations, unabashed by their novelty or his own incompetence, whether cross-country running, rambling, rowing and coxing, canoeing, lacrosse, cricket or football. As usually happens, his inaugural punting expedition proceeded in circles – he was

EDWARDIAN WAISTCOAT OF THE MYRMIDON CLUB

John Eidinow

The Myrmidon dress waistcoat now housed in the College archives belonged to Henry Henderson Monteath, who came to Merton in 1903 from Edinburgh Academy. He read Mods and Greats, rowed for the College VIII, was elected to the Myrmidons, and returned to Edinburgh to read law, eventually ending a distinguished legal career as president of the Law Society of Scotland. The club minute book which presumably recorded his election to the Myrmidons is lost, but he can be seen in photographs taken in 1906 and 1907, wearing his Myrmidon waistcoat.

The Myrmidons created their waistcoat on 17 May 1866, when rules were drawn up for the club, founded the year before, and 'the uniform chosen'. The nature of this uniform is shown by an entry from the

Dance — June 19th, 1909.

BUFFET MENU.

Foie Gras Sandwiches.

Chicken and Ham Sandwiches.

Anchovy and Cress Sandwiches.

Rolled Bread and Butter.   Fancy Pastries.

Eclairs.   Walnut Gateaux.

Trifle au Liqueurs.   Meringue Glacé.

Fruit Jellies.   Jelly Dantzic.

Strawberry and Vanilla Ice.

Iced Coffee.

Fruit Salad.   Apricot Cream.   Dessert.

Claret Cup.   Champagne Cup.   Cider Cup.

Tea.   Coffee.   Lemonade.

Soup.

following year, recording the new rule that members not wearing 'the waistcoat and buttons of the club' at wines and dinners should be fined five shillings. In April, 1881, a proposal to adopt uniform evening dress, 'expedient to the dignity of the Club', was debated and rejected. This resistance was, however, an isolated sartorial phenomenon: photographs show members of the club wearing ties (some with diagonal stripes, others horizontal), hatbands, scarves, caps, and even socks in club colours. In May, 1910, the club partially changed its mind about evening dress and agreed to 'have a coat of the Club colours as well': a committee was appointed, a tailor selected (Messrs Lomman and Lomman in the High Street), and a design approved: 'The Coat chosen was a dinner jacket, with grey (silver) moirée lapelles: brass buttons (2 on sleeve) with club monogram.' It can be seen for the first time in the club photograph for 1911, worn with a violet bowtie.

This bridge crossed, it is hardly surprising that resistance to full uniform evening dress should end as well: the poignant photograph taken at the Commemoration ball in 1914 shows members wearing Myrmidon tailcoats, but it was a short experiment. From the outbreak of the Great War until 1920 the club was in abeyance, and in 1922 the decision was taken that 'the Myrmidon dinner jacket and tie should be worn in future, though it was left optional to present members of the Club to conform to this rule, on grounds of expense. It was also decided that Messrs Hookham should be appointed as tailors to the Club for all the Myrmidon evening uniform, on the understanding that they should charge no more that £6.15. for the Dinner Jacket.'

Although it seems plausible that the Myrmidon colours were adopted as a variation on the colours previously adopted by the College Boat Club, they had within a few years acquired their own myth. A letter of June 1909, from the future anthroposophist Harry Collison (Merton, 1887), assigns their origin to the memory of an article of clothing discovered during an encounter with a dancer in his native Russia by George Bakhmeteff (Batchmetieff in the club's minutes), elected to the club at the end of Michaelmas Term, 1865, six months before the club adopted its first uniform.

It is easy to see from the club's self-consciously rakish minutes why this aetiology for the colours should have appealed to the members. Recurrent themes of the minutes before the Great War are academic idleness, difficulties with the dons, and unfortunate behaviour. The new academic year in 1878 finds the club with 'its members considerably thinned owing

principally to unsuccessful battles with the examiners … defeats hastened on if not directly caused by the too great frivolities of the Club during the preceding term'; the landlord of the club's rooms in the High Street laments that 'the floor of the lavatory and outside it was in a worse state than the deck of a channel boat', before asking if they will want the rooms the following term; W.T. Raikes 'becoming unfortunately rather excited on his way home' after a dinner in May 1913, 'knocked 3 Corpus dons off their bicycles … As a result he left the Varsity the next day'.

And the press began to take an interest in the club: *Tatler* remarked the club's existence in April 1909, and in June the secretary informed members that a reporter had been to see him: it was decided 'that the reporter if he came again should be politely consigned to a warmer climate & that nothing more should be told him before he went there'. The club decided to have its photograph taken that year in ordinary clothes instead of evening dress.

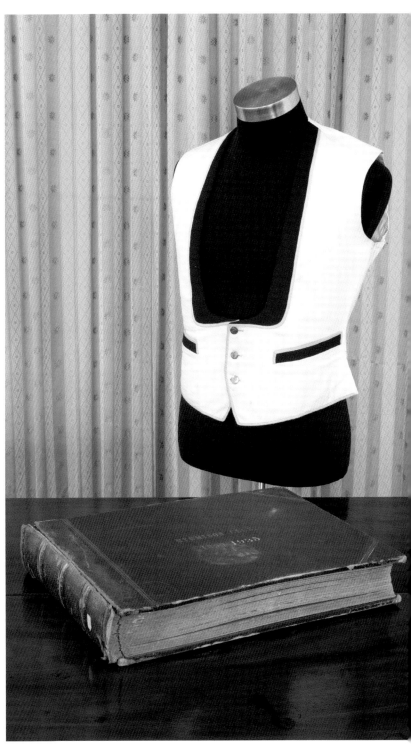

Opposite: The menu from the Myrmidon dance at the Town Hall, 1909. There were 75 dancing couples, and the Senior Tutor and Domestic Bursar brought parties.
*Above: H.H. Monteath wearing his waistcoat, 1906. **Right:** The waistcoat with the club's photograph album.*

THE T.S. ELIOT COLLECTION

Michael H. Whitworth

On 6 October 1914, an American graduate student, Thomas Stearns Eliot, arrived at Merton. He very soon ventured to one of Oxford's bookshops, where he obtained a second-hand copy of *The Logic of Science: A Translation of the Posterior Analytics of Aristotle* (1870), by Edward Poste. Harvard University, where Eliot was studying for a doctorate in philosophy, had awarded him a Sheldon Travelling Fellowship, and he

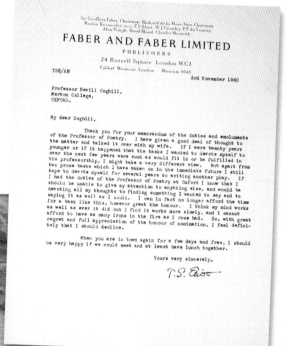

had been drawn to Merton as the college of F.H. Bradley (1846–1924), on whose works he wrote his thesis, and of Harold Joachim (1868–1938), whose *The Nature of Truth* (1906) Eliot admired. Bradley, who had been in poor health for many years, led a secluded life, and Eliot never had the opportunity to meet him. However, Eliot arranged a series of tutorials with Joachim on Aristotle's *Posterior Analytics*, and it was for this that he purchased Poste's translation. Eliot flourished under Joachim. While accounts of this period of his life have tended to emphasise his personal unhappiness – he reported feeling 'not quite alive', as well as complaining of indigestion, constipation and colds – his respect for his tutor and enjoyment of his tutorials comes across in many letters. Joachim was 'really almost a genius' in relation to Aristotle. Eliot was immediately impressed with the 'English methods of teaching', and eight days after arriving wrote that he wished he had taken an undergraduate course at Oxford. Later that Michaelmas, Eliot wrote that his tutorials had impressed upon him 'the value of personal instruction in small classes and individually, and the value of careful study of original texts in the original tongue'. On Joachim's death in 1938, Eliot was to recall the gentle, impersonal sarcasm his tutor applied when criticising weekly essays, adding that 'Any virtues my prose writing may exhibit are due to his correction'.

In March 1915 Eliot met Vivien Haigh-Wood at a lunch party at Magdalen; they married in June, and, though he completed his dissertation in April 1916, Eliot turned his back on academic philosophy in favour of a literary career. The war prevented him returning to Harvard for his defence, and he never obtained a doctorate for his thesis. Eliot's later reputation was built on the poems he had begun before coming to Merton, published in *Prufrock and Other Observations* (1917), and on the major poem that followed, *The Waste Land* (1922); but it was also supported by the authoritative literary-critical judgements in *The Sacred Wood* (1920) and later volumes.

In October 1936, 22 years after Eliot's arrival, an English undergraduate, Frank Brenchley, came up to Merton to study classics, and on his first day in Oxford went to Blackwell's. There he saw T.S. Eliot's *Collected Poems 1909–1935*, newly published, on prominent display, and although he had never heard of the author, he bought a copy; only later did he discover that Eliot had been a graduate student at his College. The chance purchase began Brenchley's lifelong fascination with Eliot and his works. Though Brenchley lost his first copy of the *Collected Poems* while serving with the Signal Corps in North Africa, he continued collecting works by Eliot while working in London in the Foreign Office from 1949 onwards, and thereafter while working as a diplomat. The collection he built up through his long career, which he left to Merton on his death in 2011, is particularly rich in first editions of books by Eliot and of books containing contributions by him, and in periodicals with contributions by Eliot. Unlike their equivalents in the Bodleian, many of these still have their original jackets. The periodicals include such little magazines as Alfred Kreymborg's *Others*, and Wyndham Lewis's *The Tyro*, and an almost complete run of Eliot's *The Criterion*. Although Brenchley did not initially seek out manuscripts, proofs or association copies, as they were beyond his means, later in his life he was able to acquire some, and the collection includes such rare items as the proofs of an unpublished quarto edition of *Ash Wednesday*, a pre-publication typescript of the pageant play *The Rock* and galley proofs of *The Dry Salvages* from its first appearance in the *New English Weekly*. From late in Eliot's life it includes an abandoned edition of his doctoral thesis, *Knowledge and Experience in the Philosophy of F.H. Bradley* – the edition was further revised and augmented before its publication in 1964 – and, from Eliot's first days at Merton, his copy of Poste's translation of Aristotle's *Posterior Analytics*.

Opposite, left: The bust of T.S. Eliot by Jacob Epstein now in the T.S. Eliot Lecture Theatre. Opposite, above: A letter from Eliot to Nevill Coghill, Merton professor of English Literature, declining Coghill's offer to nominate Eliot for the professorship of poetry in 1960. Right: Part of the Frank Brenchley T.S. Eliot Collection shelved in the Library Special Collections Room.

THE SANDY IRVINE ARCHIVE

Julie Summers

When Sandy Irvine disappeared on the upper slopes of Mount Everest, close to the loftiest spot on Earth, he became a historical cipher to the world's then most famous mountaineer, George Leigh Mallory. History by and large ignored him and dwelt on Mallory until the 1980s, when his role in the 1924 Mount Everest expedition was re-examined by climbing historian Audrey Salkeld in her book *The Mystery of Mallory and Irvine*.

However, his memory at Merton lived on after his death, first in the sculpture outside the Grove Building: a plinth with an eternal flame and with the inscription engraved by Eric Gill. Secondly in the Irvine Travel Fund, set up in 1925, which continues to give students small bursaries towards adventurous pursuits such as climbing, caving and mountaineering, and thirdly in the Library's archive. The first item to be deposited was Sandy Irvine's Mount Everest diary. It was presented by Hugh Irvine, Sandy's older brother (Magdalen, 1919–22), on behalf of their father, Willie Irvine, in 1962. The diary is a brief account of the trek through Sikkim and across Tibet on the march to Everest during April 1924 and of the climb itself with the last entry made on 5 June which reads: 'My face is perfect agony. Have prepared two oxygen apparatus for our start tomorrow morning.' This refers to the sunburn he suffered from so badly, exacerbated by wind and the pain of having to put on and take off the oxygen mask, which removed a layer of skin from his

cheeks each time he did so. The entries are sparse and for a long time historians believed it was the only written document from Sandy's Everest adventure.

Additional items such as Sandy's diary from the Merton College arctic expedition to the Norwegian island of Spitsbergen in 1923 and letters from Sandy to Merton Fellow Geoffrey Mure were added to the collection over the next few years. In 1999 Weidenfeld and Nicolson

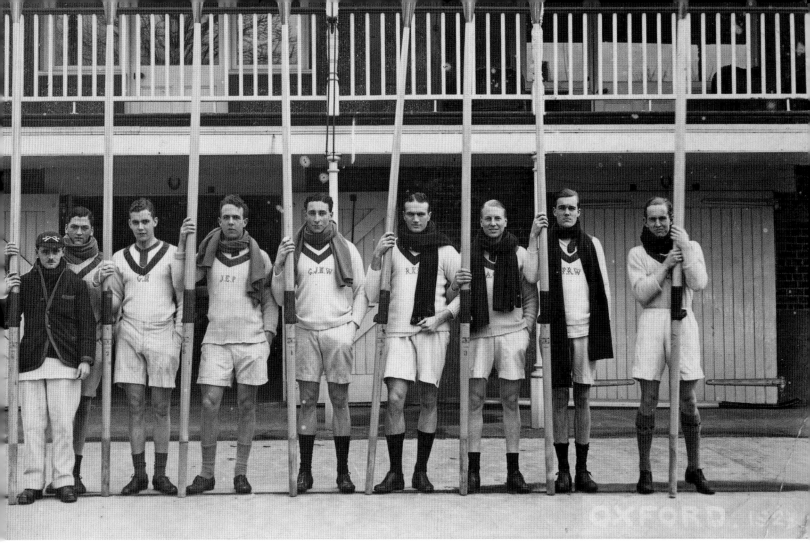

commissioned me to write a biography of Sandy, who is my great uncle. Audrey Salkeld challenged me to 'get inside Sandy's head, I want to know what he was thinking'. This was almost impossible given the paucity of material in the public domain but I became convinced that my great-grandfather would not have destroyed everything to do with the expedition, as family members had insisted, but that it would be found, all together, in one place, if only one knew where to look.

I began to nag my family and eventually my cousin, Julia Irvine, tracked down a trunk in the attic at the Irvine family home, Bryn Llwyn, near Corwen. Together Julia and I uncovered a blue foolscap folder, tied with a piece of blue ribbon, labelled 'ACI [Andrew Comyn Irvine] EVEREST 1924'. It contained 11 long letters from Everest, still in their original envelopes, photographs developed by Sandy in Tibet and sent back to his sister for printing, plus drawings of the oxygen apparatus on which he worked both at Merton during the 1923 Michaelmas term and on the trek. This exceptional find allowed Sandy's voice to be heard for the first time and, as he wrote to his mother in his first letter from Darjeeling, to add the colour to the brief diary entries. 'Please keep my letters to fill out my diary when I get home', he wrote to her. These letters revealed his delight in the unfamiliar culture, his joy at the landscape, his concerns about the fate of the Dark Blues in the 1924 Boat Race and his

excitement as they approached the mountain. More material emerged, including photographs, further letters, material and press cuttings and even a copper pressure kettle which he had commissioned in order to have a hot cup of tea on the mountain.

In 2004 the Sandy Irvine Trust, set up in 1999 to preserve the material now gathered under one roof in Oxford, approached Merton to see whether they would be prepared to house the collection on long-term loan. This was agreed between the trust's chairman John Irvine and Warden Jessica Rawson. Seven years later, in 2011, the trustees voted to gift the collection to the College as the rightful home of this important collection linked to the greatest mountaineering mystery of all time. Researchers, film-makers and exhibition organisers continue to show interest in Sandy's life and request access to the material. For the Irvine family it is wonderful to know that it is cared for in such an outstanding archive.

....

Opposite, left: Photograph by Irvine of 'Everest from the pass after Shekar', 21 April 1924.
Opposite, right: Irvine (left) and Geoffrey Milling (Merton 1920) standing outside one of the tents on the Merton Arctic Expedition to Spitsbergen, August 1923 (photograph by Noel Odell). Above: Oxford Boat Race Crew at Putney, March 1923, Irvine third from right.

THE WAR MEMORIAL

Matthew Grimley

It is easy to walk past the war memorial under Fitzjames Arch without properly noticing it, except when some of the names are picked out by occasional shafts of sunlight. Understated and unadorned (except for the College arms, added in 1947), it bears no inscription, just the dates of the two world wars, and the names of the College's dead – 109 from the First World War, 43 from the Second.

At the end of the Great War, the men's colleges had to find appropriate ways of commemorating the unprecedented number of their members who had been killed. Most erected a memorial, often in or close to the College Chapel; some also constructed larger structures such as libraries (New College and Trinity) or memorial gardens (Christ Church). Merton's Governing Body began to consider a memorial in September 1917, more than a year before the Armistice. It commissioned

a design for a chancel screen for the Chapel, intended to carry an organ, from Sir Robert Lorimer, designer of several other war memorials including the Scottish national war memorial at Edinburgh Castle. But the Fellows decided not to proceed with the screen, ostensibly because not enough had been raised in subscriptions, but also possibly because they felt that recording the names of the fallen within the Chapel would exclude non-Anglicans. Instead they compromised by commissioning two memorials from the distinguished ecclesiastical architect, Ninian Comper. The first was inside the Chapel – a plaque (since covered by carpet) in front of the altar steps, with an inscription composed by H.W. Garrod. The second, much larger, memorial was on the east wall of the Fitzjames Arch. Oak plaques commemorating individual Mertonians were also placed in their old rooms. £1,772 was donated by subscribers;

K.C.DOUGLAS. FORESTERS.
R.A.DUDMAN. OXF. BUCKS.
W.K.EVERS. R.A.
F.G.FROW. R.A.F.
A.D.HALLETT. R.N.V.R.
J.G.HALLIDAY. R.A.F.
J.A.HEAD. R.A.
T.K.HIGGS. R.A.F.
R.W.JAKEMAN. 1ST AIRBORNE RECCE

after the memorials had been paid for, £650 residue was apportioned 'for the education within some University of the British Empire of children of fallen Mertonians'.

The memorial was unveiled in the presence of the relatives of the dead in June 1922 by the lord chancellor, Lord Birkenhead (a former Merton law tutor). As a mark of the equality of sacrifice, the roll of honour included six College servants (and a Fellow's son, born in the College precincts), and did not record the ranks of the fallen, only their regiments. The names of a New Zealander, an Australian and two Americans attested to the international nature of the recent conflict. But two German Mertonians were excluded. As former Rhodes Scholars, T.H.F. Erbe and C.F.L. von Wurmb had been exempted by their commanders from engaging in direct combat against the British. Erbe died fighting the Russians in September 1914, von Wurmb fighting the French in March 1918. Merton was slower than some colleges to add German names to its Great War memorial, but eventually remedied this in 1994, after a campaign by Tom Braun, tutor in ancient history, who had himself come to Britain as a refugee from Germany in 1938.

The memorial was indirectly responsible for launching one distinguished Mertonian career. In 1921 Stephen Dykes Bower, an Organ Scholar reading English, had submitted his own memorial design. Garrod passed it on to Comper, who did not recommend its adoption, but praised its 'directness and freedom from mannerism' and encouraged the undergraduate to train at the Architectural Association. Dykes Bower went on to become Comper's foremost British rival, celebrated for commissions like the high altar and baldachin in St Paul's Cathedral.

The names of the Second World War dead were added to the memorial in 1947. Among them was John Neil Randle, posthumously awarded the Victoria Cross for bravery in saving his comrades' lives twice within three days at Kohima in Assam in May 1944, and one of three Mertonian VCs from that conflict. Three significant literary figures are also commemorated. Robert Byron, the travel writer and author of *The Road to Oxiana*, was en route to Cairo as a war correspondent when his ship was torpedoed off Stornoway in February 1941. The New Zealand novelist and author of *Man Alone*, John Mulgan, fought at El Alamein before serving with the Special Operations Executive in Greece; he committed suicide in unexplained circumstances by taking an overdose of morphia from his own medical kit in Cairo in April 1945. Another veteran of the desert campaign, as recounted in his memoir *Alamein to Zem Zem*, was the poet Keith Douglas. Though wounded by a mine in 1943, he went on to take part in the invasion of Normandy, where he was killed on 9 June 1944.

Opposite: The war memorial with wreaths laid on Remembrance Day. Above, left: The inscription for Keith Douglas, poet of the Second World War in North Africa, and Mertonians from the army, navy and air force. Above, right: A memorial wreath laid on behalf of the Junior Common Room.

E.S. GOODRICH'S ROYAL SOCIETY MEDAL

Peter Holland

Merton College has been the academic home for hundreds of distinguished scientists, including many zoologists. Much can be attributed to Thomas Linacre, physician to Henry VIII. On Linacre's death in 1524, he left lands and property to fund a series of visiting lectureships in medicine at Oxford. Merton College hosted these Linacre Lecturers for over 300 years, although according to one observer 'the happy inheritor of the Linacre bequest received his money gladly and made no pretence of work'. The year 1852 saw a rude awakening, as a sweeping parliamentary review replaced the lectureships with the Linacre professorship of Physiology. There have been 11 holders of the post, now called the Linacre professorship of Zoology, since 1860. Among the most influential was an imposing and pugnacious Victorian, Sir Ray Lankester, who argued that he was 'no longer content to see biology scoffed at as inexact or gently dropped as natural history or praised for her relation to medicine'. Lankester argued about most things with most people, and perhaps should have heeded the advice of his old friend Thomas Henry Huxley, who advised 'I wish you would let an old man, who has had his share of fighting, remind you that battles, like hypotheses, are not to be multiplied beyond necessity.' Lankester was an evolutionary biologist, as were his predecessors Rolleston and Moseley, and was succeeded by the pioneering mathematical biologist Raphael Weldon.

Perhaps the greatest of Merton's evolutionary biologists was Edwin Stephen Goodrich, who held the Linacre Chair from 1921 to 1946. Goodrich had an unconventional background, originally training as a watercolour artist at the Slade School in London. Out of curiosity, he attended public lectures on biology given by Ray Lankester and the two men quickly recognised each other's talents. In 1891, Lankester brought Goodrich to Oxford as his assistant, and enrolled him as a zoology student at Merton. As might be expected from his artistic background, Goodrich's scientific work was characterised by remarkable descriptive detail, and was beautifully and copiously illustrated. His research often went far beyond simple observation to propose bold ideas and sweeping hypotheses. Indeed, his publications on the evolution of animal segmentation and on homology are still widely cited today. The Linnean Society awarded Goodrich their gold Linnean Medal in 1932, and the Royal Society bestowed upon him their Royal Medal in 1936 'for his work on the morphology of the excretory organs of the Invertebrata and for his work on the comparative anatomy and embryology of the

Vertebrata'. Other Mertonians to have received the prestigious Royal Medal include mathematician Sir Andrew Wiles, molecular biologist Sir Alec Jeffreys and chemist Professor Bob Williams, as well as former Warden Sir Rex Richards and Linacre professors Sir Ray Lankester and Henry Nottidge Moseley.

Although Goodrich's brilliance made a lasting impression, he was a reserved and private man. Sir Alister Hardy wrote that Goodrich 'was a great zoologist, and if he had had a fraction of the vitality and force of Ray Lankester he would have been one of the dominating figures in our subject'. Nor was he a great speaker or lecturer, with one senior colleague cruelly jibing that Goodrich's lectures 'made the whole subject seem equally unimportant'. The then Warden of Merton, John Miles, painted a similar picture, observing that 'at meetings he failed as a speaker, and

often damaged a good case'. Goodrich's successor was Sir Alister Hardy, who made seminal discoveries on the biology of the oceans. Hardy invented an ingenious metal contraption, the 'Continuous Plankton Recorder', which when towed behind ships would collect a 'transect' of marine life over a distance of hundreds of miles, preserving the samples for later study. Even today, dozens of Hardy's recorders are towed across the world's busiest shipping lanes, generating data to monitor the state of the oceans. Hardy also brought to Merton, as lecturer then Fellow, the pioneering animal behaviour investigator and future Nobel Prize winner Nikolaas Tinbergen.

Merton College has always fostered academic excellence, but many of Merton's scientists have also had impact far beyond the reaches of academia. Sir Robert May (now Lord May of Oxford) came to Merton as a Royal Society university research professor and held the post of chief scientific advisor to Her Majesty's government, and then president of the Royal Society, having influence on many areas of science and technology. Former Merton biochemistry student, Sir Alec Jeffreys, invented genetic fingerprinting, revolutionising the use of forensics in criminal case work and paternity testing. And Sir Richard Southwood, Linacre professor and vice-chancellor of the University, chaired the Royal Commission into Environmental Pollution that recommended removal of toxic lead from petrol, positively affecting the lives of millions.

Opposite: Goodrich in a photograph of the members of the department of comparative anatomy, 1896; the man standing behind him is William Hine. **Right:** *The Royal Society medal bearing the head of King Edward VIII and its presentation case.*

Presentation Copy of *The Hobbit*

John Carey

It is given to very few writers to enhance the imagination of the world, and among them is a Mertonian, John Ronald Reuel Tolkien (1892–1973). *The Hobbit* (1937), originally written as a tale to amuse his children, has sold over 100 million copies and been translated into more than 50 languages. *The Lord of the Rings* was intended as a follow-up, but grew to three volumes (1954–5), and is now rated the third-bestselling novel ever published, with 150 million sales. (First and second are Dickens's *A Tale of Two Cities* and Saint-Exupéry's *The Little Prince.*)

But Tolkien was not a novelist or fiction-writer in the normal sense. He was something far stranger and rarer – indeed, unique. For his published works are only fragments of a huge background of stories, intricately imagined and interconnected, and rooted in invented languages (the elf-language Quenya, for example) that grew out of their creator's philological erudition, and out of his conviction that legends are intimately linked to the languages that give rise to them. Since Tolkien's death some parts of this personal universe have been retrieved from notes and drafts by his son Christopher and published as *The Silmarillion* (1977) and the 12-volume *History of Middle-earth* (1983–96). But had Tolkien been able to bring his great project to fruition it would have amounted, it seems, to a new mythology and a body of connected legend which, he said, though constituting 'a majestic whole', would also have left room for others to extend and build on. That, at any rate, has come to pass. Bilbo Baggins, Frodo and Sam Gamgee, the elves and dwarves and Gandalf the wizard, and all their friends and foes have inspired artists and musicians and writers. Tolkien has been credited with inventing the modern fantasy genre, and 'Tolkienian' and 'Tolkienesque' are terms recognised by the *Oxford English Dictionary*. Role-playing videogames have grown from his books, and the young utopians of the 1960s counterculture (rather to Tolkien's displeasure) seized on them for heroes. The three films based on *The Lord of the Rings* have grossed $2.9 billion from the global box office, and their director Peter Jackson is in the process of creating a three-film version of *The Hobbit.*

Yet despite this worldwide acclaim, and despite his far-flung sources – the *Eddas*, the Norse sagas, the *Nibelungenlied*, and many more – Tolkien was a very English writer. Like William Blake he was appalled by the 'dark Satanic mills' that were over-spreading England's green and

pleasant land. Fear that industrialisation will invade the Shire lies at the heart of his story, and it reflects his experience of seeing the countryside around the Worcestershire village of Sarehole and his Aunt Jane's farm Bag End, where he roamed as a child, swallowed up by the growth of Birmingham. The hobbits, brave, simple and home-loving, express his admiration for the type of English Tommy – especially, he said, 'the plain soldier from the agricultural counties' – who had served under him at the Battle of the Somme.

Norman Davis
from
J.R.R.Tolkien.

ᛒᛖᛋᛏ᛫ᚹᛁᛋᚻᛖᛋ᛫ᚠᚱᛟᛗ᛫ᚦᛟᚱᛁᚾ
ᚪᚾᛞ᛫ᚳᛟᛗᛈᚪᚾᛁᚷ

Tolkien did not retire from the Merton professorship of English language until 1959, so when I was an undergraduate from 1954–7 (at St John's, not Merton) I was able to go to his lectures. To be honest, they were very difficult to hear and even harder to understand. They seemed to be couched largely in foreign languages. Humphrey Carpenter, his biographer, says that he used to commence lectures by declaiming the opening lines of *Beowulf*, of which the first word is 'Hwaet!', and that audiences often mistook this for 'Quiet!' But I was so puzzled by what was going on that I can't say whether I witnessed this famous historical phenomenon or not. What I do recall vividly was his gown, which was covered in green mould as if he had slept in a wood. So although I learnt nothing about Anglo-Saxon, I did get some idea of what wizards were like.

Tolkien was a devout Catholic, and he and Hugo Dyson, the Merton Fellow in English literature, were responsible for converting C.S. Lewis to Christianity. All three belonged to 'the Inklings', a group that met for beer and talk in the Eagle and Child in St Giles. But unlike Lewis's Narnia stories, Tolkien's fantasies avoid specific Christian references, and this has aided their global success. The moral of the ring story – that wealth and greed and power corrupt even good people – may have been borrowed from Wagner (though Tolkien always denied it), but it is congruent with many belief-systems across the world, as well as with common observation.

Opposite: The copy of The Hobbit *from the second impression of the first edition, presented by Tolkien to Norman Davis, his successor as Merton professor of English language and literature.* **Above, left:** *The College photograph of 1954. Tolkien is in the centre of the front row. On his right is H.W. Garrod and on his left Robin Harrison, later Warden.* **Above, right:** *Tolkien's runic inscription to Norman Davis, which has been translated as 'Best wishes from Thorin and Company'.*

THE HEAD-OF-THE-RIVER BOWL

Alan Bott and Michael Stansfield

Gownsmen are recorded in the 1790s as enjoying recreation in 'skiff, gig, cutter or canoe', but the first recorded occasion of racing in eight-oared boats in Oxford is in 1815. The Oxford versus Cambridge Boat Race dates from 1829. Merton first appeared in Eights in 1838 and briefly, on 29 May 1839, went Head-of-the-River. Initially, the Merton rig consisted of a white jersey with thin blue and red stripes; the flag bore a crimson Greek cross. Then, at the College's first appearance at Henley Royal Regatta, in 1898, the official programme recorded for Merton 'colours white, magenta trimmings and cross'. This has been the official rig ever since.

Merton's rowing record up to the Second World War was unspectacular, although in 1938 the College was to build the present boathouse, on the river opposite the Oxford University Boat Club, at a cost not exceeding £1,500. After the war in 1946, normal Eights week racing was resumed over six nights. Merton's ascent was inexorable, until the zenith was reached in 1951. It was actually one of the most exciting series of races ever for the headship that year. Merton started from fourth on the first night, with New College at the head. The *Times* reported 'cold and blustery conditions' as Magdalen, ahead of Merton, bumped the second-placed Trinity, after several attempts,

THE WARDEN COACHING

outside University boathouse. On the second night Magdalen pressed New College hard for the headship, overlapping up the Green Bank, but New College survived thanks to 'some excellent coxing' (the *Times* again). Meanwhile, Merton caught Trinity to move up to third. On the third night, New College, Magdalen and Merton raced up the Green Bank all but overlapping. Magdalen eventually caught New College outside the University boathouse, only a quarter of a length away from themselves being caught by Merton. On the fourth night, Merton confirmed their superiority over New College by catching them in the Gut, setting themselves up to chase Magdalen on the fifth night. Despite a strong cross-wind, Merton gained steadily until they were a third of a length down at the University boathouse. Their chance looked to have gone but a final push saw Magdalen caught within yards of the line. On the final night, Magdalen were unable to challenge seriously and Merton's triumphant row-over was apparently accompanied from the Gut by two runners. Roger Bannister, Harmsworth Scholar, was one of them. Merton had risen 25 places in seven years, and had not been bumped during that time. The *Times* cited 'keenness and determination' as being instrumental to the success, adding that the 1951 crew had 'fair length and swing, good rhythm and plenty of dash'.

A major spur behind this triumph was the enthusiasm and the coaching provided by Warden Geoffrey Mure. He had himself been in the Merton 1st VIII in 1912, 1913 and 1914. Returning to the College after the war, during which he had been awarded the MC and the Croix de Guerre, he served as Warden from 1947 to 1963.

The success of 1951 was celebrated with the creation, by subscription, of the Head-of-the-River bowl. It is a two-handled bowl with a cover, engraved with circles of overlapping stylised rowing Eights round the foot and the central finial, which consists of a gilded mitre, in deference to Walter de Merton, bishop of Rochester. Round the rim of the cover, there is an inscription: 'This bowl was given to the Warden and Fellows by Old Merton Men to commemorate the success of the College Eights, which in 1951 finished Head of the River for the first time.' It was designed by a young silversmith, Eric Clements, made by Wakeley and Wheeler and supplied by Payne and Son.

Men's rowing at Merton has not again yet scaled the heights of 1951 in Eights. Women's rowing has, however, advanced impressively since 1983 when they first raced in Eights Week. In 2002, the 1st VIII was denied the headship by no more than a few feet on the last night and in 2003 the headship was gained in Torpids. Perhaps the best is yet to come!

....

Opposite: The bowl. **Insert:** *'The Warden coaching', a cartoon of Geoffrey Mure by Tony Stearns, a Blue of 1957.* **Above:** *The Head-of-the-River VIII in action, 1951: N.W. Sanders (Bow), K.R. Spencer (2), C.D. Milling (3), P.D. Leuch (4), R.L. Arundel (5), A.J. Smith (6), H.M.C. Quick (7), D.R. Tristram (Stroke), D.W. Bannister (Cox).*

THE CHAPEL ORGAN

Alan Bott and Benjamin Nicholas

The new organ is the eighth known organ in the Chapel. There were organs by the 1460s and on 3 March 1488 Warden Fitzjames contracted with William Wotton of Oxford for the making of 'a goode & sufficient payr off organs' in the Chapel's new roodloft. In 1577, faced with simpler services after the Reformation, the College exchanged the organ for two globes. In 1633, amid the rising tide of high churchmanship encouraged by Archbishop Laud, a very small organ was again acquired, but this was presumably destroyed in the puritan mood of the Interregnum. It was the nineteenth-century Oxford Movement that inspired a lasting return to music in the Chapel. In about 1860, Henry Walter Sargent, Fellow and vicar of the parish of St John the Baptist, replaced the harmonium then in use with an organ, a distinguished instrument built by Dr William Hill. On Sargent's early death in 1867, this organ was removed, but a new chaplain, George Noel Freeling, presided over the acquisition of another in 1872. This instrument, placed beneath the great west window, was reconstructed in 1923 by Messrs Rushworth and Dreaper.

Two important events were to occur in 1968. First, a small mid-eighteenth-century organ, which came from Hawkstone Park, a convent in Shropshire, was donated to the College by Carapict Balthazar (1912) and restored by J.W. Walker and Sons. This charming organ, with its panelling of walnut, still stands on the north side of the choir. In the same year, a new organ built by Walker, with a case designed by Robert Potter, the College architect, was acquired through the benevolence of A.W. Ackworth (1919). A condition of this benefaction was that, for a trial period of ten years, a *trompe-l'oeil* painting of the unbuilt nave of the Chapel, with a 'conversation piece' depicting former members of the College, should be placed under the west window. This painting was removed after the trial period. The design of the organ case was tied up with the presence of this painting and its removal left the organ looking narrow and oddly placed. Walker had also been at the forefront of experimenting with modern materials in organ construction and some of these did not stand the test of time, making the organ increasingly unreliable. Its tonal scheme was principally designed for the performance of baroque organ music, but the College choir sings from a broad repertoire, and regularly a large congregation needs accompanying by an organ with much more presence in the Chapel.

After a thorough search, the College commissioned Dobson Pipe Organ Builders, of Lake City, Iowa, USA, to build a new instrument. A brief tour of the US, to hear and play some eight instruments, revealed an organ builder whose warmth of tonal voicing and quality of external design are exceptional. Lynn Dobson and his colleagues visited the College on a number of occasions to hear the choir and congregation, and gain an impression of how the new instrument needs to speak effectively from its position in the Ante-Chapel and provide the range of colours required for the accompaniment of choral singing. Dobson, in consultation with the Reed Rubin Organist and Director of Music and Paul Hale, the College's organ consultant, has designed a three-manual organ of 43 stops housed in a case of American white oak. Placed against the west wall of the Ante-Chapel, the organ's great, choir and pedal divisions are located at a level immediately above the console, with the swell division occupying the upper part of the case. The attached console is fitted with mechanical key action to slider soundboards. The stop action is electric, and has a combination action with 256 levels of memory.

Lynn Dobson writes of his design: 'I believe the organ should look like an instrument from our time and not attempt to look antique. The organ should fit into its space in a handsome proportional relationship. Finally, the organ should visually take enough cues from its surroundings that it feels like a natural part of the whole experience of being in the historic Chapel. It should look like it belongs in its setting.'

The splendid organ case is an impressive tribute to the skills of Lynn Dobson and his colleagues. A particular feature is the Zimbelstern ('Cymbal Star'), which shines at the top of the case. The organist, on pulling this stop, brings on a peal of five bells adding a little aural and visual splendour to a carol service or the conclusion of an organ recital.

Opposite: The new Dobson organ. **Insert:** *The small eighteenth-century organ.*

THE *MERTON* CHOIRBOOK

Benjamin Nicholas

It is not uncommon for an institution to commission a new piece of music or art to commemorate a special anniversary. It is much rarer to find a new collection of music, all composed for one ensemble and one collegiate chapel. The *Merton Choirbook* contributes to an illustrious musical tradition.

Early Tudor anthologies, pre-eminently the late fifteenth-century *Eton Choirbook*, were substantial musical monuments in their own right and also created a rich legacy that defined the characteristic sound and style of English church music. More recently, the coronation of Her Majesty the Queen in 1953 inspired the collection *A Garland for the Queen*. Ten composers – including Vaughan Williams, Howells and Mertonian Lennox Berkeley – contributed mainly secular songs for mixed choir. For the 60th anniversary of the Queen's accession to the throne, Peter Maxwell Davies and Robert Ponsonby had the idea of presenting *A Choirbook for the Queen*. This collection of 44 pieces, including 11 commissions, not only celebrates the Queen's reign, but also the British choral tradition. Merton College choir was one of 80 cathedral and collegiate choirs asked to sing from this collection during the course of 2012.

In the *Merton Choirbook*, commissioned to mark the College's 750th anniversary in 2014, many of the leading composers of the day are represented. They include Sir Harrison Birtwistle, who has set a text by Oxford's professor of poetry Sir Geoffrey Hill, James MacMillan, Jonathan Dove and Julian Anderson. Within the collection, there are some interesting groups of pieces. Four female composers, including Judith Weir, have each set one of the Marian Antiphons; seven composers have each written one of the Advent Antiphons, with John Tavener and Cecilia McDowall heading the list. Music for Choral Evensong, the service most regularly sung by the College choir, is also included within the *Choirbook*, with *Preces and Responses* by Matthew Martin, a hymn by John Joubert and numerous new Anglican chants from composers who principally write for the church. The 'Evening Canticles' appear both in Latin and in English, and a number of anthems suitable for the different seasons of the liturgical calendar make this collection something that we will draw on throughout the year. The new Dobson organ has inspired some of the music, including David Briggs's *Messe Solennelle* and *Chorale Preludes* by John Caldwell and Gabriel Jackson.

Another distinguishing feature of the *Choirbook* is the inclusion of composers from further afield. Reflecting the popularity of choral music from the Baltic States, Rihards Dubra and Ēriks Ešenvalds have both been commissioned by the College, as has Norwegian composer Ola Gjeilo, whose setting of *Northern Lights* has been widely performed. James Lavino, an American composer renowned for his film scores, has set *Beati quorum via*, and Richard Pantcheff, currently based in South Africa, has included various African musical influences in his contribution. Although the *Choirbook* is principally a liturgical collection, Gabriel Jackson's *The Passion of the Lord*, composed for the Passiontide at Merton Festival 2014, is more likely to be performed in a concert than a service. Lasting an hour and scored for instruments, soloists and chorus, this substantial addition to the repertoire of music for Passiontide has a libretto devised by Merton's chaplain, Simon Jones, which includes texts by Mertonian poets alongside passages from the Gospels.

The process of commissioning and compiling the *Choirbook* began shortly after the establishment of the College's Choral Foundation in 2008. Thanks to Reed Rubin (the Reed Foundation) and other Mertonians, two directors of music were appointed, 18 choral scholarships were awarded, and the College choir began a new regime including mid-week services in addition to Sundays, regular foreign tours, broadcasts and recordings. A number of Mertonians who support the Choral Foundation have also made their contribution to the College's anniversary by giving one, or several, pieces in the *Choirbook*. Their generosity will ensure that the choral repertory is renewed and strengthened, not just in Merton College Chapel, but also in the institutions that have already added music from the *Merton Choirbook* to their repertories.

The range of composers represented, each with their own publishing arrangements, has made it impossible to publish the collection as one anthology. Possibly with greater practical benefit, many of the individual items are available separately, and the 'master' volume lives, quite rightly, in the Merton College Library. As befits an institution at the cutting edge of teaching and research, the *Merton Choirbook* is both a reflection of the College's dynamic role as a nexus for creativity and new thought, and a lasting musical resource.

....

Opposite, top: The College choir singing in the Ante-Chapel during the 2012 Advent Carol Service. **Opposite, bottom:** *The manuscript of John Joubert's hymn tune 'Merton College'.*

THE T.S. ELIOT THEATRE AND THE FINLAY BUILDING

Jessica Rawson

Why should a college need a lecture theatre, let alone one that seats 120 people? After all the Examination Schools are almost next door. However, even as the University becomes in some sense more centralised, colleges must also change and provide new spaces for new activities, especially for graduate students and old members, but also for undergraduates. Before the T.S. Eliot Theatre was completed in 2010, there was no place where a whole new undergraduate or graduate year group could be comfortably gathered for a talk, for example. In addition, the College needed somewhere for graduate seminars, lectures for the wider University, meetings with old members and conference presentations. And these activities increased throughout the years from 1994 to 2010. Indeed when I arrived at Merton in 1994, a new lecture theatre was already planned, though adjacent to North Lodge rather than where it was eventually built.

As so often in Oxford, there were more pressing projects and work on the new Finlay Building, supported very generously by Francis Finlay, took precedence. This accommodated the Bursars and their staffs and allowed their rooms in Fellows' Quad to be returned to teaching and residential use. For both projects the College had to be ingenious with space. After all, apart from the Fellows' Garden, there is no empty

ground at the centre of the site. However, Postmasters' Yard across the street from the Porters' Lodge was obviously under-used, with a row of garages used for storage and parking. Allies and Morrison responded to the ancient buildings of Postmasters' Hall and the Tennis Court, creating a new building in gleaming white stone that accommodated itself readily to its surroundings. And perhaps in keeping with Merton's long traditions, the College gardeners, led by Lucille Savin, made the most of the new space with four different small gardens and an innovation: a pond.

The T.S. Eliot Theatre is equally carefully and ingeniously fitted in among the existing fabric. The main part of the theatre is built into what was the garden of South Lodge and is almost completely hidden by walls and houses from Christ Church Meadow. The foyer has entrances from both the Rose Lane area inside the College and also from Rose Lane itself, so that both members of the College and others from the University have equally easy access. The foyer greets such visitors with the magnificent but thoughtful bust of T.S. Eliot by Epstein, and a group of intriguing lights, sparkling from the ceiling as small star bursts. The three clusters contain within them the constellations of the Plough,

Perseus and Auriga as they would have been seen at the foundation of the College on 14 September 1264. The light with the Auriga constellation also presents the boundaries of the College. These creative links between past and present were designed by Lucy Martin of John Cullen Lighting.

In the foyer, also, exposed stone wall and window outlines remind the visitor that South Lodge, designed by Thomas Worthington and completed in 1939, is incorporated in the theatre complex. The ample rooms of the original house, formerly occupied by Fellows and Wardens, now provide three magnificent seminar rooms and a teaching room, funded and named, like other parts of the building and its fittings, by generous Mertonians. As the number of graduates in the College has risen, so we have needed more such meeting rooms for the discussion groups founded to embrace both students and Fellows: the History of the Book, Global Directions and the Biomedical and Lifesciences Group. Leaving the foyer and passing the seminar rooms, we enter the main theatre. Here the colours change from the stone and wood of the new foyer and original house to the soft green of the leather seats and the oak of the panelling. The very fine detailing and the excellent acoustics of the theatre are a tribute to the subtle design of Graham Blackburn of Ridge and Partners. And the theatre has also been presented with a piano, so that the excellent acoustics now resonate for chamber music. The panels of the end walls can be turned to provide the hard surfaces required for such music. The College is indebted to the many Mertonians whose generosity enabled the building of the T.S. Eliot Theatre, especially the lead donors John Booth, Charles Manby and John Beard.

Future generations will take for granted the stonework and gardens of the Finlay Building. So too will they accept the texture and the acoustics of the T.S. Eliot Theatre. But as with so much in the College, happenstance and careful thought have added another layer of structure and activities to the rich architectural heritage of Oxford's most ancient College buildings.

*Opposite, left: The Finlay Building. **Opposite, right:** A lecture in the T.S. Eliot Theatre.*
Right: The foyer of the T.S. Eliot Theatre, with Jacob Epstein's bust of Eliot and the lights recreating parts of the night sky at the foundation of the College.

LIBRARY REFERENCE LIST

References for library/archive items reproduced in this volume.

Foreword: Etching of the Gatehouse: Private Collection

Introduction: Map of the manor of Malden, 1623: MCR MAL/9/1; Seal of Jacob the Jew: MCR 188; A physician's quadrant, *c.*1400–50: OB/AST/4; Vaslet portrait of Ralph Carr: MCPo/Vas; Butterfield design for Grove Building: MCD/B42

The Founder's Statutes: MCR 194

Hebrew Starrs: MCR 1146

Kibworth: Estate map of Kibworth, 1609: MCR KIB/9/1; Survey of 1280: MCR 2423

Manuscript of Aristotle's *Metaphysics*: MS 269, fol. 200r

The Hall Door and Other Medieval Doorways: Hall door drawing: Private Collection

College Seals: Bosom of Abraham: MCR 231; The brass seal matrix of the 1330s: MCR OB/SEA/2; Impression: MCR 429

The Bursars' Rolls: Roll of 1335 with its wooden tally for 'kybbworth': MCR 3669; Account roll of William de Chelesham, 1299: MCR 3628

The Astrolabes: OB/AST/2

Licence in Mortmain, 1380: The St Aldate's property marked on the Ordnance Survey map of Oxford, 1876: Merton, Mob Library Office; The Licence in Mortmain: MCR 370

***Catalogus Vetus*:** MCR 4.16

The Manor of Holywell: Estate map of Holywell, 1758: MCR HOL/9/3; David Loggan, *Oxonia illustrata* (Oxford, 1675): MER Spec 35

Fifteenth-Century Illuminated English Statutes: Caricature of F.E. Smith: Private Collection; Statutes: MS 297B, fol. 328r

The Caxton Chaucer: MER 111.C.9

Jerome's Translation of the *Chronicle of Eusebius*: MS 315, fols 125v–126r

The Chapel Tennis Balls: OB/MSC/10

The Portal of St Alban Hall and the Frontispiece in Fellows' Quad: Sebastiano Serlio, *Regole generali di architettura* [the fourth of the five books of architecture], Venice, 1543, leaf 4: MER 38.HH.13

Theodore Goulston's *Galeni Opera Omnia*: Portrait of William Harvey: MCPo 22; William Harvey, Plate from *Exercitatio anatomica de motu cordis*, in *Opera Omnia* (London, 1766): MER 48.K.9; Goulston's copy of Galen's works, *Opera Omnia* (Pavia, 1515): MER 45.B.2

The Wren Screen: Bursar's accounts, 1673: MCR 3.3, p. 379

Parker's of Oxford Sales Ledgers: Merton Blackwell Collection

The Kitchens: Eighteenth-century receptions book: MCR Accession 2006/29

Rowlandson's drawings of Merton: Top: MCD/B29; Bottom: MCD/B28

The Shute Barrington Portrait: MCPo43

The Beerbohm Room: Self-caricature: Beerbohm Collection 8.5; Oscar Wilde: Beerbohm Collection 3.83, front free endpaper

A Chinese Incense Burner: Aurel Stein, *Ruins of Desert Cathay* (London, 1912), pl. 126: MER LAEOA/STE(2)

The Letters of Kuruvila Zachariah: Portrait: Private Collection; Letter of 20 Feb. 1913: Zachariah 1/32; Letter of 15 July 1915: Zachariah 1/157

Edwardian Waistcoat of the Myrmidon Club: 1909 menu: MCR 12.1.47; Portrait of H.H. Monteath, 1906, from Myrmidon album: MCPh/A17/8; Waistcoat: MCR OB/MSC/4; Myrmidon Club photo album: MCPh/A17

The T. S. Eliot Collection: Letter to Coghill: MS F.3.48

The Sandy Irvine Archive: Photograph by Irvine of 'Everest from the pass after Shekar', 21 April 1924: Irvine 3/12; Irvine and Milling on an expedition to Spitsbergen, August 1923: Irvine 24/132; Oxford Boat Race Crew at Putney, March 1923: Irvine 24/42

E.S. Goodrich's Royal Society Medal: Portrait of E.S. Goodrich: Collection of the Department of Zoology, Oxford University; Royal Society Medal: MCR D.2.45

Presentation copy of *The Hobbit*: J.R.R. Tolkien, *The Hobbit* (London, 1937): MER 119.C.10; College photograph 1954: MCPh/G/MG272

The Head-of-the-River Bowl: Cartoon of Geoffrey Mure: MCPo72; Photo of the Head-of-the-River VIII in action, 1951: MCPh/G/BC45

The *Merton Choirbook*: John Joubert hymn manuscript: MCR 19.3

SOURCES AND FURTHER READING

General works or those relevant to several articles

Alan Bott, *The Monuments in Merton College Chapel* (Oxford, 1964)

Alan Bott, *The Heraldry in Merton College, Oxford* (Oxford, 2001)

George C. Brodrick, *Memorials of Merton College* (Oxford, 1885)

Bernard W. Henderson, *University of Oxford College Histories: Merton College* (London, 1899)

J.R.L. Highfield, *The Early Rolls of Merton College, Oxford*, Oxford Historical Society, new series 18 (1964)

G.H. Martin and J.R.L. Highfield, *A History of Merton College* (Oxford, 1997)

Merton Muniments, ed. P.S. Allen and H.W. Garrod, Oxford Historical Society, old series 86 (1928)

Oxford Dictionary of National Biography, ed. H.C.G. Matthew and Brian Harrison (Oxford, 2004)

Registrum Annalium Collegii Mertonensis, 1483–1521, 1521–1567, 1567–1603, 1603–1660, ed. H.E. Salter, J.M. Fletcher, J.R.L. Highfield, Oxford Historical Society, old series 76 (1921), new series 23 (1974), 24 (1976), 41 (2006)

R.M. Thomson, *A Descriptive Catalogue of the Medieval Manuscripts of Merton College, Oxford* (Cambridge, 2009)

Anthony Wood, *Life and Times*, ed. A. Clark (5 vols, Oxford, 1891–1900)

SECTION ONE: MEDIEVAL MERTON

The Founder's Statutes

J.R.L. Highfield, 'The Early Colleges', in *The History of the University of Oxford, volume I: The Early Oxford Schools*, ed. J.I. Catto (Oxford, 1984), pp. 225–63.

Hebrew Starrs

Peter E. Pormann, 'A Memorial to Bodley', *Postmaster* (2003), pp. 77–9; idem, 'Two New Starrs Relating to the History of Merton College, Oxford', *Journal of Jewish Studies*, 55 (2004), pp. 102–17; E. Savage-Smith, *A Descriptive Catalogue of Oriental Manuscripts at St John's College, Oxford* (Oxford, 2005), pp. 103–6.

Kibworth

Rodney Hilton, 'Kibworth Harcourt: a Merton College Manor in the Thirteenth and Fourteenth Centuries', in *Studies in Leicestershire Agrarian History*, ed. W.G. Hoskins (Leicester, 1949), pp. 17–40; Cicely Howell, *Land, Family and Inheritance in Transition: Kibworth Harcourt 1280–1700* (Cambridge, 1983); Michael Wood, *The Story of England* (London, 2010).

The Early Warden's House

Alan Bott, 'The Domus Custodis', *Postmaster* (2006), pp. 81–9; D.R. Clark, 'The Early Warden's House, Merton College, Oxford', unpublished report for Oxfordshire Buildings Record, 2012; J.R.L. Highfield, 'The Aula Custodis', *Postmaster* (1970), pp. 14–20.

Manuscript of Aristotle's *Metaphysics*

M. Camille, 'Illustrations in Harley MS 3487 and the Perception of Aristotle's *Libri naturales* in Thirteenth-Century England', in *England in the Thirteenth Century: Proceedings of the 1984 Harlaxton Symposium*, ed. W.M. Ormrod (Woodbridge,

1986), pp. 31–44; Nigel J. Morgan, *Early Gothic Manuscripts* (2 vols, London, 1982–8), ii, pp. 132–3; J.A. Weisheipl, 'Science in the Thirteenth Century', in *The History of the University of Oxford, volume I: The Early Oxford Schools*, ed. J.I. Catto (Oxford, 1984), pp. 435–69.

The Hall Door and Other Medieval Doorways

Jane Geddes, *Medieval Decorative Ironwork in England* (London, 1999).

College Seals

J.R.L. Highfield, 'Some Early Seals of Merton College, Oxford', *Postmaster* (2009), pp. 60–2.

The Treasury

The College Register 1822–1877, MCR 1.5.

The Medieval Stained Glass

T. Ayers, *The Medieval Stained Glass of Merton College, Oxford*, Corpus Vitrearum Medii Aevi Great Britain, VI (London, 2013); H.W. Garrod, *Ancient Painted Glass in Merton College, Oxford* (London, 1931).

The Bursars' Rolls

The Domestic Accounts of Merton College, Oxford, 1 August 1482–1 August 1494, ed. J.M. Fletcher and C.A. Upton, Oxford Historical Society, new series 34 (1996).

The Astrolabes

Sigmund Eisner (ed.), *A Variorum Edition of The Works of Geoffrey Chaucer*, Volume VI, *The Prose Treatises*, Part One: *A Treatise on the Astrolabe* (Norman, OK, 2002); R.T. Gunther, *Early Science in Oxford, volume II: Astronomy* (Oxford, 1923), pp. 208–10, 222–5; John North, 'Astronomy and Mathematics', in *The History of the University of Oxford, volume II: Late Medieval Oxford*, ed. J.I. Catto and T.A.R. Evans (Oxford 1992), chapter 4.

Licence in Mortmain, 1380

Elizabeth Danbury, 'The Decoration and Illumination of Royal Charters in England, 1250–1509: an Introduction', in *England and Her Neighbours, 1066–1453: Essays in Honour of Pierre Chaplais*, ed. Michael Jones and Malcolm Vale (London, 1989), pp. 157–80; Julian Reid, 'The Archives', *Postmaster* (2006), pp. 55–7; Jessica Berenbeim, *Art of Documentation: Documents and Visual Culture in England, c.1250–c.1450* (Toronto, forthcoming 2014).

Catalogus Vetus

A.B. Emden, *A Biographical Register of the University of Oxford to A.D. 1500* (3 vols, Oxford, 1959). Grateful thanks to Tim Ayers, Robin Darwall-Smith, Nigel Ramsay and Jennifer Thorp for their advice.

The Manor of Holywell

C. Bell, 'Archaeological Investigations on the Site of a Medieval and Post-Medieval Watermill at Holywell Ford, Magdalen College, Oxford', *Oxoniensia*, 61 (1996), pp.

275–95; M.G. Brock and M.C. Curthoys (eds), *The History of the University of Oxford, volume VI: Nineteenth-Century Oxford, Part 1* (1997); A. Crossley (ed.), *Victoria County History of Oxfordshire, volume IV: The City of Oxford* (1979); J. Haslam, 'The Two Anglo-Saxon *Burhs* of Oxford', *Oxoniensia*, 75 (2010), pp. 14–34.

The Sculpture over the Gatehouse
A.J. Bott and J.R.L. Highfield, 'The Sculpture over the Gatehouse at Merton College, Oxford, 1464–5', *Oxoniensia*, 58 (1993), pp. 233–40.

SECTION TWO: MERTON MATURING

Fifteenth-century Illuminated English Statutes
John Campbell, *F.E. Smith, First Earl of Birkenhead* (London, 1983); N.R. Ker, *Medieval Manuscripts in British Libraries*, III (Oxford, 1983); F.H. Lawson, *The Oxford Law School 1850–1965* (Oxford, 1968).

The Fitzjames Arch
S. Thompson, 'Fitzjames, Richard (d. 1522)', *Oxford Dictionary of National Biography*.

The Lectern of 1504
C.C. Oman, 'Mediaeval Brass Lecterns in England', *Archaeological Journal*, 87 (1930), pp. 117–49.

The Caxton Chaucer
N.F. Blake, 'Caxton, William', *Oxford Dictionary of National Biography*; Lotte Hellinga, *Caxton in Focus* (Cambridge, 1982); D.E. Rhodes, *A Catalogue of incunabula in all the libraries of Oxford outside the Bodleian* (Oxford, 1982); The National Archives, PROB 11/170/292 (William Wright's will); http://www.oxfordhistory.org.uk/mayors/1603_1714/wright_william1_1614.htm; many thanks to Julia Walworth and Julian Reid for help and advice in preparing this contribution.

The Chapel Tennis Balls
Thomas Coghan, *The Haven of Health* (London, 1584), pp. 3–4; Jeremy Potter, *Tennis and Oxford* (Oxford, 1994); Anthony Wood, *Survey of the Antiquities of the City of Oxford*, ed. Andrew Clark (Oxford, 1889–99), pp. 535–6; see also the Oxford University Tennis Club website.

The Upper Library
Richard Gameson, 'The Medieval Library (to *c.*1450)', in *The Cambridge History of Libraries in Britain and Ireland, volume I: To 1640*, ed. E. Leedham-Green and T. Webber (Cambridge, 2006), pp. 13–50; Neil Ker, 'Oxford College Libraries in the Sixteenth Century', *The Bodleian Library Record*, 6, 3 (1959), pp. 459–515; Rodney Thomson, 'William Reed bishop of Chichester (d. 1385) – Bibliophile?', in *The Study of Medieval Manuscripts of England: Festschrift in Honor of Richard W. Pfaff*, ed. G.H. Brown and L.E. Voigts (Tempe, AR, 2010), pp. 281–93.

The Library Chests
P.M. Johnston, 'Church Chests of the Twelfth and Thirteenth Centuries in England', *Archaeological Journal*, 64 (1907), p. 256; David Sherlock, *Suffolk Church Chests* (Bury St Edmunds, 2008).

The Bodley and Savile Monuments
The Autobiography of Sir Thomas Bodley, ed. William Clennell (Oxford, 2006); *Letters of Sir Thomas Bodley to Thomas James, First Keeper of the Bodleian Library*, ed. G.W. Wheeler (Oxford, 1926); David Womersley, 'Sir Henry Savile's Translations of Tacitus and the Political Interpretation of Elizabethan Texts', *Review of English Studies*, new series 42 (1991), pp. 313–42.

The Portal of St Alban Hall and the Frontispiece in Fellows' Quad
Alan Bott, 'Lost, Little Known and Unbuilt Merton (1)', *Postmaster* (2004), pp. 88–95.

The Sundial in Front Quad
M. Stanier, *Oxford Sundials* (Oxford, 2003); H.J. White, *Merton College, Oxford, The College Monographs* (London, 1906). Great thanks to J.R.L. Highfield for many delightful conversations and Alan Bott for many helpful comments.

The College Silver
Helen M. Clifford, *A Treasured Inheritance: 600 Years of Oxford College Silver* (Oxford, 2004); Philippa Glanville, *Silver in England* (London, 1987); idem, *Silver in Tudor and Early Stuart England* (London, 1989); E. Alfred Jones, *Catalogue of the Plate of Merton College, Oxford* (Oxford, 1938). Thanks to Helen Clifford, Steven Gunn, Helen Morley and Julia Walworth for their help in the preparation of this article.

Theodore Goulston's *Galeni Opera Omnia*
Martha Carlin, 'Gaddesden, John'; Roger French, 'Harvey, William'; Vivian Nutton, 'Goulston, Theodore', all in *Oxford Dictionary of National Biography*.

The Wren Screen
J.R.L. Highfield, 'Alexander Fisher, Sir Christopher Wren and Merton College Chapel', *Oxoniensia*, 24 (1959), pp. 70–82.

The Senior Common Room Panelling
J.R.L. Highfield, 'Three Little-known Benefactors of Merton College in the Seventeenth Century, William Simonson, Alexander Fisher and Peter Nicolls', *Postmaster* (2001), pp. 55–61.

The Globes
Elly Dekker, *Globes at Greenwich: A Catalogue of the Globes and Armillary Spheres in the National Maritime Museum, Greenwich* (Oxford, 1999); Sylvia Sumira, 'Secrets of the Inner Globe', *Globe Studies*, 51/52 (2005), pp. 133–9; Laurence Worms and Ashley Baynton-Williams, *British Map Engravers: A Dictionary of Engravers, Lithographers and their Principal Employers to 1850* (London, 2011).

Joseph Kilner's Coin Collection
J.D.A. Thompson, 'The Merton College Coin Collection', *Oxoniensia*, 17–18 (1952–3), pp. 188–92; Ben Zurawel, *Antiquaries, Numismatics and the Grand Tour. Discovering Ancient Rome in Eighteenth-Century England* (London, 2014).

Lewis Vaslet Pastel Portraits
Catalogue of a loan collection of portraits of English historical personages who died between 1714 and 1837: exhibited in the Examination Schools (Oxford, 1906); Neil Jeffares, *Dictionary of Pastellists Before 1800* (London, 2006); Christopher F. Lindsey, 'Hartley, David', *Oxford Dictionary of National Biography*; Rachael Poole (Mrs Reginald Poole), *Catalogue of Portraits in the Possession of the University, Colleges, City, and County of Oxford* (Oxford, 1926).

SECTION THREE: MODERN MERTON

Rowlandson's Drawings of Merton
A.H. Gibbs, *Rowlandson's Oxford* (London, 1911); Matthew Payne and James Payne, *Regarding Thomas Rowlandson, 1757–1827: His Life, Art & Acquaintance* (London, 2010); H.J. Petter, *The Oxford Almanack* (Oxford, 1974).

The Shute Barrington Portrait
James Bentley, 'Portrait of a Bishop', *Postmaster* (November 1958), pp. 12–15; E.A. Varley, 'Barrington, Shute', *Oxford Dictionary of National Biography*.

Russian Treasures
Authentic Account of the Visit of His Royal Highness the Prince Regent to the University of Oxford, June 14. MDCCCXIV (Oxford, 1815); *A Correct Account of the Visit of His Royal Highness the Prince Regent, and His Illustrious Guests, to the University and City of Oxford, in June, 1814* (Oxford, 1815); Mikhail Kizilov, 'Russkie v Oxforde: kratkii obzor istorii' [The Russians at Oxford: a short history survey], in *Russkoe prisutstvie v Britanii* (Moscow, 2009), pp. 101–16.

The Painted Ceiling of the Chapel
Anne Pollen, *John Hungerford Pollen* (London, 1912).

Holywell Meadow
A.H. Church, *Introduction to the Plant life of the Oxford District* (3 vols, Oxford, 1922–5); G.C. Druce, *Botany of the Upper Thames* (Oxford, 1926); A.G. Tansley, *The British Islands and Their Vegetation* (2 vols, Cambridge, 1965).

The Beerbohm Room
Max Beerbohm, *The Incomparable Max: A Selection* (London, 1962); Lawrence Danson, *Max Beerbohm and the Act of Writing* (Oxford, 1989).

A Chinese Incense Burner
M. Aurel Stein, *Ruins of Desert Cathy* (2 vols, London, 1912); Valerie Hansen, *Silk Road. A New History* (Oxford, 2012); Jeanette Mirsky, *Sir Aurel Stein, Archaeological Explorer* (Chicago and London, 1977).

Edwardian Waistcoat of the Myrmidon Club
Minutes and photograph albums of the Myrmidon Club (unpublished, 1865–1935).

The T.S. Eliot Collection
Frank Brenchley, 'T.S. Eliot: The Brenchley Collection', *Postmaster* (1987), pp. 49–52; T.S. Eliot, *The Letters of T.S. Eliot*, general ed. John Haffenden (4 vols to date, London, 1988 onwards); T.S. Eliot, 'Professor H.H. Joachim,' *The Times*, 4 August 1938, p. 12.

The Sandy Irvine Archive
Julie Summers, *Fearless on Everest: The Quest for Sandy Irvine* (London, 2000).

The War Memorial
Anon., 'Mertonian Victoria Crosses in the Second World War,' *Postmaster* (1995), pp. 46–8; Brian Harrison (ed.), *The History of the University of Oxford, volume VIII: The Twentieth Century* (Oxford, 1994).

E.S. Goodrich's Royal Society Medal
Gavin de Beer, 'Edwin Stephen Goodrich. 1868–1946', *Obituary Notices of Fellows of the Royal Society*, 5 (15) (1947), pp. 477–90; P.W.H. Holland, 'Embryonic development of heads, skeletons and amphioxus: E.S. Goodrich revisited', *International Journal of Developmental Biology*, 44 (2000), pp. 29–34; F. Maddison, M. Pelling and C. Webster (eds), *Essays on the Life and Work of Thomas Linacre c.1460–1524* (Oxford, 1977).

Presentation Copy of *The Hobbit*
Humphrey Carpenter, *J.R.R. Tolkien: A Biography* (London, 1977).

The Head-of-the-River Bowl
Michael Stansfield, 'Merton in Eights', *Postmaster* (2002), pp. 78–81.

The Chapel Organ
Mark Everitt, 'Merton Chapel in the Nineteenth Century', *Oxoniensia*, 42 (1977), pp. 247–55.

The *Merton Choirbook*
Daniel Grimley, '750th Celebrations – The Merton Choirbook', *Merton College Newsletter*, Spring 2010.

List of Contributors and Picture Credits

Tim Ayers is Senior Lecturer in the History of Art at the University of York, Vice President of the international Corpus Vitrearum project, and author of *The Medieval Stained Glass of Wells Cathedral* and *The Medieval Stained Glass of Merton College, Oxford*.

Jack Beatson Kt, FBA, Fellow and Tutor in law at Merton, 1973–94, and an Honorary Fellow since 1995, was Rouse Ball Professor of English Law at the University of Cambridge, and is now a judge of the Court of Appeal.

Sarah Bendall is Fellow Librarian and Development Director at Emmanuel College, Cambridge. She was Research Fellow and Librarian at Merton, 1994–2000. Her publications include *Maps, Land and Society* and *Dictionary of Land Surveyors in Great Britain and Ireland 1530–1850*.

Alan Bott OBE is a Bodley Fellow and sometime Postmaster of the College. His books include *Monuments in Merton College Chapel* (1964), *Baptisms and Marriages at Merton College* (1981), *A Short History of the Buildings* (1993) and *Heraldry in Merton College* (2000).

John Carey FBA was a Senior Scholar at Merton, 1958–9, and returned as Merton Professor of English Literature in 1976. His *William Golding, The Man Who Wrote Lord of the Flies*, won the 2009 James Tait Black Prize for Biography.

Michael Clanchy FBA read History at Merton, 1956–9. His university career has been in Glasgow and London. He is the author of *From Memory to Written Record: England 1066–1307* and *Abelard – a Medieval Life*.

Michael Dunnill, a pathologist, was elected a Fellow of Merton in 1967. He is the author of *Pulmonary Pathology, The Pathological Basis of Renal Disease* and (jointly) *Morphometry*. He has also written two biographies, *The Plato of Praed Street* and *William Budd*.

John Eidinow read Greats at Merton, where he has been Lecturer in Latin since 1992, and a Bodley Fellow since 2002. He is Fellow and Tutor in Classics of St Benet's Hall, and has published on Latin poetry.

Stefano Evangelista was Merton's first Fitzjames Research Fellow in English, 2004–6. He is now a fellow of Trinity College, Oxford, and is the author of *British Aestheticism and Ancient Greece: Hellenism, Reception, Gods in Exile*.

Anthony Fletcher read Modern History at Merton, 1959–62. His books include *The Outbreak of the English Civil War, Reform in the Provinces, Growing up in England* and *Life, Death and Growing up on the Western Front*.

David Ganz was an undergraduate and postgraduate at Merton. He was Professor of Palaeography at King's College London until his post was 'disinvested' in 2010, and is now Visiting Professor of Palaeography at the University of Notre Dame.

Matthew Grimley studied at Merton and has been Tutor in History since 2008. He is the author of *Citizenship, Community and the Church of England: Liberal Anglican Theories of the State between the Wars*.

Steven Gunn studied and was Junior Research Fellow at Merton and has been Tutor in History since 1989. His books include *Charles Brandon, Duke of Suffolk, Early Tudor Government*, and *War, State and Society in England and the Netherlands, 1477–1559*.

Yang-Hui He was Fitzjames and STFC Advanced Fellow at Merton, 2005–10. He is currently Reader in Mathematics at City University, London, jointly Chang-Jiang Chair Professor of physics at Nankai University, and continues to enjoy the pleasure of tutoring Merton mathematicians.

Roger Highfield was Harmsworth Scholar and Junior Research Fellow at Merton, 1948–51, Tutor in History, 1951–89, and Librarian, 1955–89. He is now an Emeritus Fellow. He has published on medieval English and Spanish history, as well as the history of Merton and the University.

Peter Holland FRS has been Linacre Professor of Zoology at Merton since 2002. He is the author of *The Animal Kingdom: A Very Short Introduction*.

Matthew Jenkinson read for his Master's and DPhil at Merton, and is author of *Culture and Politics at the Court of Charles II, 1660–1685*. He has been awarded Fellowships by the Royal Historical Society, the Huntington Library and the Massachusetts Historical Society.

Stephen Johnston is Acting Director of the University of Oxford's Museum of the History of Science. His research focuses on the histories of science and mathematics, and includes books such as *Compass and Rule: Architecture as Mathematical Practice in England, 1500–1750*.

Mikhail Kizilov studied at Merton, 2004–7, and published his DPhil dissertation as *The Karaites of Galicia: An Ethnoreligious Minority Among the Ashkenazim, the Turks, and the Slavs, 1772–1945*. He is now Alexander von Humboldt Research Fellow at the University of Tübingen.

Richard McCabe FBA has been Fellow and Tutor in English at Merton since 1993. His books include *Spenser's Monstrous Regiment* and, as editor, *The Oxford Handbook of Edmund Spenser*.

Kate McClune is Lecturer in English at the University of Bristol. She was Fitzjames Research Fellow in Old and Middle English at Merton, 2007–11, and has published on Older Scots literature, medieval manuscripts, and Arthurian literature.

Benjamin Nicholas studied at Lincoln College, Oxford. He has been Organ Scholar at St Paul's Cathedral, director of the Tewkesbury Abbey Schola Cantorum and, since 2012, Reed Rubin Organist and Director of Music at Merton. His recordings are on the Delphian label.

Robert Peberdy read Modern History at Merton and later undertook research on medieval urban history in the Department of English Local History at Leicester University. He has worked for the Victoria County History and has been secretary of the Merton Society.

Peter E. Pormann was a Junior Research Fellow in Oriental Studies at Merton, 2001–4, and is now Professor of Classics and Graeco-Arabic Studies and Director of the John Rylands Research Institute, Manchester. His latest book is *The Mirror of Health* (2013).

Jessica Rawson DBE, FBA, Professor of Chinese Art and Archaeology, was head of the Asian Department at the British Museum before becoming Warden of Merton, 1994–2010. Her books include *Chinese Ornament: The Lotus and Dragon* and *Chinese Jade from the Neolithic to the Qing*.

Julian Reid read Medieval Languages at Durham, before training as an archivist at Liverpool University. He worked for several years in local government archives in Norfolk and Essex. He has been archivist at Corpus Christi and Merton Colleges since 2002.

Nicholas Richardson is an Emeritus Fellow of Merton, and was Tutor in Classics, 1968–2004. He plays real tennis regularly on the Merton court.

Pippa Shirley read History at Merton, graduating in 1986. She then worked as a curator and silver specialist at the British Museum and the Victoria and Albert Museum before moving to Waddesdon Manor as Head of Collections.

Susan Skedd studied History at Merton, where she specialised in women's education in eighteenth-century Britain. She has worked as a Research Editor for the *Oxford Dictionary of National Biography* and Blue Plaques Historian at English Heritage.

Michael Stansfield came from Canterbury Cathedral to be archivist at Merton, 2000–2; he is now at Durham University Library Special Collections.

Julie Summers is a social historian and author of ten books including *Fearless on Everest: The Quest for Sandy Irvine* about her great-uncle (Merton, 1921–3). She is currently working on a book about greyhound racing.

Philip Waller, now an Emeritus Fellow of Merton, was Tutor in History, 1971–2008. His books include *Town, City, & Nation: England 1850–1914*, and *Writers, Readers, & Reputations: Literary Life in Britain 1870–1918*.

Julia Walworth came to Merton as Research Fellow and Librarian in 2001, having previously been Head of Historic Collections at the University of London Senate House Library. She has published on images in medieval manuscripts and on library history.

Michael H. Whitworth has been Tutor in English at Merton since 2005. He has published articles on T.S. Eliot in *English Literature in Transition*, *Essays in Criticism* and elsewhere. His books include *Virginia Woolf* and *Reading Modernist Poetry*.

Beth Williamson (née Jackson) read Modern History at Merton, 1988–91. She studied Art History for a Masters and PhD at the Courtauld Institute in London and is now Reader in the department of History of Art at the University of Bristol.

Katherine J. Willis has been Tasso Leventis Professor of Biodiversity at Merton and Director of the Biodiversity Institute in the Department of Zoology since 2010. Her books include *The Evolution of Plants* and *Key Topics in Conservation Biology*.

Michael Wood is a documentary film maker, writer and historian. His TV series *The Story of England* told the tale of the Merton manor of Kibworth in Leicestershire through the whole of English history.

Ben Zurawel was at Merton 2002–7, reading for a BA in Ancient and Modern History and an MPhil in Roman History. He now practises as a barrister at 9 Gough Square, London.

Principal photography by **Colin Dunn** (Scriptura Ltd).

Thanks are due to the following for permission to reproduce photographs:
Mob Library at Night, pp. 20–1: courtesy of DPA Lighting
Estate map of Kibworth, p. 26: © Maya Vision International Ltd
Kilner Coins, pp. 96–7: © Ashmolean Museum, University of Oxford
Fritillary, p. 114: photo by Geoffrey Kite
Various works by Beerbohm pp. 116–7: courtesy of the Beerbohm Estate, Berlin Associates
Ritual food vessel, Teng Hu gui p. 118: © Compton Verney, photograph by Prudence Cuming Associates Ltd
Portrait of Kuruvila Zachariah, p. 120: courtesy of the Zachariah family
Letter from T S Eliot, p. 126: courtesy of Faber and Faber Limited
Tolkien's *The Hobbit*, p. 134: © The Tolkien Estate Limited 1937, 1966, 2013
Tolkien's inscription, p. 135: © The Tolkien Estate Limited 2013
The manuscript of John Joubert's hymn tune *Merton College*, p. 141: © John Joubert; 'Light of the minds that know him' by Timothy Dudley-Smith (b. 1926). © Timothy Dudley-Smith in Europe and Africa. © Hope Publishing Company in the United States of America and the rest of the world. Reproduced by permission of Oxford University Press. All rights reserved.
The T. S. Eliot foyer, featuring the Constellation Lights designed by Lucy Martin of John Cullen Lighting, p.143: © Andrew Beasley 2010

LIST OF SUBSCRIBERS

This book has been made possible by the following subscribers.*

Mustafa Abbas	1990	Andrew and Philippa Baker	1983	John Borgars	1964	Patrick Cahill	1978
Roderick Abbott	1958	Colin Baker	1949	Patrick Boston	1943	Matthew Calvert	1960
Tim Abraham	1977	Professor J. Michael Baker		J.H. and C.J. Bothwell	1991	Mrs Kim Cameron	
Mrs Chinemerem Abraham-Igwe		Ken Baker	2002	Daniel Botsman	1992	D.J. Campbell-Smith	1969
(Eze-Uzomaka)	1999	Andrew Ball	1962	Alan Bott OBE FSA	1953	Campion Hall, Oxford	
Abigail Adams	1989	Tricia Balle (Burgess)	1989	Vis Bowatte	2011	Alison Cannon (Hands)	1988
J.D.L. Adams	1955	Douglas J. Bamber		Aubrey Bowden	1959	Edmund Cannon	1987
Rex D. Adams	1962	Marcus Banks	1987	Stephen Bowdery		Gillian Carlisle	2003
Dr Arif Ahsan	1975	Simon Banner	1980	David Bowen	1979	Colin Carmichael	1972
Gerardo Alamos Swinburn	2002	Derek W. Bannister	1948	Professor John M. Bowers	1973	Dr A. Craig Carr	2011
Rufus Aldred	2007	David W. Barber	1954	Michael Boyce	1966	C.G. Carrington	
Ivor Alex	1978	J.G.P. Barber	1950	Sandrine C.M. Boyd	2005	Max Carter	2004
C.A.H. Alexander		Jamie Barr	1979	Christopher Alexander David Boyle		Nigel Carter	1966
Richard Allan	1959	Robin Barraclough	1976	QC	1988	Avirup Chakraverty	1986
Andrew Allen	1984	Keith Barrett-Bee	1966	Emeritus Professor John Bradshaw	1958	Lawrence Challis	1951
David K. Allen	1968	Dr Christine Barrie (Wiggins)	1990	Nicholas Braime	1969	John Chamberlain	1965
John Lee Allen	2007	Amy Bartlett	2010	Dr Mario Brandhorst	2001	Christopher Chambers	1979
Richard Allen	1967	Dr Will Barton	1969	Anthony Brassil	2010	Claudia Chappell	1984
Sarah Allen and Aaron Davies	1997	Geoffrey Baskerville	1972	Dr Colin Brett	1977	Dr R.R. Charlwood	1944
Emma Allinson	2005	Caroline J. Batchelor	1996	David Brock	1974	John C. Chatham	1983
Bronwen Alty (Morgan)	1991	Colin Battell	1953	Beverley and Barry Bromham	1994	Duncan Chaundy	1981
Sudhir Anand	1967	Richard J. Baxter	1983	Tamsin Bromley-Rahlke	1991	Paul Chavasse	1983
Sir Robert Andrew KCB	1949	John R. Beaumont	1966	Professor Christopher		Paul Cheeseright	1958
Graham Andrews	1973	Will Beharrell	2006	Bronk Ramsey	1980	Ms Xi Chen	2000
David Angus	1980	Janna Katharina Behr	2008	B.H.V. Brown	1947	Dr Frederick F.-T. Ch'en	1997
Algis Anilionis	1969	Richard Jamie Bell	1990	David Brown	1982	Thomas Kin Hon Cheng	2002
Peter Annesley	1969	Clive Viegas Bennett	1975	Graham Brown	1977	Mindy Chen-Wishart	
Timothy J. Archer	1962	J.A. Benson	1943	Neil Robert Brown	2002	Matthew Cherry	1991
Ray Arkell	1950	Michael Berkson	1962	Tom Brown	1995	Tarun Chhabra	2005
Judith Armitage		Emma Bermingham Lopez	1993	David F. Browne	2012	Jeff W. Childers	1992
Robert Arnold	1988	Peter Bernie	1976	Dr A.P. Brunet	1974	Augustine Chin	2013
John Arrowsmith	1963	Dr Elizabeth Jane Beverley	1988	Arne Bruyneel	2011	Kirsten Claiden-Yardley	2003
David M.H. Ascough	2011	Rundheersing Bheenick	1964	Dr J.W. Buckee	1968	Claire Clark (Bagshaw)	1998
Dr Rhiannon Ash		Michael Bimmler	2009	Richard A. Buckley	1965	David Clark	1984
Thomas Au	1996	Adrian and Felicity Bingham	1995	Michael Bulmer	1949	James Clark	1982
Dr Norma Aubertin-Potter		Courtney Bishop	2003	Marcella Bungay Stanier	1992	Felicity Clarke (Tyler)	1999
Robert Audas	1966	James Bishop	1998	Crissy Burgemeestre	2005	Geoffrey Clarke	1949
John Augustine	1984	Nicholas I. Black	2010	Richard Burns	1964	Jonathan Clarke	1966
John Ausink	1976	Kate Blackmon		Jonathan Burr	1979	Professor Kieran Clarke	
Jack Austin	2010	Dominic Blaettler	2002	Keith S. Burton	1962	Lawrence Todd Clarke	1944
Glenn Spencer Bacal	1975	Philip Blakeley	1937	Dr E.T.J. Butchart	1995	Chris Clayton	1980
Gary G. Backler	1973	Duncan Bloor-Young	2004	Ian E. Butler	1956	Gerald David Clayton	1955
Ralf M. Bader		Leslie Bluck	1978	Dr Lawrence Butler	1957	Nicholas Clayton	1995
Jin-Hyun Bae	1997	Carl-Friedrich Bödigheimer		Catherine Byram-Wigfield		Patrick Cleary	1982
Dr Peter Mark Bagnall	1993	Margaret Bond		(Harris)	1989	William C. Clendaniel	1967
Rachel Elizabeth Bailey	2009	Nicholas Bone	1990	Joanne Cable	1997	Darren Cockburn	1987
John Baird	1966	Dr Camiel J.F. Boon	2012	Ulises Carrillo Cabrera	2002	Dr G.I.M. Coe	1979
Alexander Bajjon	2010	J.D.S. Booth	1976	Gerald Cadogan	1960	Hendrik Coldenstrodt-Ronge	2006

*Only Merton alumni have their matriculation year printed by their
names. All names have been printed as provided by the subscriber.

– 150 –

Justin Coldstream	1978	John Davidson	1972	Janet Edwards (Makower)	1982	Michael Franks	1946
E. Cole		A.S.W. Davies	1994	John Richard Edwards	1954	Professor Donald G. Fraser	1974
Professor T.J. Cole	1968	Professor Graham Davies FBA	1963	John Rogers Edwards	1953	Jim Freeman	1993
Timothy Coleman	2009	Jill Davies and Max Tse	1997, 1999	Tad Effendowicz	1950	Roger French	1966
M.E. Collier	1973	Laura Davies	1993	Elwyn O.M. Eilledge	1956	David Freud	1969
Scott Collier	2005	Philip Davies	1999	Cavendish Elithorn	1992	Professor Dr Julia Frunzke	2003
David Michael Comfort	1995	N.B.B. Davie-Thornhill	1955	Edward Ellery	1944	Changhua Fu	2005
Simon Congdon	1976	Mark Davison	1978	The Revd Geoff Ellis	1970	Tomas Furlong	2003
John Constable		Hannah C.E. Davison-Fischer		David John Ellison	1953	Dr Bryan Furnass	1945
Simon Constantine	1977	Antonio De Capua	2012	Antony Ellman	1959	Dr David A. Gabbott	1981
Richard C.M. Cook	1952	Philippe de Gentile-Williams	1984	Michael Ellman	1956	Kate Garcia (Marten)	1999
Dr John A.L. Cooke	1955	J.M.W. de la Haye and Mrs K.J. de la		David Elworthy	1959	John Gardner	1976
Peter Cooke	1952	Haye (Atkinson)	2002	R.N. Emeny	1961	John Gardner	1959
Chris Coombe	1976	Jean de Pourtales	1984	Lucy Emsden	1981	Professor John G. Garrard	1954
Dr John Cooper	1989	Antonia Deane Jones		Paul Engeham	1968	Phil Garratt	2010
Dr Suzanne Cooper (Fagence)	1988	Michael Dearden	1961	Richard England	1961	D.A.B. Garton-Sprenger	1940
Geoffrey Copland	1960	Bernd Delahaye	2001	Phil Entwistle	2009	Claire Gates (Farmer)	1983
Harry Corben	1944	Peter Dent	1995	Canon Adrian Esdaile	1954	Michael D. Gazzard	1955
Mark Corben	1989	Sarah Denton (Venus)	1981	Dr Jonathan D. Evans	1984	Michael Gelder	
Peter Corke	1961	Elizabeth Devoy D'Angelo	2004	Rupert Evans	1956	Dorian Gerhold	1975
Corpus Christi College, Oxford		Fraser Dillingham	1983	Thomas J. Evans	2004	Peter Gerrard	2010
F.N. Cory-Wright	1947	Dr Robert Dingley	1974	The Revd Mark Everitt		Professor Thomas P. Gerrity	1964
Dr Peter Cotgreave	1989	Viet Dinh	2000	Paul Everson	1965	Andrea Gewirtzman	2006
Michael Henry Cotton MA FRCS		Dr J.C. Dixon	1967	His Honour Judge Trevor Faber	1965	Deborah Ghadially	1997
FACS	1971	Jack E.G. Dixon	1949	Shengyan Fan and Stephen Lee	1997	David Giachardi	1967
Nicholas Cottrell	2004	Andrew Dodd	1990		1998	Prosser Gifford	1951
M.R. Counihan	1983	Charles Dodd	1953	Paul Farmiloe	1979	David Gilchrist	1970
Peter Cowdy	1972	Rebecca Dodson	2012	R.J. Fawthrop (Ker)	1984	Alan Giles	1972
Gillian Cowen	1995	Dr Peter R. Donovan	1957	Dr Ellen R. Feingold	2007	Martin Giles	1980
The Revd Geoffrey Cox	1953	Pauline L. Dorda	2012	Professor Allister I. Ferguson	1980	Professor John Girkin	1979
Rhona Cox	1993	Georgina Dore	2002	Robert Ferreira and Mabel Ferreira		Chio Gladstone	
Neil Craggs	1976	James Robert Doty	1962	Dr Vanessa Melanie Ferreira	2008	Michael H.R. Glover	1952
The Revd Dr Nicholas Cranfield FSA		T.E. Dougherty	2002	Mark Fiddes	1979	Eugene Goh	1996
	1974	George Drake	1957	Charles W. Filson	1966	Laura Goude	2006
Ian Creswick	1978	Simon Draper		The Revd Canon Stanley Finch	1951	J.R.B. Gould	1959
Dr Joanna Crocker	2001	Alan Drinkwater	1959	Dr M. Dominik Fischer	2012	Emma Graham	2009
Tristan Cummings	2012	John Driver	1950	Susanna Fischer	1985	Strachan Gray	2008
Andrew Curtis	1964	Maciej Dunajski	1996	Bernard Fitchett	1965	Christopher Green	1985
Susanna Curtis	1982	Dr M.S. Dunnill		Thomas Flynn	1996	The Revd E.M. Green	1985
Guy Cuthbertson		Joanne Durkin		Schuyler Foerster DPhil	1979	Amanda R. Greene	2007
John Dainton	1966	James Durrant	1998	Timothy J. Foot	2011	Pavel Gregoric	1996
Peter Dalton	1953	Graham James Dwyer	1981	Rob Forage	1976	The Revd Professor Robert Gribben	
Professor Pamela Dalziel	1985	Jane Eagan		Kathryn Ailsa Ford	1999	Clare V.J. Griffiths	1988
James Darcy	1980	David Eardley	1977	Emma Fordham (Grainger)	1988	Isobel D.A. Griffiths	1992
Graham Darrah	1954	Alan Eastwood	1962	Robin Forrest	1989	Michael Grills	1955
Robin Darwall-Smith		David H. Eccles	1955	Dr K.D. Forsyth	1959	Gerry Grimstone	1968
Professor Ian R. Davidson	1967	T.P.J. Edlin	1998	Rebecca Foulkes	1996	Erich Gruen and Ann Hasse	1957
Iona M. Davidson	2011	Andrew Edwards	1986	Patrick Francis	1972	Miss Hannah Guggiari	2009

Jim Gunton	1958	Barry Hawkey	2012	Paul Hollands	2002	Dr Andrew A. Jenkins	1986
E. Guppy	1998	Dr Martin Hawkins	1959	Dr Paul Holloway	1981	Matthew Jenkinson	2003
Monic Gupta	2008	Peter Hay	1963	Dr David Holmes	1966	Rupert Erik Jensen	1993
David Hadley	1955	Ron Haydon	1956	Natsumi Homma	2012	Vanessa M. Johnen	2009
Alistair Haggerty	2007	Peter Hayward	1959	Amber Hood and		Georgina Johnson	2009
Robert C. Hain	1976	Richard Hayward	1970	Edmund Highcock	2009	Dr Guy Johnson	1974
Catherine Haines		Stephen Hazell	1960	Simon Hooker		Peter Johnson	1951
Catherine Hale	2011	Sir Peter Heap	1956	Henry Hope	2010	Jonathan A. Jones	
David Hall	2002	Andy Heath	2005	Mark Hopkins	1977	K.P. Jones	
William Hall	1954	Barry W. Heath		David Hopkinson	1944	P.E. Jones	2000
Dr Sara Hall-Matthews	1982	David Hedges		L.B.T. Houghton	1996	Martin Jones	1978
D.I.W. Hamer	1974	Bill Hedley	1969	Stephen Howarth	1969	Michael Jones	1965
Olivia de C. Hamilton	1997	Danielle R. Hemple	2005	Edward and		Peter Jones	1962
John Hamlin	1956	Barney Henderson		Philippa Howells	1992, 1989	Samuel David John Jones	2005
Susan Hammond (Gadd)	1982	Arthur Hepher	1960	Philip Hudson	1973	The Revd Dr Simon Jones	
Keith Hampson	1977	Paul Hepher	1988	Luke Hughes	2010	Simon Jones	1971
Brian Hands	1957	Alan Heppenstall	1960	James W.J. Hughes-Hallett	1968	Michael H.R. Jordan	1954
Tom Hanna	2004	The Revd Dr Geoffrey Herbert	1957	Dr Luuk Huitink		Kate Josephs (Kelly)	1996
Anthony D.A. Hansen	1969	Keith Herbert		Nathan Hulme	2004	Sheheryar Kairas Kabraji	2006
James Hansen	1993	Michael J. Herbert	1957	David Hunt	2005	Andrew Kasriel	1963
Randall Hansen		Karin Herbst		Stephanie Hunter (Cooke)	1989	Paul Kaufman	2008
Gwyneth Hanson		Ean Hernandez MBA MSc	2006	Martyn W.M. Hurst	1962	David R. Kaye	1957
Martin E. Happs	1967	Malte Herwig MA MPhil DPhil		Dr Peter Husband	1954	Linnet Kaymer	2012
Neil Hargreaves	1972	(Oxon)	2000	Nicholas Hussey	1957	John William Keane	1962
David Harrington	1966	Florian Heupel DPhil	1993	Joseph Hutchinson	2011	Michael Keating-Hill	1940
Chauncy S. Harris Jr	2005	Michael Hewett	1988	David N. Ibbotson	1977	Declan Kelly	1993
Frances Harris (Mortimer)	1983	Michael Hicks	1971	Mariko Iijima	2000	Frank Kelsall	1961
Guy Harris	1948	Dr Raymond Higgins	1959	Dr J.F. Iles	1965	The Revd Eric Kemball	1977
Natalia Harris		Dr R. Highfield		Steven Inchcoombe	1984	Professor Graham Kemp MA DM	
Phillip Harris	1967	Mel Hilbrown	1966	Anne Cathrine Ingerslev	2012	FRCPath FHEA CSci FSB	1974
Dr Simon Harris	1954	Alan G. Hill	1954	John Ingledew	1954	Lauren Kendall	
Nicholas Harrison	1974	Dr Chris Rowland Hill	1976	Gregory K. Ingram	1965	Emily Kennedy	1996
Nicola Harrison		Dr Brian Hillyard		Jonathan Inkpin	1978	Julia Kenny	1995
Paul Harrison	1978	Christopher Hindley	2003	Jamie Inman	1993	Richard M.B. Kenyon	1956
Bill Hart	1968	John Hinds	1964	John Isherwood	1956	Ian Kershaw	1966
Laurence Edward Hart	1981	I.L. Hirst	1962	Stuart Jack	1967	Samuel Jay Keyser	1956
Dr Lorraine Hart	1987	Andrew Hitchon	1981	Michael Jackson	1954	Rory Khilkoff-Boulding	1967
Alexander C. Hartley	1996	Tony Hoare	1952	Peter R. Jackson	1952	Aan Son Khoo	2007
Dr Peter Hartman	1965	Andrew James Hockley	1994	Dr R.C. Jagessar	1992	Geoffrey Kidson	1946
Lawrence Hartmann	1958	Laura Nell Hodo	1996	Ravin Jain	2012	John Kightley	1975
John Hartnett	1960	Lionel Hogg	1986	Dr M. Jamieson	1971	L.J.P. Kilford	
David R. Harvey	1957	Emeritus Professor Les		Rex L. Jamison	1955	M.J. Kilroy	1985
Dr J.A. Harvey		Holborow	1963	Robin Jarratt	1990	Young-chul Kim	2009
Professor Laurence Marius Harwood		David Holbrook	1984	Michael K. Jary	1982	Professor Andrew King	
MA BSc MSc PhD CSci		Anthony Holden	1966	Gordon Jeanes	1975	FMedSci	
CChem FRSC		Dr The Hon. Jean Stewart Holder		L.R. Jebb	1955	David King	1954
Marc Hauert	1997	MVO CHB BCH	1955	Stuart Jeffreys	1990	David King	1979
C. Richard C. Hawkes	1958	Peter Holland		Mike Jeffs MRICS		Helen Kingsley	

John J. Kirby Jr and		Jonathon Little	1985	Rachael Maunder (Ball)	1992	Dr S. Moghaddam	1994
Susan R. Cullman	1962	Daniel Litvin	1989	Brian Mawer	1952	Siân Mogridge	1998
Malcolm Kitch	1959	Alasdair Livingston	1947	Royston Overton Maxwell JP		Johannes Möller	2010
Wilhelm Kleppmann	1970	Ieuan Lloyd	1958	Karen McAtamney	1999	Rebecca Martine Molyneux	2003
Dr Virginia Knight	1982	Keith Lloyd	1957	Jenny McAuley	1997	Lennox Money	1957
Peter J. Koe	1957	Trevor Lloyd	1953	Ian McBrayne	1968	Hugh Mooney	1956
Robert (Bob) Krueger	1959	Neil Loden	1968	Marina McCloskey	2003	C.J.V. Moore	1969
Robert Kudrle	1964	Bernard Lofthouse	1974	Colin McDiarmid	1970	Helen Mary Anne Moore	
Patricio Lahsen	2010	Stephanie Loizou	2006	Andrew McDonald	2000	Lee David Moran	1996
Dr John M. Land	1977	J. Timothy Londergan	1965	D.B. McDowell	1988	Stewart Morgan	1968
Toby T. Landau QC	1987	Alexander Long	2003	Charles McEvoy	1991	Daniel Morley	
Carlos Xabel Lastra-Anadón	2002	Alan Longmore	1947	Professor Ian McGowan		Helen Morley	
Dr A.J.H. Latham	1959	Charles Lonsdale	1984	DPhil FRCP	1991	William Morris	1977
Roger Laughton	1960	S.L. Lord	1974	Robert G. McKelvey	1959	Dr James Morrow	1987
Daniel Jacob Lavenda	2010	Professor Graham Loud	1971	Ian D. McMichael	1952	David W. Moskowitz MD	1974
David S. Law	1952	Stephanie Rhiannon		James McMillan	2007	Russ Mould	1987
Sophie Law (Hamilton)	1999	Lovell-Read	2012	Anna Della Frances McVey	2003	James G. Moxness II	2008
Lisa Lawrence		Michael Graeme Lowe	1968	Dr R.J. Meadway		Peter Moyes	1959
Alexander le Druillenec		Tony Lowman	1965	Sally E. Mears (Collings)	1980	Peter Mulberry	1977
Raulin Le Mière	1998	David Lund	1972	Roger M.A. Medill	1952	Martin John Munden	1956
Hannah Leadbetter	2006	Lawrence D. Lyle MBE FHA	1941	Mark Christian Medish	1985	Sebastian Munden	1986
Dave Leal		Dr Peter Lyne	1975	Bob Meier	1992	Jaron Lloyd Murphy	2010
Paul Ledger	1948	Dr Stuart Lynn	1955	Jena Meinecke	2011	Tucker Murphy DPhil	2005
Robert Ledger	1974	Andrew J. Macarthur	2012	Brian Melican	2003	J. James Murray	1951
Geoffrey Francis Lee	1976	M.C.A. Macdonald	1967	Guy P. Melin		S.V. Murray	2003
Keith Lee	1965	Ian Maclachlan		Nicholas Menon	1958	John Myatt	1973
Ken T.C. Lee	2009	Ian Macpherson	1949	Kristine Roberta Merriman	2008	James Edward Nation	2008
Dr Michael M. Lee	2008	Sir David Madden	1965	Deyan Mihaylov	2009	Peter Neary	
Richard Lee	1984	Chris Madell	1974	Ray Miles	1965	Tristan Needham	1976
Malcolm Leflaive	1958	Helen Mallalieu	1999	Michael Millard	1948	Richard Nelson	1959
Professor I.S. Lemos		Charles Manby	1976	Christopher D. Miller	1980	New College, Oxford	
Matthias Lenz		Gareth Mann	1995	Natalie Miller	1980	Mark Newbery	1974
The Revd Sebastian Leonard		Peter Mann	1953	Paul Miller	1991	The Revd Canon John	
OSB	1963	Richard Manning	2007	T.P.X. Miller	1997	K. Newsome	1969
Brandon Leong	2008	André Marques-Smith	2009	Tony Millns	1969	Tom Newton-Lewis	2003
Julian Leslie	1968	David Marsh	1955	John Mills CBE		Dr M.C. Ney	1981
Markham Lester	1988	Christopher Martin	1972	John Angus Mills	1958	Benjamin Nicholas	
Sir Brian Leveson	1967	Christopher Martin	1976	John Peter Mills	1981	Helen Nicholas	2003
Anthony Levy	1976	Dr David Martin	1968	Stephen Mills	1971	Dr and Mrs Michael Nicholas	
Heather J. Lewandowski		Mrs Janet Martin		Martin Milton	1978	Andrew Nicholson	1969
Bryan Lewis	1958	Matthew Martin	2007	Dominic Minghella	1986	Toby Nicholson	1988
Cathy Lewis		Professor Paul R. Martin	1972	David Mitchell	1975	Henry Charles Nickerson	
C.P. Lewis	1975	Ines Marusic	2011	John C. Mitchell OBE	1955	Robert Joseph Nickerson	
Lionel Lewis	1946	Charlotte Mason	2009	Robert B. Mitchell	1974	Susan Nickols (Willcox)	1996
The Rt Revd Michael Lewis	1972	Donald J.A. Matthew	1950	Ruth Mitchell	2010	John Nightingale	
Robert Lewis	1973	James C. Matthew	2012	John M. Mitnick	1985	David Norbrook	
W.W. Li	1980	Philip Matthews	2002	The Revd Canon Peter Moger	1982	Mark Norman	1978
Dr Gregory B.S. Lim	2006	An Maudens RA	1999	J. Moghaddam	1997	Stuart Norman	1998

Liesl Nunns	2006	Martyn J. Peters	1977	Frank Rae	1974	D.H. Roscoe	1958
Daphne O'Connell		Victor Petrov	2006	In memoriam,		Matthew Rose	1990
Peter O'Connor		Andrew Pettegree	1976	Robin D.T. Raikes	1953	Alexandru George Rosoiu	2008
John A. Oetjen	1983	Susanne Pfeifer	2007	Hinesh Rajani	2001	Donald Ross	1970
Anthony O'Halloran	1955	Natalie Tienelle Phillips	2001	Nick Rampley	1978	Julian Ross	1985
Dr Sue O'Hare (Allcock)	1983	Peter Phillips	1981	Dr Frances Ramsey (Davies)	1983	Peter Ross	
Yuuki Ohta	2008	Robyn Lynch Phillips	2012	Aditya Rana	1983	Philip Rosser MA	1966
Jonathan Oldfield	1979	T.N. Phillips	1976	John W. Randall	1964	Miss Kirsten Rulf	2003
Edward Olleson		Tim Phillips	1960	Gursharan Randhawa	1988	Michael Ryan	1979
Eric Olson	1986	Charles M. Phipps	1986	Cyril Randles	1957	Richard Ryder	1982
Nathaniel F. Olson	2005	Praab Pianskool	1979	Dr P.R. Rastall	1970	Stephen E. Sachs	2002
Dr Chern Ein Oon	2007	Stephen Pickett	1972	Professor R.G. Ratcliffe	1971	L.H. Sackett	1949
Oriel College, Oxford		Robert Pitt	1972	Peter Neil Ratoff	1974	Robert Sackett	1950
David Owen	1976	Terrence J. Piva	1988	Dr Georg Rau	1993	Mehrunissa Sajjad	2011
Oxford Conservation Consortium		Professor Fran Platt		Professor Dame Jessica Rawson		Andrzej Henryk Sakaluk	2011
Oxfordshire History Centre		Hugh Podger	1949	Matthew Ian James Raybould	2012	Professor Paul Salzman	
John R. Pagan	1973	Chris Pogson	1963	Dr Martin Read CBE	1971	Albert Sampson	2007
David Page	1963	Alastair Porter	1949	Tim Reading	1977	Michele Jeanette Sanders	2012
Edward Paine	1979	Jean-Pascal Pouzet	1998	Martin Redfern	1955	Nigel Sanders	1948
Simon Pallett	1973	Stephen Powell	1968	Laurence John Reed and		Martin Sands	1967
J.R. Palmer	1962	Jonathan W. Powell-Wiffen	1963	Barbara Anne Mercer	1980	Angel Sarmiento	2007
Jeremy Palmer	1976	Crispin Poyser	1975	Anthony Reeve	1958	John Saunders	1970
Nyrie Joy Palmer	2004	Jonathan Prag		Jocelyn Retter	1995	Kevin Saunders	1972
Dr Peter Palmer	1968	Charlotte Prather		Tom Reusch	1992	Terence John Saunders	1957
Charanjit S. Pangali	1971	Michael Prather	1969	Carter Revard	1952	Simon Saville	1977
Matthew Paradis	2004	David Preest	1956	Martin Reynolds	1948	Daniel Schaffer	1986
J.H.M. Parry	1958	Katherine Preiskel	1996	A.J. Rhodes	1946	Dr Peter Scharbach	1970
P.J. Parsons	1958	Nigel Prescot	1981	D.S. Richards	1953	Alexander Schekochihin	
Christopher Pascoe	1955	Barry Press	1968	Derek Richards	1948	Paul Schofield	1973
Alix Patterson	2006	Maria Pretzler	1996	Sir Rex Richards		A. Truman Schwartz	1956
Dr Jim Pattison	1981	Gareth Price	1985	Clive Richardson	1967	Professor A.B. Scott	1955
In memory of Revd A. Paxton	1895	Katherine Magdalene Price	2001	Peter Richmond	1967	Ian W. Scott	1950
Dr Catherine Paxton		Mark F. Price	1964	Rita Ricketts		Marcus Scott	1978
Jennifer Payne		Dr Nicholas Price	1964	Michael Riddle	2003	Patrick Scott	1963
Richard Payne	1990	Rebecca Price	2007	Michael Rines	1954	Hugh Scott-Barrett	1977
Professor Ceri Peach	1958	Robert Price	2011	Dr S.J.S. Rippon	1951	Charles S.K. Scudder	1971
Roy Peacock	1953	Lester Pritchard	1964	E.R. Roberts		Robert Sears	2000
Thomas Pedrick	1989	Enrico Emanuele Prodi	2007	Dr Kelvin Roberts	1968	Professor David J. Seipp	1977
David Pelteret	1968	Ben Prynn	1985	Nick Roberts		Mr E.I. Selig	1956
The Revd Canon Jeremy C.B.		Dr Simon James Pulleyn		Dr Paul Robinson	1981	Sandeep Sengupta	2006
Pemberton	1974	John Purkis	1951	Peter Robinson	1965	Emma Senior	1990
R.W. Penman	1974	Kerry Purnell (Jones)	1989	John and Marion Roche		Mr J.D.C. Seymour	1983
Rose Pennells	1999	Andrew Quartermaine	1973	Phil Rock	1951	Clive Shackell	
David Pennock	1963	The Queen's College, Oxford		Christopher J. Rogers	1962	Daniel Shapiro	1994
João Pereira da Silva Melo Lima	2012	Mrs Julie Quinn (Smith)	1989	David Watson Rogers	1964	Jack Sharman	2008
Alex Perry	1988	Saeed Ahmad Qureshi	1956	Carl Rohsler	1988	Tony Sharp	1970
Ben Perry	1992	Sir George Radda	1956	Susan Roller (Harris)	1983	Arthur J. Shartsis	1967
Robert Perry	2002	Daniel Radice	1986	Leonid A. Romanenko	2006	James A. Shaw	2004

Michael Shaw	1958
Katie Sheehan	2002
John Shimwell	1980
David Shipp	1959
Dr John Shore	1953
Pamela Shorney	1998
Dr Paul C. Shrimpton	1971
Henry Shue	1961
John and Veronika Simms	1958
Alistair Simpson	1958
Keith Singer	1977
Mandeep S. Singh	2009
Ian Skeet	1949
Nick Skinner	1970
Tom Skinner	2000
Hannah Skoda	
Eugene B. Skolnikoff	1950
Dr Dimitrios Skrekas	2002
His Honour Stuart Sleeman	1966
Alan Slomson	1961
Glenn C.Th.M. Sluijter	2012
Barbara Mitchell Small	1981
Karen Small (Reynolds)	1984
Paul Smeathers	1958
Alan Smith	1965
Anna Smith	1991
C. Craig Smith Jr	1964
Chris Smith	1966
His Honour Judge David	
Smith QC	1957
Jeannette Smith	2011
Peter R. Smith	1963
R.S. Smith	1973
Roger A. Smith	1980
Sarah Smith	2001
Tyler Jo Smith	1990
Graeme P. Smyth	1993
Christophe Snoeck	2010
Gilberte Snoeck-Wyckmans	
Derek Snoxall	1952
A.L. Sockett	1932
Bob Spears	1964
Mark Spillman	2006
Robert Spray	1961
Ian Spurr	1957
Adrian T.J. Stanford	1955
Chris Starr	1967
G.M. Stead	

In memoriam,	
Anthony H. Stearns	1954
James Steckelberg MD	1976
Julia Steinberg	2010
Dr Sergej and Tatjana Steinberg	2010
Sir Howard Stringer	1961
John Stephany	1967
L.C. Stephens	1948
Gary G. Stevens	1968
Robin Stevens	1992
Roy Stevens	1962
Hedley Stone	1969
Turlough Stone	1992
Peter John Stubbs	1969
Robert Summerfield	1987
Daniel L. Sussman	1991
Duncan I. Sutherland	1972
Philip Suttle	1978
T.J. Sutton	1970
Angela Swift	1991
David Swinnerton	1989
John Sykes	1974
Michael Szonyi	1990
Amber Tallon	2012
Kenneth Y.H. Tan	1986
Charles Target	1975
Lady Taylor	
Brek Taylor Tamblyn	
Ian R. Taylor	1975
J. Christine H. Taylor	
James Taylor	
Dr John W. Taylor	1978
Sir Martin Taylor	
Michael Taylor	1963
Dr Michael A. Taylor	1976
Tim Taylor	1997
Dr Andrew Taylor-Castillo	1999
Neh Thaker	1992
Archondia Thanos	1999
Bryony Thayre	1999
E. Donald Thibodeau	
Alun P. Thomas	1951
Amanda L.R. Thomas	2012
Miss Laura Thomas	2000
Richard Thomas	1956
Simon Thomas	1992
Steven Thomas	1979
Richard Hugh Thompson	1960

Professor R.M. Thomson	
Halldór Benjamín Þorbergsson	2010
Katy Thorneycroft	1995
Dr Patricia M. Thornton	
R.H. Thornton	1942
Dr Philip Tibbs	1974
Dr Henry S. Tillinghast Jr	1982
Mark Tiner	2000
My Chi To	1996
Sarah Tobin	1992
Edward Tomme	1997
N.C.E. Tongue	1963
Adrian G.J. Toutoungi	1991
Neil Towers	1969
Dr Christopher Townsend	1993
Professor Sir Richard Trainor	1971
Michael Trevanion	1956
John Trott	1958
Andrew Trotter	1972
Dr Tony Trowles	1985
P.J. Truesdale	1976
Chin-Yin Tseng	2008
David Turner	1984
Gareth M. Turner	2007
Jonathan Turner	1997
Kevin John Turner	1977
John Turvey	1952
George F. Tusa	1953
Dr A.D. Tustian	1999
R.E. Underwood	1950
Dr Nicholas Unwin	1972
James Upcher	2006
William Upcher	2008
Michael Sy Uy	2009
Frits van Hout	1978
J.Z. van Rookhuijzen	2009
Kenneth W. and	
Renee L. Van Treuren	1991
Robert Venables QC	1966
Michel Vennat	1963
Anthony Verdin	1953
Dr Geraldine Verschoor	
(Houston)	1989
Dirk Llewellyn Vertigan	1988
Dr Rupert and Laura Vessey	1983
Adrian and Emma Vickers	1958
Emanuel Viebahn	2008
Chris Vile	1980

Mrs Jane Vile	
Dr O. Villalobos Baillie	1972
Desmond Vowles	1942
Mladen Vranic	
Victor Vu	2009
Keith Waddell	1955
Keith Wade	1967
Lauren Kay Wahl	1997
Helen Wain (Bray)	1995
Peter Wakefield	1980
Paul Andreas Walker	2007
Ralph Walker	
The Revd Dr Robert T. Walker	1969
Philip Waller	
James Anthony Walmsley Lowe	2006
John Walters	1971
Paul Walton	1974
R. Walton	1997
Joy and Frank Walworth	
Julia and David Walworth-d'Avray	
Fanxi Wang	2006
Tira Wannamethee	1981
Samuel Ward	2011
Robert Lloyd Ware	
Jeremy Warren	1974
Ben Warth	1997
David Warwick	1976
Angus Gavin Watson	1962
David Watson	1954
David Lowes Watson	1958
John Watson	1959
Dr Trudy A. Watt	
Dr Cory Way	2003
Alexander Weate	2012
Anthony Webb	1999
Elia Weinbach	1967
Michael Weingarten	1965
Nicholas Weller	1982
A.L. (Bert) Wells	1978
Dr E.M.P. Wells	1981
Mike Wenger	1982
Tristan West	2004
Guy Westwood	2004
Peter Westwood	1954
Gordon Whatley	1963
Peter Whibberley	1981
Philippa (Edwards) and	
Sam Whipple	1984, 1983

Chester White	1952	Paul Woodruff	1965
David Whiteley	1964	Brett Anthony Woods	2012
Juliana Widjaja	2012	A.D. Wood MBE	1957
John Wilkinson	1949	Jo Woods (Brindley)	1985
Mark Wilkinson	1996	W.R.T. Woods	1959
Tom and Polly Willett	1986	Jonathan Woodward	1989
A.J.T. Williams	1946	Patrick Worsnip	1966
Dr Andrew N. Williams		Lord Wright of Richmond	1951
PhD MRCP FRHistS	1984	Allan Wright	1978
David Nash Williams	1951	Howard Wright	1957
G.A. Williams	1957	Jonathan Wright	1960
John Carey Williams	2003	Nicholas Wright	1967
Robin Williams	1975	J.B. Wroe	1962
Steve Williams	1973	John Wrout	1965
Elizabeth Williamson	1999	Brian Wyatt	1977
Hanneke Wilson	1981	Lucy Wyles	1989
Nigel Wilson		Peter F. Wyles	1955
Sarah Frances Wilson	2007	Szymon Wylezol	2008
Dr Stephen Wilson	1975	Anthony Wynn-Evans	1956
Mr Justice Herman J.		Jurei Yada	2008
Wilton-Siegel	1971	Eleutherios Yalouris	1971
Andrew Wingate	1996	David M. Yates	1953
Professor Brian N. Winston	1960	Ian Yates	1966
Christine Winzor	1986	Gabriel Shih Chung Yiin	2011
Roger Witcomb	1965	S.A.L. Tross Youle	1974
Brian Witherden	1969	George Zachariah	1991
David Witt		J.M. Zamet	1965
M.B. Wolf	1963	Joseph Ziegler	1990
Lisa Jun-Pei Wong MD MS	1999	Professor Nicole Zitzmann	
John Wood	1960	Dr Eldon Zuill	1967
Dr Anna Woodman	1996		

The chalice engraved by Laurence Whistler with a line from T.S. Eliot's 'Little Gidding', given to the College by Barbara Rees in Eliot's memory and used once a year in the Chapel.

INDEX

Italics indicate captions for images.

Treasures of Merton College

2013 © Merton College, Oxford and
Third Millennium Publishing Limited

First published in 2013 by Third Millennium Publishing Limited,
a subsidiary of Third Millennium Information Limited.

2–5 Benjamin Street
London
United Kingdom
EC1M 5QL
www.tmiltd.com

ISBN: 978 1 906507 96 1

British Library Cataloguing in Publication Data
A CIP catalogue record for this book is available from the British Library.

Project Manager	Neil Burkey
Design	Susan Pugsley
Cover design	Matt Wilson
Principal Photographer	Colin Dunn (Scriptura Ltd)
Production	Bonnie Murray
Reprographics	Studio Fasoli, Verona, Italy
Printing	Gorenjski Tisk, Slovenia

Above: The sports ground with a cricket match in progress.

Endpapers: An allegorical depiction of Merton College from the Oxford Almanack *of 1737, drawn by W. Greene and engraved by George Vertue. The perspective view of the College is taken from David Loggan's* Oxonia Illustrata *(1675). Below it, in the centre, is the founder, Walter de Merton. On his right is Bishop Rede of Chichester, benefactor of the Library, a plan of which is held by a putto at his feet. Next to him are Elizabethans and Jacobeans. The laymen are perhaps intended for Sir Thomas Bodley, Sir Henry Savile or John Chamber, Fellow, founder of two postmasterships. The cleric may be Griffin Higgs, who endowed the post of Librarian, or Thomas Bickley, Warden, though one contemporary commentator on the print thought he was the fifteenth-century cardinal and archbishop John Kemp. Beyond them stand more recent donors, some of them the patrons of a young student wearing the gown of a Postmaster. On the right, Mercury and Education present a boy to the founder. Mercury points to Immortality, who holds a crown over Walter de Merton's head. Alongside flies a putto with a scroll inscribed with the names of famous Mertonians. Some are genuine: Bodley, Harvey, Jewel, Savile, Wyclif and the now largely forgotten John Hales, author of the widely read* Golden Remains *(1659). Others had been speculatively adopted in earlier centuries: Bacon, Ockham, Duns Scotus. On the left, Charity, depicted as a nursing mother, endorses the College and its assembled benefactors.*